IN GOOD COM

IN GOOD COMPANY

by

Norman Bearcroft

First published in 2010
by The Salvation Army Trading Company

ISBN 978-0-85412-826-6

Cover design by Jonathan Carmichael

Cover photograph:
Norman Bearcroft explaining a new work about to be played
at the Royal Albert Hall

SALVATION ARMY
TRADING
COMPANY

Contents

Foreword

It is a pleasure to accede to my friend Norman's invitation to write the foreword to this book. During the years we have worked together we have shared deep concerns and visions about Salvation Army music, especially its place in the varied facets of the Army's mission and worship and its social implications, under the guidance of the Holy Spirit. The Army music scene has inevitably changed during the period covered in these pages so that we have a personalised historical record of public events and a view behind the scenes. The author is a gifted, dedicated and determined man; his humour accompanies a strong sense of fairness and moral principle. He is a man who has fought his corner on more than one occasion.

Norman and I first met in the late 1940s – he a visiting cornet soloist, I the local bandmaster. We found that we had much in common, including armed forces experience. We both became Salvation Army officers. The cost of officership, not always recognised, is pointed up by a comment by Norman's first wife, Jill. My wife-to-be, Joy, was a new officer and our marriage was imminent. Joy told Jill (an officer cadet) that she was looking forward to us getting our home together. To which Jill replied, 'That's what we have just given up.' This will partly explain their wholehearted acceptance of a variety of appointments and overseas assignments.

Sometimes, too, the accolades which accrue to a musically creative officer tend to overlook his or her primary calling as a minister of the gospel. While music has been a major factor with the Bearcrofts, early in their service I visited their centre at Gosport to conduct a meeting and found them deep into a period of revival.

The year 1960 saw Norman appointed National Bandmaster, taking him into a field in which he has uniquely made his mark.

An appointment in Canada, during which he reformed the Canadian Staff Band, occupies significant book space. General Arnold Brown – who had been Norman's supremo in Canada – recalled him to the UK in 1977 as National Secretary for Bands and Songster Brigades. General Brown, a former PR man, keenly appreciated and exploited the value of music in the Movement. Consequentially, Norman and I, as the Head of the International Music Editorial Department, were often on call. It was during this period, when Norman had charge of the British music scene, that he afforded me immense opportunities for composition in connection with concert events in the Royal Albert Hall and elsewhere.

Mention must be made of Norman's leadership of the International Staff Songsters, to which I believe there was a prelude. As far back as 1972 I had directed two LPs of Army songs in popular-type arrangements. General Brown liked the arrangements and broached with me the possibility of such a group continuing. This was not practical without official backing but the idea obviously stayed in his mind. In 1979 he sent for Norman and me to discuss an official choral group which would function in parallel with the International Staff Band. Norman was made the founder-conductor – a sound move. A change for Joy and me was already on the cards and we were appointed to Australia. The 1986 song book was in process and I had begun work on the companion tune book. Norman's representations helped ultimately to bring us home, leading to my co-ordination of that project. These snippets hint at the extent to which the author has been an effective influence in the realm of Army music. His concerns have been both cultural and spiritual. We have sick-visited together and he mentions precious moments which we spent with Eric Ball in his last days.

As a composer, Norman has been in the enviable position of directing highly talented groups which have stimulated the writing and performance of his music. His band output has an immediacy, from the fun of 'Just Like John', through the brilliance of 'Golden Slippers' to the heart-reaching 'Word Of Grace'. His workroom walls are a travelogue of photographed events and people. After Norman married Kathie he moved to New York, where happily they have the sense to use him.

The book is not only about Norman but also a first-hand account of his Army world, its personalities and occasions. It makes a humorously-laced, informative and inspiring read.

Lieut-Colonel (Dr) Ray Steadman-Allen OF

Chapter 1

REFLECTIONS

Early Days

I have always been grateful for open-air meetings. My father Albert Bearcroft – who had been an officer in The Salvation Army before home circumstances caused him to resign – was leading a Saturday night open-air meeting in the town of Evesham when he first saw Alma Stanford as she watched the progress of the meeting. Alma, a Methodist, later became his wife and I was the fourth child of the marriage. My father had been a military bandmaster in the First World War and, following his discharge, was reinstated as a captain in The Salvation Army and my mother, who had never had training as an officer, became Mrs Captain Bearcroft, serving along with her husband.

Their appointment in 1925, now with their daughters Nancy and Margaret and son Bramwell, took them to Wallsend-on-Tyne Corps in the Northern Division where, in 1926, I was born. Obviously, I do not remember the next few appointments (a different one every year) but I still remember that my mother would sing me to sleep every night, and always with the same song, the first verse being:

> There were ninety and nine that safely lay
> In the shelter of the fold,
> But one was out on the hills away,
> Far off from the gates of gold.

There were three more verses which, speaking of the peril of the lost sheep, took quite some time to sing but, long though it was, I had to know that the sheep made it home safely. I rarely went to sleep before the last verse, which is:

1

But all through the mountains, thunder-riven,
And up from the rocky steep,
There arose a cry to the gate of Heaven,
'Rejoice! I have found my sheep!'

Now I could go to sleep knowing the lost lamb had been found. Even today, when I see sheep, I remember her singing. My mother never got old – at 93 years of age she still liked fun and it was always a joy to be with her.

In latter days she was very cautious about the many claims made on the television. It so happened that she was with us at a Canadian music school on the date that the men first landed on the moon. Having arranged for the students to watch this on television, I asked my mother if she would like to join us. She declined and I thought that perhaps such a crowd of young people might have been a bit daunting. When it was all over and I took her to tea, I said, 'What a wonderful thing that those men could be on the moon and that we could see it on the television.' After a few moments she replied, 'Yes, if they really were there.' To my reply that we actually saw them on the television, she said, 'Well, they can make anything look real on television!' I then asked what she liked on television, to which she replied, 'Oh, the news, and that old Benny Hill, if he doesn't get too vulgar!'

I have a photograph of my sister Nancy pushing me in a pushchair during the time my parents were stationed at Great Yarmouth and vague memories of the Yorkshire towns of Shipley and Heckmondwike before we went to London when my parents were appointed to Norland Castle Corps in West London. This corps had a good band that did counter-marching (that's what my dad called it) on the forecourt of the hall on arrival from open-air meetings. To the small boy I was, this was fascinating!

Incidentally, it was about this time I went with my mother for a two-week holiday in the country village of Broom, near Stratford-upon-Avon, where my grandmother lived. Sunday evenings saw us in the local Methodist chapel where, before electricity was installed, I was enlisted to pump the church organ. The pump was situated in a cellar below the organ and was operated by a long wooden handle, which I had to push up and down. The amount of air being pumped could be checked by a weight on a string that went up and down. There was a line to indicate when the air was getting low and it was great fun to see how near to the line one could go before the organ began to lose pitch. Considering I received sixpence each week for my work, I suppose I could claim that this was my first professional job!

The next appointment was to Southall 1 Corps, also in the West London Division, a corps which was to have very special meaning for me in the years to come.

I have a picture of Southall Band dated September 1933, numbering some 35 players, along with their bandmaster, Captain Eric Ball, who is seen standing between my parents on the front row. Eric, then working in the Music Editorial Department at Salvationist, Publishing and Supplies in Judd Street, King's Cross, led this very hard-working band in three open-air meetings every Sunday, each followed by a meeting in the citadel. In those days, headquarters prescribed the times of the meetings as follows: 11 am holiness meeting, 3 pm praise meeting and, at 6:45 pm, a salvation meeting, all preceded by an open-air meeting – and from this standard there was never any deviation!

Also at Southall, there would be a Monday night open-air meeting held in a street near to the hall, Tuesday night was songster rehearsal (Eric was the songster organist), band practice was on Thursday night and there was an open-air meeting on Saturday nights, often followed by an indoor meeting before the coming Sunday. This really was The Salvation Army at war!

One evening, while walking with my father to the hall, I saw Eric Ball's father-in-law Mr Dorset who, my father told me, had vowed to preach the gospel in every street in Southall. There he was, standing in a street on his own, holding an Army flag and reading loudly from the Bible. I suggested to my father that someone should at least go and hold the flag for him, to which he replied, 'You could do that.' The flag was far too large for a seven-year-old boy to hold, so Olive,

3

Eric's wife, gave me her sessional flag, which was much smaller. This meant I could be with her father and hold the flag while he preached the gospel. I also remember that sometimes Mr Dorset would stand in a testimony period and sing in a very shaky voice, 'Running over, running over, my cup's full and running over.' Then, after catching his breath, he would add, 'If your cup is not full ⋯⋯ over, you need to seek the Lord afresh!'

It was in those early days at S⋯ ⋯ Lister. The occasion on which I fi⋯ ⋯ of those so-called National Days ⋯ ⋯ve. The Scout Troop, the Life-Sav⋯ ⋯ts but for girls) the Chums (younge⋯ ⋯s (younger Girl Guards) were giving a⋯ ⋯ had been removed and the parents and fri⋯ ⋯ sides of the hall to observe the young folk a⋯ ⋯ drills.

Came the turn of the S⋯ ⋯ Lister was a member, their contribution to the e⋯ ⋯ he form of a marching display. There they were in ⋯ ⋯ orms ready to obey the commands of their leader. A⋯ ⋯ quick march!' was closely followed by an even louder 'Rig⋯ ⋯ t which all the girls turned to the right except Jill, who t⋯ ⋯ o the left! I can remember thinking, 'There is a girl with a mi⋯ ⋯ her own!' Some 15 years later, we married.

Wandsworth, my parents' next appointment, was where my father used to have a Saturday afternoon open-air meeting in the neighbouring town of Putney. For this meeting there would just be my mother, my father (with his concertina), my brother Bram and me. In order to get a good crowd, he would put Bram and me on a stool to sing duets. Many's the time some kind lady would give me a packet of sweets! One could ask, was this my second professional job?

A few times I heard my mother and father discussing where their next appointment might be and my mother would always say, 'Anywhere but Battersea.' It so happened that, when the Divisional Commander (Colonel Bertie Rolls) came to our house for a meal, he asked me where he should send my parents in the coming May. In my innocence I replied, 'Anywhere but Battersea!' 'Why do you say anywhere but Battersea?' asked the colonel. 'Because that's what my mother says,' I replied amid much laughter.

Farewell and marching orders brought us to Kingston-on-Thames Corps, where the corps sergeant-major – an official in the police force – was quite spectacular as he directed the traffic while the band marched down the main street every Saturday and Sunday evening, following an open-air meeting in the town's marketplace. It was in the marketplace that large crowds gathered to hear the band and the message of salvation, that order being correct in that it took the music of the band to attract a crowd to hear the message of The Salvation Army. It was also at Kingston that I was commissioned as a member of the junior band and became a second cornet player, sitting next to my brother Bram, who was on first cornet. I wondered, 'Can anything be better than this?'

It was while we lived at Kingston that my sister Nancy fell in love with Alfred Bowen, a bandsman and songster at nearby Staines Corps. Alf, as we knew him, would cycle over to Kingston on a night when my parents would be at the Kingston Corps hall and Bram and I should have been in bed. Of course we were not asleep and used to peep over the top of the stairs to see what courting was all about. A sharp word from Alf and we were back in bed – temporarily!

My first opportunity to play with the band was while out Christmas carolling. I had learned the second cornet part to a tune called 'Sawley', to which northerners used to sing 'While Shepherds Watched Their Flocks By Night' (the music being in the old carol sheets). Unfortunately, it didn't get played at every lamppost so I just went round with the band until 'Sawley' was chosen. Lip fatigue was not a problem!

It was at Kingston that my brother Bram got his first bicycle. I am not sure if it was a brand new one but he treasured it as if it were made of gold. I longed to have a ride on it but such a luxurious experience was not on the horizon – well, not until one day when he was away from home on a school outing. We lived in a house very near to a park called Canberry Gardens, on the banks of the River Thames – just the place for a quiet bicycle ride. The temptation overcame me and I made my way, with Bram's bicycle, to the riverside. Cars were not permitted there so, with confidence, I mounted the bicycle and, after a few yards, rode straight into the River Thames! A man pulled me out and then very kindly rolled up his trousers and waded into the river to rescue the precious bicycle. It was a very subdued Norman that had to face his brother who, after a very detailed inspection, forgave me on the promise that I would never, ever touch it again.

Cheap violin lessons became available at the Kingston school and my father thought it would be good for me to learn how to play one. It did mean he had to buy a violin from the school, which he gladly did, in the hope that I would become a good violinist. I have to admit that I was a failure – mostly because I would rather be playing my cornet.

The next corps was Sutton in the county of Surrey, which had a very good junior band. I was delighted to become the soprano cornet player and loved every moment of marching and playing with this band. Alas! it was here that I suffered suspension for two weeks owing to my disobedience. It happened like this. It was harvest time and we were playing the harvest song 'Bringing In The Sheaves', in which it is possible to give a 'cuckoo' effect following the first line of the chorus, thus, 'Bringing in the sheaves, cuckoo!' The band leader, having heard it a number of times, gave the instruction, 'No more cuckoo sounds', but, on the march back to the hall, I succumbed to the temptation and one more 'cuckoo' was heard. The two weeks of marching behind the band seemed an eternity, especially when my brother, now in the senior band marching in front of the junior band, kept looking round and laughing!

Govan, in Scotland, was our next home and, for a boy, life there was quite different to that in England. I found the school in which I was enrolled to be difficult, mostly on account of my English accent. The history class, where the English were constantly looked on as the bad people, was a problem in that the teacher would always single me out as if I were part of the English oppressors by saying, 'And you and your lot should be ashamed of yourselves!'

The corps had a splendid band (led by Bandmaster Dry), with a long tradition of high standards. The year 1938 was a special Exhibition Year for the Scottish people and, as part of the celebration, there were the Sunday afternoon Glasgow Exhibition festivals. It was here that I first became acquainted with some of the Army's finest musical compositions, such as 'Songs Of The Morning', 'King Of Kings' and 'Army Of The Brave', to name but a few.

Being only 13 years old I was still in the junior band but, having made some progress as a player, I was invited to play a cornet solo in one of these festivals. So, with pianoforte accompaniment by George Brown (then the corps pianist and later the corps bandmaster), I stood to play a solo entitled 'Long, Long Ago'. It must have been all right because I was asked to repeat the solo a month later. In those now far-off days, I had no idea that, in years to come, I would be in the Royal Albert Hall conducting an 800-voice chorus in the singing of this same melody to Herbert Booth's immortal words, 'Lord, through the Blood of the Lamb that was slain, cleansing for me.'

The house in which we then lived overlooked a bowling green and it was funny to hear my father shouting advice to the players, even though they could not hear him! It was here that I wondered if I should forget the cornet and become a percussionist. I had learned the basic rules for producing drum rolls but the temptation soon left me.

Second World War

My parents' next appointment was back in England, to Barrow-in-Furness Corps, then in Lancashire. The year was 1939 with much of Europe at war and, just a few months later, Britain declared war against Germany. The boys' school I attended was near to a railway station so the authorities decided that, seeing the railway might be a target for bombing by the enemy, we should be transferred to a girls' school on the outskirts of the town. Unfortunately, this did not mean that we would mix with the girls, because it was decided that the girls would use the school from early in the morning and the boys from the afternoon until evening.

I can still remember my father and a group of bandsmen pasting black paper over all the windows in the Barrow Corps hall following an instruction from the Government about the need for blackout to hinder the German planes on their bombing raids.

By now, at 14 years of age, I was playing in the senior band but was still required to attend Sunday morning Sunday school before the senior meeting at 11 am. It was in the junior meeting that the leader, Sergeant-Major Plumb – who had lived for some years in America – used to celebrate anyone's birthday by requiring the said person to put as many pennies as years lived into a small tower, that would light up as each penny fell, while singing a chorus with these words: 'Dropping, dropping, dropping, dropping, hear those pennies fall, every one for Jesus, he shall have them all.' He then invariably added, 'It is always better to give than to receive.'

From Barrow-in-Furness we went to Ilford in London and to a very different life from that which we had so far known. It was now 1940 and Ilford, being east of London, was where bombing from enemy planes was maintained night after night and often through the day. Ilford Corps kept up its open-air meeting activity, and the Sunday evening meetings were held under the balcony in the hall, which was considered to be the safest place. Sometimes on Sunday nights, at a period when the bombing made the evening meeting impossible, my father would take my brother Bram and myself to various air-raid shelters in Ilford, where we would hold cheerful salvation meetings with the people who were taking shelter from the bombing raids.

One Sunday morning, while walking to the open-air meeting, my brother Bram, swinging his arms, dropped his cornet and it was very badly damaged. On arrival at the chosen place, the temporary bandmaster (Colonel Arthur Bristow) wanted to know what had happened. On hearing Bram's excuse, he took my cornet and gave it to Bram and then handed me the broken one!

It was at this time that my brother had a serious girlfriend and, providing no air raid was in effect, would walk her to her home following the evening meeting. He really didn't want to leave me out of this arrangement so suggested that I follow at a distance, far enough for her not to see me, so that we could then walk back home together!

On leaving school, I went to work at the Men's Social Work Headquarters in London, where my job consisted of taking letters and correspondence to and from International Headquarters in Queen Victoria Street. In those days, all personnel wore Salvation Army uniform, and I was supplied with one where the yellow trimmings identified me as a messenger. There was a Men's Social Work Headquarters Band in which I played for one engagement before it was disbanded. It was here I met a number of well-known composers working at this headquarters, including Brindley Boon, Charles Skinner and Arthur Goldsmith. My direct boss was a lady called Miss Van Rossum who looked after me like a mother! She taught me how the filing system worked and, if I were not on a journey to other headquarters, I was required to do the filing for the Cashier's Department.

The bus journey from my home in Ilford to this headquarters took about 40 minutes but, when the bombing started, it could take hours. I then decided to do the journey by bicycle, which proved to be much quicker than the bus. This was because, when I came to a road that was now impassable by bus, I could carry my bicycle through the rubble until it was possible to ride again.

The headquarters was situated very near to an Underground station where people, trying to find safe shelter from the bombing, could go and spend the night. Two or three nights a week some of the headquarters staff would take tea and whatever else could be obtained to the people seeking shelter and I was very happy to be included in this. I still remember seeing all the people sleeping on the platform, which they would have to leave by six o'clock the next morning because the trains would be running.

One morning I arrived at the Men's Social Work Headquarters to find that it had been bombed and now lay in ruins. As we stood looking at the smoking remains, and as I wondered about all the filing I had done (and that which I had not done), someone offered a prayer, we sang a verse of a cheerful song and then were sent home to await further instructions. Not long after this International Headquarters in Queen Victoria Street also lay in ruins.

My last move with my parents was to Tunbridge Wells, a lovely town in the heart of the Kentish countryside and away from the constant bombing of London. On arrival at the corps my brother Bram and I were told that the members of the band were expected to do what was called fire-watching at the hall in turn with other bandsmen.

Fire-watching duty meant staying at the hall all night to report any incendiary bomb activity that may have hit the hall. A snooker table was placed in the band room for entertainment during the long hours of the night, during which one was required to stay awake. The hall did not suffer from any enemy action. It seemed a strange occasion when, on the nearest Sunday to 11 November, we observed a two-minute silence for those who had lost their lives in the First World War. I was required to be the trumpeter who would sound Last Post and, two minutes later, Reveille – a forerunner to my future life! In the summertime, despite all the problems of the war, the band would hold late-night open-air meetings in the town and large crowds gathered for these occasions.

The town of Tunbridge Wells was well known for its auction rooms and these had a very strong attraction for my father. We were overjoyed when he came home and said that he had obtained a grand piano. When it arrived we thought we were in Heaven.

It was while we lived in Tunbridge Wells that my brother Bram joined the Royal Air Force and became a flying officer. Sadly, it was on 2 January 1944 that he was killed in operations over Germany. When the war was over I accompanied my mother to a British cemetery in Hamburg where we found his grave. My mother placed some flowers there with the quotation from the New Testament found in Romans 8:38 and 39: 'For I am persuaded, that neither death, nor life, nor angels, nor principalities, nor powers, nor things present, nor things to come, nor height, nor depth, nor any other creature, shall be able to separate us from the love of God, which is in Christ Jesus our Lord.'

I left Tunbridge Wells and went back to Southall to live with my sister Margaret and her husband William Barnett. Although the war was far from over, many of the Southall bandsmen had employment that prevented them from being called to military service. This meant that, at a time when so many corps bands were depleted, Southall Band still had a full complement, and more. I was very pleased when told I was to be the soprano cornet player. This was exciting news and I was now with a band that was able to play all of the *Festival Series* music that had been published before the war. (The series was suspended during the war.)

I was transferred to the solo cornet section and played a few solos with the band. I think the most popular solo was 'Maoriland' (a solo written by Henry Goffin, whose son Dean I was to know in years to come). The solo is mostly triple tonguing (producing three notes to every written one) and finishes with an exciting ending on a very high note. This solo appeared on every programme until I begged to change to an Erik Leidzén solo entitled 'Tucker'. This solo attracted me by the lovely harmony in the first presentation of the theme, the tune called 'Tucker'. This is the melody to which we sing, 'Thou Christ of burning, cleansing flame, send the fire' – for me, and many others, the only melody for these words!

Military Service

I was now almost old enough to volunteer for military service and went to the recruiting centre to do my part in ending the war! The recruiting sergeant thought I should join the Regiment of Guards and suggested that I would like being in The Life Guards – a regiment brought into being in 1660 to guard the life of the king or queen but now engaged in warfare on the battlefield. In peacetime the regiment is horse-mounted and seen on every formal occasion when royalty is present. When told all this, I signed a paper which meant that I would serve for seven years with the Colours and five years on the reserve. I felt a little more resolved about it when the recruiting sergeant expressed his thought that the war would last another seven years!

I soon made my way to Combermere Barracks in Windsor (one of the two barracks used by The Life Guards) to help in winning the war, but it wasn't many days before I began to wonder if I had done the right thing. A visit to the regimental barber was an unexpected occasion considering that, as he was running his electric clippers back and forward over my hair and forming a cross, he asked, 'How would you like it done?' I left the barber's with just signs of hair growing! The next thing that troubled me was the endless shouting by the sergeants (known in the cavalry as Corporal of Horse) and by almost everyone in the place! I understood that an order had to be clear, but did it need to be so loud?

One day, some weeks after my initial entry and while doing some parade drill, I heard a band playing in the distance. Following the order to 'Dismiss' I made inquiry as to the source of the music and was informed that it was the Life Guards Band in rehearsal. I wondered if this could be the way for me. I made an application to join the band once the recruits training was over and was quite surprised when I got the order to go for an audition.

Came the day when I went to the band room with my cornet only to be greeted by a corporal-major who asked me, 'Why is it still in the box?' A wink from an older man sitting at a desk made me understand it was best not to reply but just to get the cornet out of its case, ready to meet the Director of Music, Captain Albert Lemoine. Once in front of the director, I was asked, 'What are you going to play for me?' My reply, which was met with a completely puzzled look by all in the room, was, '"At The Cross Where I First Saw The Light".' 'At the what?' yelled the corporal-major. I repeated my answer, adding that it was a cornet solo written by a very prominent composer called Erik Leidzén from the United States of America. The stony silence which followed my announcement was broken with, 'Well, get on with it then!' which I did, now thinking of the words of the principal melody in the solo, 'At the cross, at the cross, where I first saw the light, and the burden of my heart rolled away' (*SASB* 395). There was another stony silence, which was a bit unnerving, but it was followed by words conveying I was accepted and an instruction to report to the band room the very next day. (The solo was later published with band accompaniment under the title 'Happy All The Day'.)

The first welcome change was that I no longer had to sleep in the barracks. This meant that I could now return to my sister Margaret's home in Southall and travel in daily to Windsor for rehearsal. This also meant that I could now resume my place in Southall Band when not on duty with the Life Guards Band.

Southall Corps had a very vibrant youth group called Torchbearers, which used to meet on Monday evenings at the citadel. It was on one such evening that I saw a girl with whom, at sight, I fell in love! A very quick inquiry from a friend told me that she was Jill Lister – the girl I remembered from the Sunbeams! It took a couple of weeks before I plucked up the courage to ask for a date and, when I did, was turned down with the request, 'Don't ask again!' Jill didn't wear uniform but did attend the Sunday night meetings. Fortunately for me, her mother had taken a shine to me and would, at the close of the meeting, keep Jill waiting until I had left the band room and was available for a chat. It was hard to get into conversation with Jill and she found all sorts of excuses to avoid a date with me.

I then discovered that she worked in an office for London Transport so, with the help of her mother, I obtained her telephone number. Jill was somewhat surprised to hear me on the telephone and told me that she would be in serious trouble if discovered accepting private calls. My reply was to the effect that if she would come out with me I would not phone her again at the office. After a short break she agreed to a visit to the cinema (not looked on in those days as a place a Salvationist should be!). I have to say that it wasn't a hand-holding occasion but she did agree to another cinema visit on the following week. This time, when I took her home, her mother appeared at the door and said, 'Bring him in for a cup of tea before he has to make the journey home.' That did the trick! Now I felt that she was my girlfriend. Jill joined the songsters at the corps and all went well for many months until we had a disagreement and stopped seeing each other.

The corps officer, Major Stephen Henderson, invited me to his house and, in conversation, said he was sorry that Jill and I had broken our friendship. I replied that I was more than sorry about it but didn't know how to repair the situation. He had a word of prayer with me and then asked if I would collect a certain road for the Self-Denial Appeal. I agreed that I would and, came the night to collect in the envelopes, saw that Jill was also there collecting Self-Denial envelopes! Major Henderson conducted our wedding on 11 September 1948 in Southall Citadel. The house in which we went to live was in a street next to the one we collected for the Self-Denial Appeal!

D-Day, 6 June 1944, was the day that allied troops landed in France to begin the liberation of Europe.

On 19 August 1944, orders came for the Life Guards Band to go to France and the first step was a move to a camp near Gosport. The following day the band boarded an American tank landing craft, with Ops Neptune painted on its bow, manned by British seamen. At 9 o'clock the craft was packed with tanks and lorries, the only passengers on board being the Life Guards Band. Six or seven hours later the craft moved a little way off Portsmouth, where it waited for the convoy to assemble and, by midnight, it moved off round the Isle of Wight.

Landing on Juno Beach at 6.45 pm on 23 August, the band's first task was to help with the loading of British casualties and wounded German prisoners on to the boat in which we had arrived. We were then transported to St-Aubin-sur-Mer (a rest camp for soldiers from the front). On Saturday 26 August the band moved to St-Germain-du-Crioult, only to find we were not expected and we had to sleep under the hedges with our greatcoats for bedding.

The following day instruments were unpacked, oiled and later played in a concert given at Condé for the Guards Armoured Division. Saturday 2 September was spent travelling to Flers and very rough accommodation in a very recently vacated German barracks. A brief period of comparative luxury was spent in the Three Merchants Hotel in Les Andelys. After playing for local civilians, the band provided music for an inspection parade of the Scots Guards followed by a long journey to give a concert the same evening for the Grenadier Guards.

One of the reasons for the band being in the war zone was to play concerts, as a goodwill gesture, in towns just liberated from the German occupation.

Although in the middle of a world war, time was still found for a football match between the Grenadiers and the French Army. The next day was spent entertaining at the local hospital and, the following evening, we played at a sports meeting. After the liberation of Brussels, which had been led by a troop of the Second Household Cavalry Regiment, the band played a part in the freedom celebrations.

One humorous incident concerned the Trumpet Major who, during his travels in France, had somehow acquired a leather-covered armchair. The chair became his great comfort when travelling, while the rest of us were seated on hard wooden seats in the back of the three-ton lorries. One day, in the absence of the Director of Music, the Trumpet Major had to ride in the cab with the driver so, seizing the opportunity to give vent to their feelings, some of the bandsmen threw the chair out of the lorry and into a river over which we were passing. Considering there was no comeback from the Trumpet Major, we all wondered how he had come by the chair in the first place!

Two or three days after arriving in the Belgian capital, the band gave a concert at the Royal Opera House in Brussels. Then, on 24 October, we left for similar duties in Holland.

Here, it was the Welsh Guards' turn to sample the music of The Life Guards on an inspection parade at their Divisional Headquarters. Not to be outdone, the Coldstream Guards held a similar parade the next day at the same venue. During the evening the band played for their own regiment very near the front line, which was 'rather noisy'. On Saturday 11 November, the main event was in the presence of Her Majesty Queen Mary, the then Queen Mother.

On Friday 17 November we were on the road bound for Asch, Belgium, with a corporal-major detailed as navigator. Captain Lemoine (Music Director) insisted that he was in charge and would therefore navigate. Some hours later the musicians were asking why all the road and shop signs were in German. When the driver heard this, the Life Guards Band's tour of Germany came to a very speedy end as we headed back to Belgium as fast as possible!

On arrival in Brunssum we were billeted with civilians who, having no choice in the matter, were only required to provide bare accommodation. My billet, along with Corporal Jimmy Buck, was an uncovered stone-floor kitchen. There was nothing to eat and the toilet facilities were down the garden. Six days were spent under these conditions, which also included eating in a café two miles away, playing in a cinema six miles away and having a bath down a coal mine!

One date easily remembered was 15 December when the dance band played for the US Air Force on the night Glenn Miller's plane went missing over the English Channel. A concert on 19 December was cancelled five minutes before starting time when the regiment, as part of the Guards Armoured Division, was ordered up to assist the Americans at the Battle of the Bulge. The band returned to England on 9 March 1945.

While on the tour it was always a great joy to meet liberated Salvationists who now were able to wear their uniforms (something that had been forbidden during the years of occupation).

Peacetime

The Life Guards Band returned to Paris in August 1945 for the liberation celebrations, and I have a picture of the band marching down the Champs Élysées, celebrating the end of the war.

Celebrations were also held in England, the first one on a Sunday known as VE Day (Victory in Europe) with a thanksgiving service in St Paul's Cathedral. As one of four State Trumpeters, I had been sent to a place where all the state dress clothing had been kept during the war and fitted with a gold knee-length tunic, a black jockey-style hat, white leather riding pants and thigh-length black riding boots. Then, with three other trumpeters, I stood on the steps of St Paul's to sound fanfares for special guests.

The fanfares were reserved for the British Royal Family, Heads of State and royalty from other European countries. The then Prime

Minister, Winston Churchill, among deafening cheers from the massive crowd gathered around the cathedral, received a fanfare and, after waving to the crowd, made his way up the steps. Seeing me in the state uniform (which had not been seen since the declaration of war), he said, 'Well, trumpeter, the gold has kept well!' He then continued on his way to the service of thanksgiving inside the cathedral.

Some time later we were called back to St Paul's, this time to celebrate the victory in Japan, which is known as VJ Day. It was decided that there should be eight trumpeters to sound the notes of victory and the Trumpet Major should be there to conduct the fanfares. The powers that be did not want the conductor to be seen by the waiting crowd so it was decided that he would stand inside the railings around the statue of Queen Anne (situated at the bottom of the St Paul's steps) to do the conducting. All went well at the rehearsal with the Trumpet Major behind the railings but, on arrival on the Sunday morning of the thanksgiving service, we discovered that the small gate in the railings was locked!

Representation was made to the caretaker of the cathedral who knew nothing about a key to the offending gate, which resulted in us having to lift the Trumpet Major over the sharp, pointed railings. All went well with the welcoming fanfares but getting the Trumpet Major back over the spiked railings at the end of the service was impossible! Our transport arrived and we had to leave him looking very cross and having to wait for someone with a key to set him at liberty. The next day we thought it best to keep out of his way!

Among other state occasions to which I was assigned as a trumpeter were the official opening of the first Olympic Games since before the war by His Majesty King George VI at the Wembley Stadium in 1948 and the announcement of the first Secretary-General of the United Nations, Trygve Lie, at the Mansion House in London (in 1946).

Another trumpeter and myself were selected to play a fanfare for Queen Mary (the present Queen's grandmother and wife of King George V) when she came to open a Garden of Remembrance in Piccadilly, London. A large crowd had gathered and several minutes before the Queen arrived we, in state dress, took our places either side of the entrance to the garden, which meant that she would walk between us as we sounded a royal salute. It was then that I realised I was without my white gloves! What to do now? Film cameras were everywhere and this event would be on the front of tomorrow's newspapers! A young lady standing near to me was wearing very fancy white lace gloves and, at my urgent request, gave them to me to wear. By pulling my sleeve down as far as possible, little of the gloves could be seen and the next day's newspapers showed no sign of incorrect dress. Phew!

Following the end of the war, news concerned the return of the horses to The Horse Guards and Life Guards Regiments and the first to ride would be the Trumpeters. Word came that we were to report to the riding school for training, where we were introduced to the horses chosen for our training. The horse chosen for me was called Pegasus and was the largest horse I had ever seen! The first requirement was to secure a saddle on the horse. This seemed an impossible task seeing that the straps which went under the horse appeared to be far too short. The instructor inquired as to the problem and, following my complaint about the shortness of the straps, took them in his hands and with a quick movement of his knee against the horse's belly (causing the horse to take a sudden breath) secured the straps that held the saddle in place. His parting words were, 'Use your head!' I was about to reply that it was your knee you needed and not your head, but thought better of it!

It seemed to me to be a good idea to make friends with Pegasus by giving him something sweet but confectionery was not available during the war or the following months. Discovering that a form of liquorice could be obtained from a chemist shop, I bought a packet to seal a friendship with my horse. On arrival at the riding school I saw a large notice saying 'Feeding of horses is strictly forbidden', which meant that my horse should not have the liquorice that I had bought for him. Wanting Pegasus to be my friend, I decided to ignore the instruction and gave him the liquorice, which he was very pleased to receive. Having saddled up, we were required to lead the horses to the parade ground for inspection. As I stood beside Pegasus waiting for the inspecting officer, I noticed long dribbles of liquorice coming from the horse's mouth! Now what to do? With a very speedy action, I took out my handkerchief and wiped his nose and mouth just in time to get past the inspection!

The riding part seemed to go all right until the morning when some repairmen were working on the riding school roof. Just as I was riding past, one of them lit a gas lamp which made a loud hissing sound, causing my horse to make a run for it. For that morning's instruction we were without reins, which left me at the mercy of the horse who, with me clutching his mane, went straight out of the door and into the sports field. I held on for dear life as he circled a couple of times before I was thrown off. The final insult came when he placed his hoof on my shoulder just to let me know who was in charge!

A few days later I learned that it was now possible to purchase a discharge from The Life Guards so I paid the money and was then told that I must hand in all clothing belonging to The Life Guards, including underwear, socks and boots. My pleading to at least keep the underwear did not help one bit, but I was told that I could keep it until the next day. This meant I would have to come all the way back to Windsor, which I didn't want to do. They handed me my civilian blue suit, which no longer fitted me, and a pair of old shoes (that had been at the barracks with the suit since I first joined). Having handed everything in, I made my way out of the barracks wearing just the blue suit (which I could no longer button up) and the old shoes. As I got on to the train (without shirt or socks) I was aware of the other passengers who were wondering how a tramp got the money for the journey. I then had to walk a mile to my home. Was I pleased to arrive!

Early Days

Captain Albert Bearcroft and Mrs Alma Bearcroft (Norman's parents)

Norman as a child collecting for the Self-Denial Appeal

The Bearcroft family: (back row) Nancy and Margaret; (front row) Alma with Norman, Bram and Albert

Peacetime

Norman as a State
Trumpeter returning to
barracks following the
VE Day Thanksgiving
Service at St Paul's

Opening Ceremony of the first Olympic Games at Wembley following the
Second World War (1948)

The International Training College

The band of the Ambassadors Session of cadets (1950)

Corps Officers

Alderney Band on the march, with 'Colonel' Gavine carrying the flag (1951)

Corps Officers

Norman and Jill as corps officers at Waltham Abbey with sons Bram and Norrie

Bram, Norrie and Mark

Chapter 2

THE CALL OF CHRIST

The International Training College

I left The Life Guards in 1948 when both Jill and I received the call to become officers in The Salvation Army. Jill had no problems with this but, for me, it meant giving up what I had hoped would become a professional career in music. I knew a lot of musicians from my military days and I very much wanted to be in a symphony orchestra, which then, to me, would be the climax of my ambition.

In Southall Corps, the officer would often choose a song written by Sidney Cox, the chorus of which was as follows:

Follow thou me, he calls again,
And I will make you fishers of men;
As in the days by Galilee,
Jesus is calling you and me.

It was the 'me' in the last line that I found to be a constant problem. The 'you' was fine, but the 'me'? There was no getting away from it, because the call was certainly for me! Following some interviews with a very understanding (and godly) candidates secretary, we packed up our little home and made for the International Training College at Denmark Hill, London, to join the Ambassadors Session (1950-1951).

Now, strange though it may seem considering my career in The Life Guards as a State Trumpeter, our sessional song (words by Catherine Baird and music by Bramwell Coles) began with the words:

Sound the trumpet!
Wake the nations!
Men have turned their hearts from God.
See, they faint, truth refusing,
Shunning light, blindness choosing.
Sound the trumpet!
And speed the warning now!

Seeing that Jill and I were cadets from a London corps, we were recruited to be at the front entrance of the college to welcome the cadets who had travelled long distances, help them with their luggage and show them to their rooms. One such person was Cadet Eva Burrows from Australia, who had been a delegate at the International Youth Congress a few weeks before and who was a member of the sparkling Australian Timbrel Group which had made such an impression with its presentations. (Timbrel groups the world over have copied the colourful drills it displayed.)

The noticeboard, which we were required to consult several times every day, stated that there would be auditions held in the band room for men (no women) who could play a brass instrument and to report to Captain Albert Drury, bandmaster of the Cadets Band. I duly arrived for an audition given by the captain, who then said, 'I am very sorry, but I have had word to say that you will not be in the band' (adding that someone else would tell me the reasons why!).

The next day, I was told to report to the Training Principal, Commissioner John Bladin, for a personal interview. The commissioner greeted me and ordered me to a seat at a table opposite him. He began by telling me, 'Forget all about music!' Then, in a more determined voice, he repeated, 'Forget *all* about music!' He went on to say that my candidate's papers had revealed that my life up until now had been all about music and now it was time for change! I plucked up the courage to say that most of my music-making had been in the service of The Salvation Army, but this got no response.

He went on to say that he thought I needed to be humbled and that I would discover what that meant in a few days' time. He then took my hand across the table and began to pray for me. I was a little uncomfortable holding the commissioner's hand for so long and opened my eyes for a quick look, only to see that he had his eyes open and was looking at me! He then warmly shook my hand and said he expected to see a real change in me. As I left his office wondering about what my 'needing to be humbled' was all about, his secretary told me to report back to Captain Drury.

Captain Drury greeted me, apologising that he had to give me the news that I would not be playing in the band but, instead, would be carrying the lamp for the band on the weekly half-mile marches to and from Camberwell Citadel. The marches started in a couple of weeks and I found myself in the middle of the band, holding the much-needed lamp on a long pole. Knowing the marches the band would play, I tried to hold the lamp nearer to the most important parts but then, realising the power I was wielding, would move away from the most important parts on the pretext of helping the lesser ones!

My period of carrying the lamp came to a halt when I tried to emulate Cadet Bramwell Moore who, being the Sessional Flag Bearer, would give a very wide, impressive swing with the flag when coming to a corner. Alas, the movement caused a draught under the glass covering and blew out the light. The light going out did not stop the gas (with which the lamp was powered) from flowing freely – the result being black smoke over the marching cadets! The next week I was on song book duty at the entrance to Camberwell Citadel! A few weeks later I was appointed to the band.

Commissioner Bladin had been in meetings when the International Staff Band was on duty and noticed that the bandmaster, Major Bernard Adams, conducted the bandsmen as (without music books) they played their instruments to accompany the choruses in the prayer meeting. In an interview, he told Captain Drury that he wanted the Cadets Band to do the same. Captain Drury explained to the commissioner that what the Staff Band could do was not always what the Cadets Band could do. Undaunted, the commissioner insisted on his request and, having a great sense of musical pitch, would turn to the Cadets Band naming the chorus to be used and adding in which key the band should be playing.

Very few of the bandsmen could play without music copies and, although the commissioner's instruction about the key was all right for the B flat instrument players, some of the E flat-pitched instrumentalists (not understanding the theory of transposition) did not fare so well. It was a particular problem for the bass section and Cadet Leslie Condon, though he was the bass trombone player, had to play the E flat bass for the prayer choruses. This he did with one hand, while attempting to show the fingering for the B flat basses with the other. The trouble was that Leslie needed to think ahead with his B flat hand while playing an E flat bass with his other hand – it was almost impossible. His frustration with the B flat bass players tested his patience and willingness to a very high degree. It certainly did not put him in the mood to be blessed by the choruses!

Being the only cornet player who could manage to play the tunes without the music, I was a bit surprised one night when the commissioner turned to me and said, 'Put your cornet down and go fishing!' (help the undecided in the congregation to get saved). Even as I put my cornet on the floor, Captain Drury (who was trying to hold the music-less band together) said in a very commanding voice, 'Pick it up and play!' Obeying the last command, I did so but, a few moments later, the commissioner said to me, 'I thought you were told to put down your cornet and go fishing!' Again, as I was putting my cornet on the floor, I heard the bandmaster's voice saying, 'Pick it up, pick it up and play!' At the close of the meeting the commissioner and Captain Drury were having a few warm words together! The playing of the band for the prayer choruses without copies of the music became a thing of the past!

Along with a large number of women cadets, Jill had been taking lessons from Cadet Eva Burrows, who as mentioned earlier was proficient in the Australian method of timbrel playing. Twenty or thirty of them would prove their recently gained dexterity as they marched behind the band to and from, and occasionally in, the Thursday night holiness meeting at Camberwell Citadel. A favourite march for the timbrel players was Erik Leidzén's 'In The King's Service'.

A never-to-be-forgotten day was the one known as Personal Initiative Day. This was a day when you could show your initiative in doing something special to attract people's attention to the work of The Salvation Army and, in so doing, it would help to get rid of any shyness you may have. Some cadets showed a remarkable facility in getting ideas about what to do and how to go about doing it! One cadet decided to run, with another cadet dressed as the devil chasing him! Another decided to climb half a dozen lampposts in the busiest streets in Camberwell and give his testimony. All sorts of ideas were floating around but none seemed to suit me.

Cadet Chris Jorgensen from Denmark, knowing that I was without any ideas, said that he had a great idea but it was an idea that needed two persons to make it work. He went on to say that we should go up to the centre of London, with me in uniform and him in civilian clothing, then get on a bus going to Marble Arch. Here we were to climb to the upper deck where I was to go to the front of the bus and he would stay at the back. He then said that he would shout some questions to me from the back of the bus and would expect me to answer from the front, adding, 'This way, everybody sees and hears us.' To my, 'Well, I'm not sure', answer he enquired if I had a better idea. He already knew I had no answer and so together we made our way to the bus stop.

Knowing that I was less than thrilled at the idea, he kept saying, 'Don't worry, it will be great!' (I was far from sure!) When the bus came we got on board and climbed the stairs to the upper deck, which in those days was a smoking area. Chris found a seat right at the back and I found one right at the front amid the density of the smoke. I sat there hoping against hope that he would change his mind when, suddenly, I heard loud and clear, 'Hey there, Salvation Army!' My nerve wasn't at its best so I just kept looking out of the front window as if nothing had happened. A couple of minutes later, in an even louder voice, there came, 'Hey there, Salvation Army!' Now, in those days, buses had an attendant called the bus conductor, whose job it was to tell you the cost of your journey and give you a ticket for the same. Addressing me, he said, 'Is that man annoying you?' After a short pause, ashamed as I now am to confess it, I said, 'Yes he is' – at which point the conductor stopped the bus and threw him off! As I looked out of the window I could see Chris shaking his head at me! It was rather difficult to fill in the report sheet on arrival back at the training college. Strangely enough, Chris became my best friend!

Spiritual Days were high points in the training college. They were sometimes led by the Training Principal and, at other times, by special guests. I well remember the one led by General Albert Orsborn, then the active leader of The Salvation Army throughout the world. His very appearance was impressive and his voice, especially when he quoted one of his wonderful songs, was an inspiration. It was hard for us beginners to understand how he could write words that would immediately strike home, bringing us to a realisation of our true need if we were to become the effective officers of the future. Even now I can remember his voice as he quoted his song:

> My life must be Christ's broken bread,
> My love his outpoured wine,
> A cup o'erfilled, a table spread
> Beneath his name and sign,
> That other souls, refreshed and fed,
> May share his life through mine.
>
> My all is in the Master's hands
> For him to bless and break;
> Beyond the brook his winepress stands
> And thence my way I take,
> Resolved the whole of love's demands
> To give, for his dear sake.
>
> Lord, let me share that grace of thine
> Wherewith thou didst sustain
> The burden of the fruitful vine,
> The gift of buried grain.
> Who dies with thee, O Word divine,
> Shall rise and live again.

What better challenge could come to a cadet than this? I wanted so much to have this happen in my life.

The concertina (a smaller version of the piano accordion) was a very prominent musical instrument in my early days in the Army and most officers had one. Colonel Arthur Knapman, Chief Side Officer for Men at the training college (a wonderful man, much-loved by the men cadets), thought it would be good for the cadets to be able to play the concertina so, in one of his classes, he introduced us to the great value of this instrument. He straightway confessed to his being only able to play in three keys but then added, 'Most songs can be managed in these three keys.' He then revealed to us that one side of the instrument was the 'treble side' and the other the 'bass side'. He went on to explain that holding down three selected keys on the treble side would give a nice sound and that by pressing one key on the left side (which would give the bass note) a satisfactory chord would be produced.

He then began to sing an Army chorus and, halfway through, added some chords on the concertina. As he finished the chorus he waited for some response, which resulted in loud cheers and hand-clapping! His next move was to ask for the name of a chorus, which brought a swift suggestion of 'Climb, Climb Up Sunshine Mountain'.

'Right!' he said, 'I think that will be in the key of... er... C, so I will need the following three chords.' He then added the notes of C, E and G (which he quickly found with his right hand) and a C from the bass hand. 'Next you need the chord of G, this time adding the notes B and D and a G from the bass hand, then the third chord which,' he added, 'you can sometimes do without, but it is better if it is available and it is the chord of F (F, A, C) with an F from the bass hand.'

Having played all three chords, he then started to sing, with the chord of C, 'Climb, climb up sunshine mountain, heavenly breezes' – then explained that the next word, 'blow', would need the chord of G. He continued singing, now in G, 'Climb, climb up sunshine mountain, faces all a' – now saying, '"Glow" will need to be back in C.' He then started the second half of the chorus – 'Turn, turn your

27

back on doubting, looking to the' – another stop and a change to F for 'sky', in which chord he remained while he sang, 'Climb, climb up' – now back to C for 'Sunshine mountain', back to 'G' for 'You and', then C for the last word, 'I'. He then added, 'There's really nothing to it!' The London Symphony Orchestra never got a better reception!

It was on another occasion when Colonel Knapman, having asked all the men to sit quietly and think about things, suddenly heard the women cadets singing from their room. He then said, in a soft reverent tone of voice, 'My, the hens are clucking well tonight, lads!'

Cadets were assigned in brigades numbering about 20, with an officer to whom one was responsible. Captain Gordon Cox, the officer of the brigade to which I was assigned, was a very gifted and seemingly fearless man who would set tasks that we cadets thought impossible, always adding the words, 'Nothing is impossible with God!' You could be sent into a Woolworth's store in the high street to 'give your testimony' or left on your own to 'sing a verse of a song in the marketplace'. The captain had such a way with him that one would always try to accept the challenge. I must confess to one occasion when, on entering one very large Woolworth's store to give my testimony, I lost my nerve and simply bought a tube of toothpaste! The following interview was not an easy one as he kept saying, 'Courage is what you need – "Courage, brother, do not stumble!"' I had the greatest admiration for the man!

A party of us were with Captain Cox for a weekend in Winchester where, on the Saturday night, the drummer, seeing that there was no bandmaster, insisted on playing the drum in his own time. After the second verse, Captain Cox asked for an increase in tempo. The drummer ignored the request and the captain asked again for more speed. There was still no change until the final chorus, which the drummer took at such a speed it was impossible to sing the words. Then, before the captain could offer any further requests, he was immediately on his knees ready for the prayer. Following the close of the meeting, Captain Cox was seen shaking hands with the drummer and thanking him for coming to the meeting. On the Sunday morning, the drummer kept his eyes firmly fixed on Captain Cox and at one point even asked if he was playing at the desired speed. We then realised that the kindly word to the drummer was much better than any words of complaint.

When we had completed a few weeks of special training in children's work, Captain Geoffrey Dalziel unexpectedly appeared in a Joy Hour (meeting for children) that I was leading. The children were very noisy and paying little or no attention to me. At the disastrous close of the meeting, and knowing I had already had completed my young people's training, he said, 'When are you having *your* young people's training?'

Near the end of our time at the training college I was asked if I would write a song to be sung by the cadets at their commissioning in the Royal Albert Hall in London. I had, previously, been sent some words from a lady with a request that I write some music to them and which, to me, now seemed perfect for this occasion. I wrote some music to these words with the hope that the song would prove to be what was required and handed it to Colonel Gordon Mitchell, from whom the request had come.

In an interview later that day, the colonel said that they liked the music, but 'someone on the building' should write the words. He then said that he would copy the music and place it on the noticeboard, so that anyone in the college – cadets, officers, secretaries or workmen – could submit words to this given melody. To my surprise, a couple of hundred sets of words were submitted by cadets, secretaries, workmen and officers! The ones written by Captain Gordon Cox (of the above Woolworth's fame) were accepted (and sung) by the newly commissioned officers. The song, entitled 'At Thy Throne', was eventually published in the September 1952 edition of *The Musical Salvationist*, the second verse and chorus being:

> Gladly, my Lord, at thy throne I am offering
> All I possess; claim and cleanse and refine,
> Take thou my life, whether joy, whether suffering;
> Transcending glory, all Heaven is mine.

29

Come, Holy Spirit, on this hallowed day,
Strengthen my weakness, illumine my way;
Help me to honour thee in all I say,
Let every deed reflect thy holy sway.
Here as I covenant always to be
Thy true ambassador, sanctify me;
Use thou my life to win men back to thee;
This my ambition, and this my one plea.

Jill and I were commissioned as 2nd lieutenants and appointed to Alderney Corps in the Southampton and Channel Isles Division. The only way to get there by public transport was to go by airplane. This became the first of the many plane journeys I have made in the succeeding years as an officer of The Salvation Army.

Chapter 3

SHOUT ALOUD SALVATION!

Corps Officers

Alderney (our first appointment) is a small island in a group known as
the Channel Islands. The island is about three miles long and about a
mile wide and we wondered, as our seven-seater aircraft approached, if
there would be enough room to land. As it was, the aircraft headed
straight for the side of the cliff and Heaven-sent air pressure lifted the
craft on to the airstrip.

Alderney's inhabitants had been evacuated before the island was
taken over by the German forces in the Second World War. All
furniture and belongings were moved around by the occupying forces
and, following the liberation, all such goods were placed on a field and,
at the sound of a pistol shot, the returning inhabitants had to run and
claim what was theirs. One man (the corps drummer) got inside a
wardrobe to make sure he kept it, only to discover that he was being
carried to a house that was not his own!

On our arrival we discovered that the corps had about 30 soldiers,
which included a band of 14 players. The lady who met us at the airport
expressed her hope that we would not have any children while we were
in Alderney, which would 'allow the wife' to be fully engaged in the
work of the corps! In fact our first child – a son – was born, not actually
on Alderney, where the medical resources were very limited, but back
in England. This left me on my own for some time in a house that was
reputed to be haunted. I cannot vouch for this but I do know that, in
Jill's absence, my cat – sleeping at the bottom of my bed – suddenly, in
the middle of one night, arched his back and spat at something!

It was on a Sunday evening, as I was about to enter the hall, when
I got a telephone message with the news that I was now the father of

a baby boy called Bramwell (named after my brother Bramwell who was killed in the war). To say there was new life in the meeting is to put it mildly!

An open-air meeting was held every Saturday evening and always attracted a crowd of people. One man, known as Colonel Gavine – who was usually the worse for drink – always came to the Saturday night open-air meeting and most weeks would seek me out and promise to be at the meeting on Sunday. I learned that he was a ship's pilot, and was always being sought to bring vessels into the difficult entrance to the Alderney harbour. Came another Saturday evening open-air meeting and the Colonel, as everyone on the island knew him, assured me once again that he would be at the meeting on Sunday evening. To my surprise (O ye of little faith) he did arrive at the meeting and, coming straight to the mercy seat, was wonderfully saved! The next Saturday he was back in the public houses, but this time wearing an Army cap and selling *The War Cry* (the Army's weekly paper). He always made sure that his papers were sold in time for him to march back to the hall with the band and he always marched beside me. He kept saved and was a wonderful witness to Jesus and his keeping power. The Colonel died some years after we had left the corps, but a friend sent me the epitaph on his gravestone. It was, 'He sailed straight to Heaven.'

During the war, the German troops had used the Salvation Army hall as an ammunition storage centre with hundreds of cannon shells being placed upright all over the floor. Following the liberation, it was found that the round marks made by cannon shells standing on end completely covered the floor. This was an unacceptable situation in the House of the Lord and so the ladies of the corps worked week after week in an effort to obliterate the offending marks. We had a special thanksgiving meeting to celebrate the success of their splendid effort.

Bandsmen will know that Dean Goffin wrote a march called 'Alderney' as a reminder of his visit to the faithful soldiers of that corps. Incidentally, Alderney Band had a very fine trombone player for whom I wrote a solo called 'Harbour Light', which, in later years, I revised as a euphonium solo with the same name.

The first of our other two corps appointments in the Southampton and Channel Isles Division was Fordingbridge. It was at Fordingbridge that we were able to work with the gypsy children in the beautiful New Forest. A lady who was closely related to Cecil Frances Alexander (the writer of many hymns including 'There Is A Green Hill' and 'All Things Bright And Beautiful') opened her immaculate home for The Salvation Army to come and teach these children about Jesus and his love for them. They were beautiful children and very responsive to our teaching.

The corps had a tuneful band which was always ready for any demands made upon it and a songster brigade whose contributions to the meeting always proved to be a blessing. Both sections could be seen in the Saturday night open-air meeting, always drawing a crowd of interested listeners.

Gosport, a naval town just across the harbour from the city of Portsmouth, is where the Lord blessed us with a time of real revival. I found the band, songsters and soldiers of the corps ready and willing for some real, vigorous outreach. We made an attack on the public houses with the Salvationists going into these and actually bringing people out and into the Salvation Army hall, where a salvation meeting would be in progress. Many came to the mercy seat and some joined the corps. At the next attack, it was very encouraging to see those who had been converted during the first raid taking part in this one.

The Gosport bandmaster, James Findley, was not only a good bandmaster, but he was also a good concertina player. This proved most useful in our street meetings as well as in leading some singing between the playing of the band on the way back to the hall.

It was while I was looking at the nearby Bridgemary estate with the thought of commencing a Sunday school that a lady, standing at her gate and seeing my Salvation Army uniform, asked me if I was looking for her husband. I asked what her name was, to which she replied, 'I'm Mrs Lewis.' I quickly checked my visitation book but the name Lewis was not there. Not wanting her to know this, I said, 'Oh yes, and will your husband be home soon?' In the ensuing conversation she told me that her husband, Dennis, used to go to the Army Sunday school and that his mother had been a regular attender at the meetings. When she said, 'I am sure he would like to meet you,' the seed had been sown. Both Dennis and Betty started attending the meetings and got soundly saved.

Dennis, who had been a dance band leader and a saxophone player in the Marines Band, proved to be a very good musician and, before very long, was made the songster leader of Gosport Corps. Three years later Dennis and Betty entered the International Training College and became officers. And yes, we did start a Sunday school in Bridgemary.

The Divisional Commander, Colonel George Badley, informed me that Gosport had been chosen by the training college as the venue for a ten-day campaign and that the officer leading this would be Captain Gordon Cox! Needless to say, the captain was not expecting me to be just an onlooker. This kind of salvation warfare became the norm for the two years we were at Gosport.

Another reason for remembering Gosport is that our second son, Norman (Norrie), was born during our stay in this remarkable town. In those days it was usual for a mother to give birth in her own home and the appointed midwife had given me instructions about what to do when the birth was imminent – this just meant calling her in good time. In those days we had no telephone, which meant that I had to get on my bicycle and ride to her house with the news. When getting the bicycle out of the shed at one o'clock in the morning, I woke all the dogs in the neighbourhood, which, in turn, awakened their sleeping owners! The midwife seemed not to be in a hurry and just told me to go home and get some water boiling and that she would follow in a while. Was I glad to see her when she arrived!

My two-year-old son Bram was awakened by her arrival and, having been told that he could not go up to his mother, started rushing about with a little wooden horse (which had come in some jumble) and making as much noise as he could! A couple of hours later he was looking at his new baby brother and trying to introduce him to his wooden horse.

Most corps in the Southampton and Channel Isles Division were invited, in turn, to be responsible for the weekly Thursday evening holiness meeting that was held at the Boscombe Corps hall. A note from the divisional commander informed me of the date Gosport Corps would be leading the meeting. On the given date, we – the band, songsters, supporting soldiers and I – made our way to Boscombe in very high spirits. Just before the meeting started, General Albert Orsborn appeared at the door and made his way to the platform. My first feeling was that we had come on the wrong evening and I was about to apologise to my people when the General himself greeted us and said he was looking forward to us leading a good, wholesome holiness meeting. Well, we did our best, and the many hallelujahs and loud amens that escaped from the General's lips gave us great encouragement.

When the appeal was given for anyone present to seek and find the blessing of holiness, the General left the platform and made his way to the back of the hall where a man was sitting close to the wall. The General beckoned the man to come forward but the man shook his head so the General would know that he was not going to move. This all happened a second time, with the same response from the man, whereupon the General pushed his way past the row of people, took hold of the man and brought him to the mercy seat. Some few minutes later the man was up on his feet thanking God, and the General for his action.

One Christmas, while we were still at Gosport (and our own personal funds were very low), Jill suggested that we should take Bram's wooden horse and give it a coat of paint and add a mane and proper tail so that he, not recognising it, would think he was getting a new horse. This we did, using the fur from an old coat that we found in a jumble sale. On Christmas morning Bram saw his new wooden horse. With a puzzled look he observed the horse but was not sure what to think. An hour later he returned to the mystery of the horse and started to pull the fur off. When all the fur was gone, he looked again at the horse and with truth dawning on him he exclaimed, 'Ah, gee-gee. It's my dear old gee-gee!' The first person to ride it was his brother Norrie. Never was a Christmas present so precious!

Our next appointment, to Camberwell Citadel in south London, was a complete surprise. As stated earlier, Camberwell was the central training corps for officer cadets and our only contact with the corps was when we had been cadets ourselves. I knew that every Thursday evening there would be a full hall for the central holiness meeting, led by the college staff and cadets, with the songs being accompanied by a 25-piece band and with some great singing from the united cadets. A letter from Commissioner Frederick Coutts (then the Training Principal) containing my appointment to Camberwell did not say what to expect when the cadets were not present.

The following is the story of my first open-air meeting as the corps officer of Camberwell Citadel. Ronald Thomlinson also recorded the account in his book about General Frederick Coutts, *A Very Private General*.

Now appointed to Camberwell and not knowing quite what to expect, I arrived at the appointed place for the Sunday morning open-air meeting to find just three people standing there. They were Commissioner Coutts, the corps sergeant-major (wearing a red tunic) and the colour-sergeant, holding the flag. As I was looking round to see if a band or other comrades were on the way, the commissioner inquired, 'Are we going to make a start, lieutenant?' I was a bit taken aback by this but was able to say, 'Yes, commissioner, right away.' I quickly found a song, which I asked the commissioner to lead, following which I asked, 'Is there someone who would lead us in prayer?' Following a moment's silence, the commissioner prayed. I then thought it time that the sergeant-major should take part so, looking directly at him, asked if anyone would like to testify. This was apparently something which neither the sergeant-major nor the colour-sergeant were about to do. So, once more, the commissioner stepped forward to give a testimony and, as he was doing so, would occasionally stoop to pick up a few coins which had been thrown from the windows of the nearby houses. Then, after adding an invitation to attend the indoor meetings, the commissioner turned to me and said, 'Shall I close in prayer?'

The open-air meeting over, the problem was how to get back to the hall. Seeing my puzzled expression, the commissioner again took the initiative, 'We are going to march, aren't we, lieutenant?' 'Oh yes, certainly,' I replied, in a not too convincing manner. The corps sergeant-major, who had been very silent up to this point, suddenly took command and, looking at us as if he were counting how many we were, said, 'We'll march in – er – threes and I'll direct the traffic!' So, with the commissioner at one side of the colour-sergeant and me on the other, we began marching down the street and out into a very busy London road on which the traffic had been brought to a complete halt by the corps sergeant-major. I wondered what else could happen, when to my utter amazement the commissioner then started to sing, in two parts, 'If the cross (if the cross) we boldly bear (we boldly bear), then a crown (then a crown) we shall wear (we shall wear).' On arrival at the hall, the commissioner said to me, 'You won't forget this morning, will you?'

Commissioner Coutts (as he then was) would always be at Camberwell Corps on any Sunday when he was not engaged with training work. His willingness to play the small portable pedal-driven Triumph De Luxe organ proved very helpful seeing that there wasn't a band at the corps. He used to sit behind us on the platform at the little organ ready (and able!) to accompany any song or chorus, without music if necessary. The platform had a shiny surface and I noticed that when the commissioner was pedalling the organ it would tend to shift in a forward movement, so that he had to keep adjusting his chair. One Sunday, following a lot of singing, the commissioner was found to be halfway across the platform! At the close of the meeting he said to me, 'Now you know what the term "a travelling commissioner" means!'

The Camberwell hall was too large for our corps meetings so a series of high screens were placed about halfway back, which made our congregation more comfortable, but a certain group of ladies would always sit behind the screens with their knitting needles in full operation! Colonel Albert Mingay, the Chief Side Officer at the training college, was always a great support and would bring his euphonium to the open-air meetings, which meant, with me being the cornet player, the size of the band was doubled. Mrs Colonel Mingay became the home league secretary and worked very hard for the goodly number of ladies who attended on Tuesday afternoons. Our appointment to Camberwell also gave us the great privilege of attending the training college for the cadets' Spiritual Days, under the leadership of Commissioner Coutts – an experience never to be forgotten!

Our next appointment was to Waltham Abbey, so called because there was a lovely, quite ancient abbey in the town – a quiet place bordering on the beautiful Epping Forest in Essex. The corps had a fine band led by Bandmaster William Jackson and a very musical songster brigade. The corps folk were a little surprised at my suggesting a public-house raid in this quiet town but they all accepted the challenge and went out to bring the people in.

The corps had a very nice suite of buildings but, as was usual in those days, had no central heating. The sergeant-major's comment was, 'If we have the fire in our hearts we won't need central heating in the hall!' As an officer, I had to agree but it did mean that I would have to light the large coal stove in good time to get the hall warm in the winter. I decided that an early Sunday morning prayer meeting (called knee-drill in the Army) would be the order of the day, at which time the fire could be lit in the stove as well as in the hearts of those who were in attendance! Not only was the hall warm for the meetings, but the attendance at knee-drill was much improved!

Then followed an appointment to the coal-mining town of Maltby in the South Yorkshire Division, with a very active band and songster brigade who would lead open-air meetings on a Saturday evening and give great support to all the corps activities. One very interesting aspect here was that, every month, a coal truck would appear at our quarters and deposit a half-ton of freshly mined coal on the road outside our front door! I was told that, for many years, the coal company had provided this very welcome gift to the local Salvation Army captain. So, once a month, the coal came and I would have to remove the coal from the street to the shed at the back of the house. It was the nearest thing I ever did to being a coal miner!

Maltby is not too far from the city of Sheffield where, in those days, Wilfred Heaton (a name now famous to brass bandsmen throughout the world) had a brass instrument repair shop. It was my very real pleasure to meet him when I took one of the Maltby Band's instruments in for repair.

A year later, in 1959, we were back in London and appointed to Twickenham Corps, where our third son, Mark, was born. The corps had an excellent songster brigade, which, more often than not, I asked to sing more than once in a meeting. Among some very gifted musicians at this corps were Retired Bandmaster George Crane (who had band and vocal music published by the Army) and, later, Retired Bandmaster Stan Raikes, who wrote the much-loved march 'Cairo Red Shield', which had the refrain, 'Salvation Army, Army of God, onward to conquer the world with fire and blood.' (Stan wrote this march when he was serving in His Majesty's Forces and was stationed in Cairo, where he formed a band for Salvationists in the same circumstances.) This piece was always so suitable for a Sunday morning march from the open-air meeting to the hall.

It was while we were at Twickenham that Brian Bowen, son of my sister Nancy, would bring me his early manuscripts to look over and Jill would bring us a cup of tea if she sensed that we were not in agreement.

For a one-week corps outreach campaign we had a number of guest speakers, including Lieutenant Dennis Lewis (a convert from the Gosport days), Captain Ray Steadman-Allen, Captain Dean Goffin and Captain Brindley Boon. Each came on a different night to help with the campaign, which was an inspiration for the soldiers of the corps. The hall itself was quite new and considered modern at that time.

The officers' quarters had a very old piano that was suffering from a serious attack of woodworm and Jill decided that it must go! Our neighbour, a very friendly person, helped us to get it out into the garden in order that we could dismantle it. He asked if he could help in the process and, at the word 'yes', ran into his house and reappeared with a large axe with which he made a dedicated attack on the piano. The effect was that the strings (which were under real tension) were flying everywhere and, although I was concerned for his safety, he continued in the same vein until the whole thing was just a heap of rubbish. 'Oh,' he said, 'I needed that!' Then he disappeared back into his house. We became very good friends!

Chapter 4

THE GREAT ADVENTURE

National Bandmaster (British Territory)

A letter from the British National Headquarters dated 20 October 1960 stated:

'It has been decided to appoint you as the National Bandmaster of the British Territory, and we extend to you a welcome to this Headquarters. Captain Dean Goffin is the National Secretary for Bands and Songster Brigades. You are required to report to the Staff Secretary at National Headquarters on Friday, 4th. of November, at 9.30 a.m. With kind regards to Mrs Bearcroft and yourself.' (Signed by Colonel Horace Mead, the Staff Secretary)

I arrived at Headquarters at exactly 9.30 on Friday 4 November and was taken by the Staff Secretary to meet Captain Dean Goffin, who introduced me to Celestine Skinner, the secretary of the Bands Department. Celestine was near to retirement age but was one who, I was to discover, was so invaluable that retirement would have to be constantly postponed!

A cup of tea was the next requirement, followed by Miss Skinner showing me the office I would be sharing with her. I was promptly told to always call her Cissie! Dean had been the National Bandmaster prior to his becoming the Secretary for Bands and Songster Brigades and he had made a deep impression on the British band and songster scene.

My Memorandum of Appointment stated the following:

1. Two weeks to be spent within a Division, visiting one Corps on each night of the week. Conduct meetings at a Corps during

the weekends. The following week to be spent in London – one or two days at home, the rest at National Headquarters to make out reports and prepare for the next tour in another Division, the following Saturday.

2. During visits to Corps, conduct Band and Songster rehearsals, and not public meetings or festivals, except a Saturday Divisional festival or, as agreed by National Headquarters.

3. Accompany the British Commissioner and Secretary for Bands and Songsters when conducting Band and Songster Councils and share the conducting of united Bands and Songsters in National and Inter-divisional events.

A final statement made the work clear when it said, 'To train Bands and Songsters as an evangelical force and to speak of the urgent need for Candidates to replenish the ranks of Officership.'

A Minute by the Chief of the Staff, Commissioner Erik Wickberg, confirmed my appointment as a member of the International Music Board.

Captain Dean Goffin came with me for the first night of my first tour as National Bandmaster to Potton Corps in the Northampton Division. Dean rehearsed the band in 'The Great Crusade' and I rehearsed the band in Dean's 'The Shepherd Psalm'. We shared the billet (the first of hundreds I had in the following years) and Dean left for London the following morning. I was now launched in the kind of work that I was to do for the rest of my active service, and even after that!

My second tour was to the Northern Division where I first met Bobby and Rene Quinn. Bobby was the very active band secretary of Monkwearmouth Corps and if I were ever 'up north' he would insist that I stayed with them. (When, following retirement, I was invited to accompany Sunderland Monkwearmouth Band to Canada, Bobby, then retired himself, came with the band to look after me and make sure my shoes were polished!)

Roy Horrabin, then bandmaster of Monkwearmouth Band, took me to meet Mrs George Marshall, known to all as Jenny. It was just a few months after her husband George (the composer of some very stirring music published by the Army in the 1920s and 30s) had gone to Heaven and the house still had the feeling that George would arrive at any moment. While being shown the room in which George wrote his music, I noticed that his pen was on the top of a part-finished manuscript and that the inkbottle was already open and ready for use. Jenny, who had cared for George ever since his crippling accident in a coal mine just a few days following their wedding, offered a prayer for me. I really was standing on holy ground.

As the National Bandmaster I was required to write a detailed report of my visits to bands and songsters and any other information that would be considered important to the musical fraternity for publication in *The Musician* (a much-loved weekly paper containing reports, news and anything to do with Army bands and songsters, of which Captain Brindley Boon was then editor).

Councils (devotional and technical instruction) for bands and songsters were considered to be most important and regarded as essential for the wellbeing of our musicians. Councils could be for a single division or several divisions. My first involvement was in an All London Bandsmen's Councils held at Clapton Congress Hall in January 1961 and led by General Wilfred Kitching.

The General, himself a composer who had written lovely melodies for the words of General Albert Orsborn as well as music for bands, had also been, many years before, the National Secretary for Bands and Songster Brigades and instinctively knew what inspired our musicians.

This was the first of such occasions I attended and, after being introduced as the new National Bandmaster, I was invited to give a 45-minute technical talk for which I used the duty band for demonstrating the points I wanted to make. The music used was a new and very popular selection by Erik Leidzén entitled 'A Robe Of White'.

The morning and evening meetings were purely devotional, the General seeking to help his listeners in their service and devotion to Christ. The very next day he wrote me the following letter:

My Dear Captain,

You must have felt very gratified with the manner in which your name was received by the bandsmen yesterday afternoon. I bespeak for you a time of great blessing and believe that your service will have some impact upon your own life. You will need much wisdom and I pray that you may become a blessing to many.

Signed, Wilfred Kitching

Then, in his own hand, he wrote at the bottom of the letter: 'You will know where to go to get this wisdom.'

The four bands performing for the Saturday evening festival were from Croydon Citadel, High Wycombe, Luton Temple and Tottenham Citadel. A feature of these festivals was the playing of united items in what used to be termed Massed Bands. I was chosen to conduct the first massed item, a new march from the pen of Donald Osgood (my Southall bandmaster friend) entitled 'Motondo'. This was followed by the cornet solo 'Tucker' (theme and variations on the beautiful melody of William Booth's song 'Send The Fire'), played exquisitely by Bandsman Deryck Diffey (then quite unknown to me but who was to play an important part in my later life).

Dean conducted the last item of the evening, the new piece 'A Robe Of White'. All bandsmen present were given the words of the songs that appeared in the selection and were required to stand and sing in unison as the music unfolded.

My next introduction to new responsibilities was when I first made an appearance at a meeting of the International Music Board. The members of the Music Board were all people having close association with bands and songsters and were as follows: the Head of the Music Editorial Department (Colonel Charles Skinner), the National Secretary for Bands and Songster Brigades (Major Dean Goffin), the Bandmaster of the International Staff Band (Colonel Bernard Adams), the National Bandmaster (myself), the Secretary for Trade, a corps officer and a corps bandmaster. The British Commissioner was the Chairman.

The Music Board exists to approve music for publication by The

Salvation Army and, before the new International Headquarters building was completed, used to meet in some very old property near to the site of the old International Headquarters at 101 Queen Victoria Street. The International Staff Band would play the music from one floor and the members of the Music Board would listen in a room downstairs, leaving the door open so we could hear. The band would play the prescribed number of pieces, then leave the building while we remained to discuss what we had heard. It was important that we did not know who had written the music until it had been approved for publication. Discussion could get hot and opinions were freely expressed. It was not too long before we were in the new headquarters and the Music Board met in a room adjacent to that of the Staff Band. It was here that we even got a cup of tea and a biscuit!

In the Bands and Songster Brigades Department it was understood that the General would always conduct the yearly councils for bandmasters and songster leaders. In his book *Play The Music, Play*, Colonel Brindley Boon records:

> The first Councils for Bandmasters were held on January 17 and 18, 1903. There was no associated festival on the Saturday, when delegates met in the Laura Place hall at Clapton for an informal 'get together'. On the Sunday morning the International Staff Band marched the 320 Bandmasters and Songster Leaders to the Manor Assembly Rooms, Mare Street, Hackney, where the Chief of the Staff (Bramwell Booth) led the day's meetings. When Bramwell Booth became General he continued to meet the music leaders in council in London at intervals, and ever since the Army's General has reserved the right to conduct similar gatherings.

When Evangeline Booth became the General she decided that the International Training College for Officers should be the venue for the bandmasters and songster leaders councils, a decision continued up to the present time. In 1959 it was decided that there should be separate councils for songster leaders, and these were alternated with those for bandmasters, but in the 1980s the councils were again united and held every year. The councils are preceded by a festival of music, the venue being the Royal Albert Hall in London.

Dean Goffin, then Secretary for Bands and Songster Brigades, was responsible for the entire organisation to do with bandmasters and songster leaders councils and festivals, and this would include the choice of bands, soloists, music and 101 other details for the festival on the Saturday night at the Royal Albert Hall. Dean was very creative in his approach to the content of these festivals and was always aware that not everyone in the audience would be musically informed. The largest chorus the risers on the stage could hold was a must and the invitations to solo bands, soloists, etc, very carefully considered.

Just following the 1961 councils and festival, Dean and I met to discuss the 1962 festival and our discussion was along these lines:

Obviously, the International Staff Band would be there and a quick decision was made to have an all-male chorus – comprised of bandsmen from the Greater London area – three corps bands and three soloists. A few weeks later it was decided that the three bands would be Coventry City Band (Bandmaster Bramwell Jacobs), Boscombe Band (Courtney Bosanko) and Tottenham Citadel Band (James Williams). A few more weeks and Dean announced the names of the soloists: Deputy Bandmaster Charles Dove of Stapleford (cornet soloist), Deputy Songster Leader Jean Hammond of Derby Central (vocalist) and Songster Leader Maisie Wiggins of Cannock (trombone soloist).

It seemed no time at all that we were again in the Royal Albert Hall, where Coventry City Band played 'Gems From Mozart' (arranged by Frederick Hawkes), Boscombe Band chose 'When They Crucified My Lord' (Ray Steadman-Allen) and Tottenham selected 'Song Of Courage' (Eric Ball). The International Staff Band played an unpublished work, 'The Kingdom Triumphant' by Eric Ball. This work made a profound impression on the assembled audience and has become an international favourite. Jean Hammond sang Haydn's 'With Verdure Clad', Charles Dove played Eric Ball's cornet solo 'The Challenge' and Maisie Wiggins premiered a new work by Ray Steadman-Allen entitled 'Immortal Theme'.

Ray told me that the night before this festival he dreamed that, in the middle of the solo 'Immortal Theme', the General stood up and stopped the soloist playing this item, saying, 'It is too long and is not suitable for an Army programme.' Ray was worried that this might actually happen at the festival and was feeling very apprehensive the whole time the solo was being played. At the end of the programme General Kitching signalled to Ray that he needed to speak to him. Fearing the worst, Ray came face to face with the General who said to him, 'Ray, I was deeply moved during the playing of your new solo, so much so that I want to have it played again tomorrow afternoon at the Councils and, not only that, I want you to talk about the piece before it is played.' Ray was a bit overcome and went on to explain that the afternoon programme was already arranged. 'Then it will have to be rearranged,' replied the General, in no uncertain terms. It was a very appreciative company of bandmasters that sat and listened to Ray speaking about his new solo and, in Maisie's absence, Staff Bandsman Arthur Rolls playing his 'Immortal Theme', with its glorious second movement based on the old song 'Some Day I Shall Be Like Him'. It was one of those never to be-forgotten moments!

> Some day I shall be like him,
> Some day, like him,
> Changed to heavenly beauty
> When his face I see,
> Some day I shall be like him,
> Some day, like him,
> Hallelujah! this wonderful promise
> He gives to me.

In March 1963 Dean and I were in Birmingham, where no fewer than seven divisions had united for Bandsmen's Councils with the British Commissioner, Edgar Grinsted. These were held in Birmingham Town Hall, a wonderful building for such an occasion and filled with 1,500 bandsmen. The Saturday night festival included united and solo band items, as well as instrumental and vocal solos.

On the Sunday morning, music had already lent its valuable aid to the outcome of the day for, while the bandsmen were settling in their seats, Birmingham Citadel Band (Bandmaster Bram Williams) played two of Erik Leidzén's devotional gems, 'Sweet Hour Of Prayer' and 'Secret Prayer'.

A very powerful meeting was followed by a mammoth march by the 1,500 delegates (headed by Birmingham Citadel Band) to an establishment just less than a quarter of a mile away, which had been chosen to provide dinner for the hungry delegates. It was announced that the commissioner would be 'taking the salute', standing on a low bridge under which the bandsmen would be passing. Those of us who had been in the forces (that being the majority on the march) were used to hearing the command 'Eyes right!' or 'Eyes left!' according to where the saluting officer happened to be. There was much laughter when the instruction 'Eyes up!' was given as we approached the said bridge. Brindley Boon (who was there for the weekend to write a report for *The Musician* and was now with us on the march) looked up and, thinking that the commissioner was leaning over too far, shouted, 'Don't jump, Guv'nor, we are all coming willingly!' – even more laughter!

For the afternoon session, I was invited to give a technical demonstration with Birmingham Citadel Band and, for this, I had again decided to use the new Leidzén selection 'A Robe Of White'. Some weeks before, I had written to Erik Leidzén telling him that I was to do a technical talk and wondering if he would give me a few comments on the piece. He replied with a seven-page letter in which he wrote about his leaving the Army and how, by the care and prayers of Captain Richard Holz, he had come back to the Army. He then sent me three or four lines about 'A Robe Of White' and finished by saying, 'Norman, you will know what else to say about it!' We actually had a good deal of correspondence after this and I recently found a copy of his letters and my answers in the National Headquarters archives in America.

Dean's pièce de résistance was in 1963, the year he decided to present a Festival of Gospel Song. He was convinced that, on this

48

occasion, only words and music that would proclaim the gospel of Jesus Christ should be used. We had long discussions about this and how best it could work. After a visit to the Royal Albert Hall (and to the stage in particular), Dean came up with the idea of packing the stage with a 1,000-voice chorus, with the International Staff Band being right in the middle. 'This should make a great sound,' he said in a very confident voice. Included in the Chorus would be the National Songsters, the London Male Chorus and the girls of the National School of Music.

We realised that it would mean that all the songs to be sung by the 1,000-Voice Chorus would need new musical arrangements, some with fanfare trumpets as well as the Staff Band. A few days later, Dean had decided which songs to use and who to ask to do the arrangements. His list was as follows: 'All Hail The Power Of Jesus' Name' (Dean Goffin), 'Shout Aloud Salvation' (mine), 'He Hideth My Soul' (Eric Ball) and 'Crown Him With Many Crowns' (Charles Skinner) (all now published by SP&S).

Other special arrangements for this Festival were 'Are You Washed In The Blood Of The Lamb', sung by the National Songsters conducted by Muriel Packham (now Muriel Yendell), 'I Think When I Read That Sweet Story Of Old', sung by Kevin Platts (boy soprano soloist) and arranged by Ray Steadman-Allen, 'Beneath The Cross Of Jesus', arranged by Donald Osgood and sung by Joan Clothier (now Joan Cook) and 'Though Your Sins Be As Scarlet', arranged by Dean Goffin and sung by Kevin Platts with the London Male Chorus.

It was the London Male Chorus (several hundred singers) accompanying boy soprano Kevin Platts that I was conducting when, during the last verse of the song, General Kitching passed me a folded handwritten note which said, 'Sing the last verse again!' Being so far from the actual singers I wondered how to get this message to all these singers without saying a word. You can't just shake your head to the General as if the request were an impossible one, even if at the time I thought it might be! So, when the time came and the song had come to its end, I waved my arms in a big circular movement and hoped for the best. Well, it came out just as the General's note had requested and just as if we had rehearsed it many times! It was a most telling silence that followed this item, with its message, 'Though your sins be as scarlet, they shall be as white as snow.'

Songster Leader Marjorie Ringham was the pianoforte accompanist and Bandmaster Michael Clack was at his usual place at the Grand Organ.

Dean had contacted the EMI recording company who, after some persuading, thought that it would be worth their while, and so came and recorded the evening. They were delighted with the result and the recording made the event a memorable one, not only for those present, but also for the thousands of people who were unable to attend the festival in person.

My lasting memory of this festival is this: it was one minute to starting time, the General and his party had already arrived in their appointed seats at the side of the stage and, as Dean and I made our way to the stage, he said to me, 'Well, Norm, in two minutes we shall know if we have done the right thing, or if we should head for the bush!' In the many times I entered the stage in the following years at the Royal Albert Hall to conduct the opening item I always thought of his words, 'Well, Norm, in two minutes you will know if you have done the right thing, or if you should head for the bush!'

The time had come for Celestine Skinner to retire after so many years of faithful service and a tea party was held in which to thank her for the love and care she always had for us both. Major June Kitchen became the Bands Department secretary.

Billets

I must have had hundreds of billets during my days as the National Bandmaster and I really appreciated the kindness and care shown towards me by all those who offered me the hospitality of their homes. I did sometimes find it difficult at the end of two weeks, with a different bed every night, to remember all the people with whom I had stayed. Prior to my visit, the divisional commander in whose division I was to be would inform the corps officer of my visit and ask that a billet be found for the night in question.

One humorous incident occurred when one lady officer, at the close of the rehearsal and not quite understanding this request, said, 'Well, I hope you won't be too late getting home tonight.' Considering that I was about 200 miles from home, I had to reply that I thought a billet had been arranged. 'Oh, no problem,' she replied and then went on to tell me that she knew someone who might just take me in for the night.

A telephone call proved she was right and I was driven to the house in question. The officer introduced me to the lady who had responded to her request and I was invited to enter. As I was shown into a room where half-a-dozen men (all smoking) were sitting round a very small television set, she asked me if I was hungry. Thanking her for her inquiry, I added that I was very tired and would like to get some sleep. 'No problem,' she assured me and asked me to wait a couple of minutes. As I stood at the bottom of the stairs, a man, obviously just having been awakened from his sleep, appeared and the lady announced, 'The room is now ready.' It was certainly a warm bed from the previous occupant!

The very next night, following the rehearsal, it was a very different experience. A chauffeur, resplendent in his uniform, who had come to drive me to a mansion, said, 'His Lordship was expecting us five minutes ago.' On arrival, I discovered that a few guests had been invited by His Lordship to meet this 'Musical Man' from The Salvation Army!

On looking back I realise that life for Jill must, at times, have been hard. In those days we didn't have a telephone at home and often, with no addresses of the billets I would be in, it would be quite some time before she had any word from me. No car was made available for my constant journeying, so it was bus and train until the day I was able to buy a car myself and for which I was then allowed to charge the train or bus fare. (Things are different now!)

The National School of Music

The 1961 National School of Music was my first contact with music schools and a wonderful experience it was. Dean Goffin was the

Musical Director and I was invited to conduct what was known as the A Band, which was formed by the older and more advanced students. Tylney Hall (which was then a school for boys situated in a lovely mansion in Hook, Hampshire) had been the venue for a few years but, at the last minute, was not available for the 1961 Salvation Army week. After much scurrying around looking for accommodation, the offer of Clapton Congress Hall was accepted. Clapton had been the site of the Army's Training Garrison in years long past and, apart from accommodating a few occasional visitors, had been empty for years. The main hall (Clapton Congress Hall) was a superb building, seating many hundreds of people and used by the local corps.

The sergeant-major of Clapton Congress Hall Corps grasped the situation and persuaded the music camp director that the five bands, now at the Congress Hall for a week, should each be out leading open-air meetings on the Sunday morning. Each bandmaster was instructed as to which road to occupy and where to be precisely at 10.36 am so that all the bands would be able to play together for the last part of the march back to the hall. It was quite spectacular!

The music staff (all colourful characters) were as follows: Bandmaster Alf Springate (Gillingham), Bandmaster George Snook (Swindon), Bandmaster Jim Hopkin (Romford), Bandmaster Reg Jobson (Sutton) and Bandmaster Michael Clack from Chalk Farm (plus Dean and me).

To many men, the name Tylney Hall rekindles memories of a 19th-century mansion situated somewhere between Basingstoke and Reading where, as boys, they attended the National School of Music. The yearly miracle was the arrival of 150 such boys, laden with brass instruments ranging from soprano cornets to B flat basses and some with loads of percussion instruments, all eager to make music.

Before this could begin there was the ordeal of an audition. Queues of boys could be found tootling away outside the audition room as they waited to display their ability, some wanting to play the latest and most difficult solo and others just a simple hymn tune. Whatever the standard the boy had reached, he was sure of a warm welcome at Tylney.

The National School of Music in those days catered for boys up to the age of 16 years and Dean, in giving me the A Band, had stipulated that all music had to come from the *Triumph Series* (music for smaller bands). There was no shortage of good music to be found in this series, but Dean wanted one boy, a certain Leslie Piper who was in the A Band, to play Erik Leidzén's solo 'Concertino For Band And Trombone', which was published in the *Festival Series* (advanced music for bands). Dean reminded me that this was a 'one-off' special concession. Leslie gave a superb rendering and I thought this would now open the way for the bands to play more advanced music.

The following year (1962) found us back in the lovely surroundings of Tylney Hall. A few days before the Music School began, Dean asked me what music was I thinking of using (while reminding me that it needed to be from the *Triumph Series*). Seeing the look of disappointment on my face, he asked me what I had in mind. 'Well,' I said, a bit sadly, 'I was thinking of doing your arrangement of "Themes From The Italian Symphony" by Mendelssohn.' After a few moments of silence, Dean said, 'Well, it would do the boys good to play music by Mendelssohn. Yes! Go ahead.' His decision opened the door to more advanced music and we never looked back!

One year, Dean, wanting the boys to be at their best for the final festival, announced that no late-night feasts were to take place on the Friday night. I was a little concerned when my wife Jill told me that she had already been invited to such an event. The food had been obtained and she was invited to cut the ribbon and declare the feast open so, having a mind of her own, she did just this! Arriving back at our room (just after midnight) she told me that the 'ribbon' was an unravelled toilet roll which she had ceremoniously cut with a pair of beribboned scissors. Then, sounding like a mayoress, Jill had declared the feast 'well and truly open!'. Seeing Dean never mentioned it, we decided that either he did not hear about it or secretly wished that *he* had been invited to cut the ribbon.

The midweek cricket match in which the boys played the staff was always a big event. The staff team, handpicked from the instructors and sergeants, had to face the boys' team – who always managed to have good bowlers (usually very fast) and stylish batsmen.

One year the headmaster of Tylney Hall School offered to play on the staff side. We were delighted when he duly turned up wearing his white gear and county cricket cap. Dean, also in whites (and looking as if he had been left behind from a New Zealand test match series), decided that he and the headmaster should open the batting for the staff team.

There was a strange hush as the two batsmen made their way to the crease. Seeing that the headmaster was our special guest, Dean thought it right and proper to ask him to receive the first ball. The headmaster took quite some time looking around to see the field placing of the student team then, after tapping the ground a few times with his bat, gave the signal that he was ready. The first ball of the match came from a very slight student who, after making a run which seemed all of 100 yards, delivered a fearsome ball which knocked two of the stumps right out of the ground!

The umpire, Bandmaster Alf Springate, regretfully realising the headmaster was well and truly out first ball, raised a very reluctant finger to denote the same. Knowing that the headmaster's goodwill was crucial to us being at Tylney, we wondered if the raucous merriment being shown by the boys was going to injure our future chances.

Thankfully, the headmaster did not know the words of the tune the boys started humming. It was from 'The Great Crusade' (which one of the bands had been rehearsing), which concludes with the words 'Never quit the field'! We were delighted when the headmaster behaved like a true cricketer and was pleased to hand out the trophy to the winning side. (Yes, it was the boys' side!)

The summer of 1962 was very hot and the boys were looking very despondently at the swimming pool which, according to the National Youth Secretary, could not be used by Salvationists on a Sunday. Alf Springate made an impassioned appeal on behalf of the boys and, following a telephone call to somewhere, permission was given for the boys to swim. The boys were all called to the main hall and Alf gave the following speech: 'It has been decided at the highest level at the International Headquarters in the City of London that you can all have a swim today but,' long pause, *you must swim slowly!*'

Another year, Brigadier Denis Hunter (then Youth Secretary for the British Territory) and I went to see the headmaster to discuss the possibility of inviting the girls from the vocal school of music held at Sunbury Court to come to Tylney for a day. Denis felt it was important for Army boys to meet Army girls and that their coming to Tylney would be a good idea.

The headmaster greeted us in a very cordial manner and, over a cup of tea, asked the purpose of our visit.

'Well, Mr Headmaster,' began Denis, 'we are hoping that this visit may be the beginning of a few Salvation Army families.' Hoping the headmaster would not take his suggestion the wrong way, Denis continued, 'We are going to take the boys up to Sunbury later in the week so that any would-be friendship that might have commenced here at Tylney Hall will have an opportunity to flourish in due time.' The headmaster understood the request perfectly, and it was a humour-filled journey that Denis and I had back to London.

I have met men all over the world who have the fondest memories of Tylney Hall. My last year at Tylney (at least for a few years) was in 1968, when the final programme was held at Clapton Congress Hall. By then I had received farewell orders and been appointed to Canada. The united bands (conducted by Bandmaster Bram Williams) ended the programme with 'The Canadian', a very popular festival march that contains 'O Canada' (the Canadian national anthem), which Bram suggested I should stand and sing!

Chapter 5

1965 – DAY OF JUBILEE

The Army's Centenary

The year 1965 was the one in which The Salvation Army celebrated 100 years of service and music in abundance was to be needed in the Centenary Celebrations. The inaugural meeting was held on Thursday 24 June in the Royal Albert Hall in the presence of Her Majesty Queen Elizabeth II. The first Sunday meetings were held simultaneously at Regent Hall, Clapton Congress Hall, Wood Green, Croydon Citadel and the Royal Albert Hall. It was here that General Frederick Coutts conducted three meetings, the first of these being the Sunday morning holiness meeting supported by the International Staff Band and the Congress Chorus of 700 voices (which Dean and I had spent many months preparing for this milestone in the Army's history).

Being before the days of computers and the ease with which we can now print music, all newly composed and arranged music for the Congress was written by hand with pen and ink! This then had to be copied on to a skin that would be put into a duplicating machine and (if you were lucky) could produce a hundred or so copies. Some arrangements would need seven or eight pages to contain the required song and, seeing that we would need seven or eight hundred copies, a lot of patience and hard work had to be expended before the music was sent out to the songsters!

It is all a big contrast to today's technical procedures. Nowadays, I would just send the manuscript copy to my very good friend Retired Songster Leader Terry Nielsen who, with his skill and knowledge of the computer, would have a printed copy of the music back to me the next day! Moira, his very understanding wife, would frequently supply him with tea and coffee in order to keep him happy and get the job done at top speed!

For the Sunday morning holiness meeting, Dean had asked me to do an arrangement of my own choice of an Army holiness song, so I chose Herbert Booth's words to the secular melody 'Long, Long Ago', which Herbert Booth had captured for the Army and which made a perfect melody for his inspired words:

> Lord, through the Blood of the Lamb that was slain,
>   Cleansing for me;
> From all the guilt of my sins now I claim
>   Cleansing from thee.
> Sinful and black though the past may have been,
> Many the crushing defeats I have seen,
> Yet on thy promise, O Lord, now I lean,
>   Cleansing for me.

The reason I had selected this song was that I had read that William Booth liked to use it at the commencement of a holiness meeting. Seeing it was the centenary of his bringing the Army into being, it seemed to me to be the right choice for this occasion. I sought to make the arrangement a little different to the one in the Army's tune book but wanted it to be a simple statement of the song. A most emotive and moving point was when all the voices in unison loudly sang, 'Jesus, thy promise I dare to believe,' followed by, 'And as I come thou wilt surely receive,' sung very softly in harmony.

The complete and utter silence which followed the singing was an indication that the message had found a place in many hearts.

In retirement I have visited Kensico Cemetery in New York where a stone cross marks the place where Herbert Booth's body was laid to rest and I have thanked God for the many unsurpassable songs which he wrote for the Army and for the influence they continue to have.

Dean also asked me to do an arrangement of an Army war song for the afternoon meeting and I chose one whose melody had its beginnings with secular words, the American Civil War tune

'Marching Through Georgia', to which another early-day Salvationist, George Scott Railton, had written 'Shout Aloud Salvation'. The arrangement had a substantial introduction sung by the Congress Chorus and interludes between the verses leading to a higher key which made them sing all the better!

In one event, in which the Congress Chorus had just sung the third chorus of another arrangement, 'Happy Song', Leopoldville Band (Bandmaster Captain Ray Munn), who were sharing the platform, broke out in their own language with, 'Then awake, happy song.' This was followed by people all over the hall standing and singing the same chorus in their own language! I let this go on for a quite a while before bringing the whole congregation in for twice more through the chorus.

The song comes to an end with an extended 'We'll work till Jesus calls' (ending on a high A flat) to be sung by the Centenary Chorus, but the congregation were not about to be left out and insisted on singing along with us a very, enthusiastic, 'We'll work till Jesus calls'! It was quite a few moments before the loud *hallelujahs*, *glories* and *amens* quietened down and the meeting was able to continue on its course.

Looking through some of Jill's scrapbooks I came across this letter (which I had never seen) from James Wilson of Leighton Buzzard, printed in *The Musician* and headed 'Happy Song':

> Beyond all the Centenary excitement I looked forward especially to the Royal Albert Hall Festival of Praise.
>
> On the platform that day would be a whole collection of friends, relatives and Army acquaintances; the band (in which I had served for years as a bandsman) and local officers; the band with which we had enjoyed fellowship when touring Sweden; the band from the city which I once called home; the songster brigade from the corps at which we were currently nominal soldiers. Whatever the experiences to be undergone, strangeness would not be one of them that day. The festival took its highly polished course and then my moment came.

'We are marching onward, singing as we go,
Then awake, then awake,
Shout for joy, shout for joy...'

The most thrilling moment of the whole Centenary had arrived. 'Happy Song' was the title and so it was, no doubt about that. But I was the loneliest man in the thousands there that day.

Festivals are finished, they say. This festival marked my restart; this I know. The exuberance of the music and singing underlined my remoteness from Army service. After five years of doing nothing we had to get back. Uniform is being worn again, full-time service is becoming a reality – all triggered, understandably, wonderfully, by 'Happy Song.'

Joy Webb

The year 1965 saw the transfer of the Joystrings from the training college to National Headquarters in Queen Victoria Street. This meant that Captain Joy Webb, the founder and driving force of the group, became a member of the Bands Department. It also meant that Joy now shared an office with me, with a portable organ for her desk! We all made her very welcome in the department where she stayed until her retirement in 1992. As the years went by, Joy became very good at finding occasions when more than a cup of tea could be the order for a mid-morning break. Joy did not keep her songwriting just for the Joystrings. Our publications have many beautiful songs written by her and the inspiration does not show any signs of diminishing. Many of her songs have found their way into instrumental solos and many recordings of these are available. I was present at the Gospel Arts Concert when Joy received the Order of the Founder. Her song 'Share My Yoke' seems to reflect its author.

When I'm tired and nothing's going right for me,
When things I've counted on just do not come my way,
When in my mind the thick grey folds of doubt arise,
It's then I seem to hear him say:

Share my yoke and find that I am joined with you,
Your slightest movement I shall feel and be there too!
Share my yoke and come the way that I must go!
In our 'togetherness' my peace you'll know;
The world beholding us will see it so!

Bands change pitch

The year 1965 marked other happenings in the Army world, one of them being the announcement that brass band instruments were to go into a slightly lower pitch. British brass bands had for many years used instruments in a slightly higher pitch than that of orchestras, etc. The instrument makers Boosey and Hawkes had decided not to make any more brass instruments in high pitch so The Salvation Army, which had its own instrument factory, decided that it should follow suit and an announcement was made to this effect. Both Boosey and Hawkes and the Army's factory agreed to offer a temporary change to the pitch of existing instruments by adding a small amount of tubing which would lower the pitch to the universal one.

Bands were very good in accepting the news and instrument makers everywhere were made busy in effecting this change. The alteration to existing instruments was really only a temporary solution to the problem. The National School of Music encountered some difficulties with the change in that some boys arrived with the new low-pitch instruments while others came with their high-pitch ones. As stated, it was possible to make a temporary lowering of the older high-pitch ones by pulling out the tuning slide to its fullest extent and making some adjustments to the valve slides. Jill and I spent quite a few hours adjusting the main and valve slides to the required length, with Jill taping the slides to prevent them from reverting to their original pitch.

Commissioner Edgar Grinsted

Commissioner Edgar Grinsted, a very colourful character, liked to have some humour of the right kind and at the right place in his

61

meetings – including Officers Councils, then held every year in a lovely part of the country called Swanwick. The conference centre there was not large enough to take all the British field and headquarters officers at the same time. The solution was to take several divisions for two-and-a-half days and then change on the Wednesday afternoon for a few more divisions until the Friday. This would go on until all officers had the opportunity to attend and this would take two or three weeks to complete.

One year, Commissioner Grinsted said that he wanted me there for all the sessions to tell my story about my cadet days and the bus incident (previously referred to in Chapter 2). 'To cheer the folk up,' he added. Well, for one session there was no pianist available and so I was enlisted to play for the songs that would be used. Following one song, the commissioner said, 'Well, it is good to have a real pub-pianist with us today.' His remark caused much laughter and I took a long, demonstrative bow to it!

At the end of the meeting, Mrs Grinsted brought her husband over to me and said to him, 'Edgar, do you have something to say to Norman?' After a little hesitation and with a puzzled look on his face, he said, 'Er, I don't particularly think so.' 'Oh, I think you do,' replied Mrs Grinsted. 'Well, in what connection?' asked the commissioner. 'Could it have to do with the piano and what you said about Norman playing it, perhaps?' 'Oh well, that was just a bit of fun,' was the reply. 'Edgar, don't you think an apology is needed?' At this point I interjected, saying, 'No, no, it was just a bit of fun and I did get a round of applause.' This did not get the commissioner off the hook so, with a bow of humility, he rather overdid his apology, to which dear Mrs Grinsted said, 'Edgar, I do hope that was a sincere apology!' A wink from the commissioner was followed by an invitation to join them for dinner! Actually, after having been with them so many times in music events, I must say it would be hard to find two more lovely people with whom to work than Commissioner and Mrs Edgar Grinsted.

A few years later, when I had received orders to go to Canada, I had a call from Commissioner Grinsted inviting me to their retirement home in Brighton. The commissioner had been the Territorial Commander in Canada at one time and thought a few words about my new appointment would be helpful. I accepted the invitation and took a bus down to Brighton, where it was pouring with rain. The commissioner was there at the bus stop waiting for me and told me that his car was in the next street and that we could 'make a run for it' – which we did, but I had a job to keep up with him!

Major Dean Goffin returns to New Zealand

In 1966 it was announced that Major Dean Goffin was to be appointed back to New Zealand, where he became a divisional commander and, eventually, the Territorial Commander.

The last time Dean and I met was when, as the Territorial Commander for the New Zealand Territory, he came to London for a meeting of the High Council to elect a new General. Prior to leaving New Zealand, Dean wrote and said he would like to spend a few days with us, and we were delighted to be able to have him in our quarters and to go over the happy days we had spent together.

In particular we remembered the return from a weekend councils when the car, which I was driving, got into a collision with another car. It so happened that there was a snowstorm on the day we were travelling back to London and, while we were climbing a hill, a car coming in the opposite direction appeared at the top of the hill quite out of control and smashed into us. The offending car did not stop but left us covered in oil and grease and with a car that was never to go again! In the flurry, Dean lost his glasses and we both started to walk for the nearest town looking a very sorry pair.

One or two cars slowed down as if to pick us up but, seeing how dirty we were, just drove on. Then a car slowed down and even stopped and we were delighted to see that it was the British Commissioner, Edgar Grinsted, who had been the leader of the bandsmen's councils from which we were returning. We were duly invited to get in the car, which was being driven by the commissioner's driver, Major Joe Evans. A few miles down the road and the commissioner thought it time to stop for some lunch. Dean thought that he and I should just stay in the car seeing that we were looking so dirty after the accident, but the commissioner insisted that we go with him for a meal. Dean whispered to me that he thought the customers in the restaurant would think we were a couple of vagrants which the Army captain had just picked up!

The excitement of the day did not stop there. We were nearing London and it was still snowing. The commissioner, getting a bit nervous of Joe's driving, saw we were getting too near to a car in front and kept saying, 'Joe! You're going to hit him, Joe! You're going to hit... Oh, you've hit him, Joe! Oh dear!' Seeing this was our second car accident in one day, Dean and I concluded our journey by London Transport!

Another incident I recalled was that of a walk in St James's Park, which was very close to the temporary National Headquarters in Vandon Street. Dean and I, joined by Brigadier Wesley Evans (who has a number of songs published in *The Musical Salvationist*), were suddenly surprised by a man jumping out of a bush holding a microphone and asking, 'Do you know anything about poetry?' He then explained that he was from the British Broadcasting Corporation and was conducting this survey. He repeated, '*Do* you know anything about poetry?' Wesley looked surprised and I looked the other way, so Dean thought he should be the spokesman and began, in a somewhat pompous voice, 'Long my imprisoned spirit lay, fast bound in sin and nature's night...' 'Er, thank you!' said the man and quickly disappeared back into the bush. Both Wesley and I were laughing when Dean, in a somewhat resentful voice, said, 'It's called casting your pearls before swine!'

Major Brindley Boon welcomed as National Secretary for Bands and Songster Brigades

The 17 September edition of *The Musician* announced the coming of Major Brindley Boon to National Headquarters as the National Secretary for Bands and Songster Brigades. Brindley, so well known by musicians the world over, was welcomed into the department with the customary tea and cakes. His songs (there are around ten of them in the Salvation Army song book) have proved to be an inspiration on so many occasions. Brindley was in the department from 1966 until 1972. I will never forget his coming to the Bandmasters Councils a number of years after retirement and leading the delegates in the singing of his 'I Would Be Thy Holy Temple', the dedication song he wrote for the cadets of his own 1949-1950 session, the Standard Bearers. (The verses are now in the song book, number 786.)

I would be thy holy temple,
Sacred and indwelt by thee;
Naught then could stain my commission,
'Tis thy divine charge to me.

I dedicate myself to thee,
O Master, who has chosen me;
My every selfish aim denying,
I give my all, on thee relying;
Take thou my life and use me at thy will;
In deep submission I dedicate myself to thee.

Brindley and I travelled to many divisions, including a weekend in Scotland where we had the privilege of meeting bandmasters and songster leaders of that territory which, in those days, was separate from the British Territory.

The following appeared in *The Musician* – though I didn't know that it was going to happen:

I MARRIED A MUSICIAN! By Mrs Captain Jill Bearcroft
Continuing the second series of intimate close-ups of some of the Army's outstanding musical personalities, written from 'the other side of the fireplace'

Life with my husband has been hectic, to say the least; we were married when he was still a musician in the Guards and I was a songster at Southall Citadel.

Music has always been a part of him and I naturally accepted this from the beginning. Every day there was the ritual of scales and practice, a habit that was never a burden to him although at times I could have wished for more melody. On occasions he would go over the same few bars again and again, and when I was forced to plead for the neighbours he would just smile sweetly at me and continue as before.

IMPORTANT SCRAPS

I sometimes destroyed scraps of paper which had five lines and a few notes scribbled on them, thinking that he had been doodling, but learned after hard experience that the scruffy envelope with its few notes often held the key to a problem which had disturbed him for days and was more valuable than gold.

My husband is not a very good odd job man, and does not like trying his hand at interior decorating. If I wait until he is out of the way, then strip the room which wants renovating and do as much as possible to it while he is away, in desperation he will tackle the wallpapering so that the mess is cleared as soon as possible.

At one house where we lived an old disused fireplace was a particular eye-sore, and in his absence I managed to wrench it out of its position. No sooner had it come away than I heard the familiar sound of the rag-and-bone man calling in the street, so it was down, out and away in a very short time. My husband's disgust with me was soon replaced when he surveyed the good job he made at boarding up the hole! His favourite weapon is an axe, with which he fondly imagines he can mend most things. He is an expert at handling it now, for everything except chopping wood!

EASTER MEMORIES

Although he is not a moody person by nature, there are times when his music affects all our lives. Three Easters ago, when his mind was so possessed with the Good Friday story and he was trying to translate his feelings into music, the whole family became depressed. I think I realised that year the despair and desolation of the disciples more than ever before. What joy we all felt on Easter Sunday morning, and how my husband tried to express this, too! He called the result 'The Cross, The Victory' and we felt we had shared in it.

Our boys have grown used to the idea of their father becoming preoccupied with his music and now when he fails to hear someone speak to him they say he 'has gone away again'. We have what we call a 'coming home' tea to celebrate the completion of a piece.

My husband is very forgetful at times, hardly ever remembering a birthday; he never remembers the dates his sons were born or how old they are, or for that matter how old he is himself! Somehow he always thinks he is younger than his actual age but fortunately he takes six years off mine, too, which evens it up a bit!

Sometimes his preoccupation is rather dangerous, such as the time when, driving our old car, he arrived at a busy junction of five roads, and instead of giving the intended hand signal, he opened the door.

As a corps officer my husband's main time for music was after ten at night, or before nine in the morning, which made a rather long day. Just before an examination he was taking I decided to cook an extra nourishing meal, and make the housekeeping money stretch to a steak and some fresh fruit and vegetables which were out of season. Imagine my disgust when, after the meal was over, he could not remember what he had just eaten and was quite surprised when I told him.

PET AVERSIONS

He has strong likes and dislikes, one of his pet aversions being chiming clocks, and thinks that all budgerigars should be fitted with silencers. He likes plain food (for which I am grateful) and shakes his head sadly if I attempt some exotic dish. He is passionately fond of his three sons, who enjoy nothing better than to have a noisy romp with him, but one of his peculiarities is his love for his old tabby cat who rejoices in the name of Clarinet and will go down the road to meet him.

My husband is obviously much more at ease with a baton than a gardening fork (although he likes to see a nice garden), but is equally at home in a public-house raid and in a festival.

There are many things which contribute toward making ours a very happy home, the most important being a common interest in the Kingdom of God and a desire to serve Jesus Christ in the best way we can.

Chapter 6

GOOD CHEER

Butlin's – Holiday-plus-Fellowship

The date of the commencement of the first Holiday-plus-Fellowship series to be held at Butlin's Holiday Camp at Clacton-on-Sea in Essex was 24 September 1966. The then British Commissioner, William Cooper (what a man!), had an idea that there were lots of Salvationists and friends who would like to have a holiday with like-minded people who otherwise would not have a holiday.

He called me to his office and outlined what he thought might work, adding that an announcement that this was going to happen could bring a lot of people to join in the fun and fellowship. He then said that the announcement could say that there would be a band and songsters (formed from the customers) and that anyone who wished to could bring their instruments and join in the fellowship. Having said this, he immediately commissioned me to run these two sections. But then he added, 'I don't want you saying that people who would like to be part of the band or songsters must attend rehearsals. Remember,' he repeated time and time again, 'these people are on holiday and will not want to be told what they can or cannot do.' Then he added, 'Do you understand?' He then went on again to say that nothing had to be organised and to remember that these people were on holiday.

I saluted, and added in a quiet voice, 'Well, let's hope they don't expect meetings every day.' There was something about the way he pointed to the door that made it clear to me that the interview was at an end.

Regardless of what the commissioner said, I thought there would need to be some direction or it would be chaos! The commissioner must have been psychic because, before the afternoon was over, a phone call summoned me to his office and he repeated again, 'Nothing has to be prearranged.' He then added, 'I hope you do understand what I mean.' I assured him that I did and said, 'I will be at Butlin's as instructed and ready for anything or nothing as the case may be.'

My thinking that I would just be required to lead a couple of band and songster rehearsals turned out quite differently when on 24 September we set off for Butlin's with no idea of what we would be doing.

Having never been to Butlin's I had no idea what to expect. On arrival I found a massive complex with a huge theatre called the Gaiety in which the meetings, and whatever, were to take place.

I also found about 50 bandsmen waiting and wanting to join the Butlin's Band and all were expecting to be auditioned before doing so. 'Hands up all who play solo cornet in the corps band,' I said, and a goodly number responded. I continued in this style until I had covered all the instruments in the brass band.

Remembering the commissioner's words, I began explaining that no pressure would be brought to bear regarding their attendance. At this point, one of the men stood to his feet and said, 'Look here, captain, if we're in the band – we're in the band. You just have to say what you want and we'll do it.' Then, wondering if he had been a trifle hasty in committing all the others, he turned to them and said, 'That's right, isn't it, lads?' Seeing no one disagreed, I took it that, so far as they were concerned, what I said was law!

The first happening was the 'flag break' where, quite reverently, the yellow, red and blue flag was raised by the then Chief Secretary of the British Territory, Colonel Fred Griffin, as the band played 'So We'll Lift Up The Banner On High'.

A prayer and a 'Three cheers for the commissioner', who informed us that there were people present from 24 churches and Salvationists from more than 300 corps in the British Isles, followed this. The first Holiday-plus-Fellowship was now under way, with a total of 1,830 guests!

Some 200 singers were enrolled as the Butlin's Songsters for the week and, after giving the same words about not having to be present on every occasion, I got the same kind of response as that given by the band, although some ladies thought they might have to bring their children with them.

The next day (Sunday) we welcomed General Frederick Coutts, who had come to be the 'special' for the day. No one was going to miss this, so a huge crowd gathered for the Sunday morning meeting in the Gaiety Theatre. (I thought how easily we turn a theatre with its tinsel trappings and coloured lights into a house of God. Here were certainly shades of the pioneering early-day Army.)

The afternoon meeting was held outdoors with some items from the children, lots of hearty singing and words of encouragement from the General. The final meeting in the Gaiety Theatre was the place where we heard, 'You can't just take a holiday from sin.' Many folk knelt at the improvised mercy seat.

On Monday morning Commissioner Cooper told me he wanted me to lead the talent competition and to 'be ready to entertain the folk at night'. I was just about to remind him that 'nothing was to be arranged' when a nudge from Jill made me think better of it!

That afternoon, as we walked on to the stage to lead the talent competition, we were aware that the loud cheers and accompanying applause was for the entertainment the audience of 1,500 people were expecting us to give! Realising it was no use panicking, I began to sing, with a long pause on the first two words:

> Oh, I do like to be beside the seaside,
> Oh, I do like to be beside the sea;
> Oh, I do like to stroll along the prom, prom, prom
> Where the brass band plays tiddly-om-pom-pom.

(I knew the words from my days as a member of the Life Guards Band and the summer tours of holiday resort bandstands, when the director of music, complete with white gloves and ceremonial sword, would invite the people to 'let yourselves go!')

There were about 40 contestants waiting to display their abilities to the judges (these being Commissioner and Mrs Cooper and Colonel and Mrs Griffin). I quickly worked out that if each item took five minutes, and allowing for applause, we would be there for about four hours! So, explaining that the judges were well trained in their work and that just two minutes of each item would be sufficient for them to name the winners, we began.

I'm a bit hazy now about the content of that afternoon, but as we finished and the prizes had been awarded the commissioner (looking very happy and with his glasses high on his forehead) said, 'Good, now go and get some tea. You'll be on again at 7.30!'

One instinctively knew that it was not a fruitful exercise to argue with Commissioner Cooper, so it was in for tea with a notepad and pencil and a hope that some ideas would come.

As I was finishing a second cup of tea, Colonel Griffin offered to recite 'Albert And The Lion', adding, 'Only if you get stuck.' At this point, Commissioner Cooper, probably feeling a bit guilty, said, 'If you want, me and the missus will sing a duet.' It was with some sense of power that I replied, 'Well, I will let you know!'

That evening, realising I had nothing else, I used both the items and judging by the prolonged applause they had to be recorded in the 'great success' category!

Both band and songsters were pressing for some real rehearsal, following which both groups added greatly to the now twice-daily shows.

After the first weekend, Commissioner Cooper thought Jill and I should lead the evening epilogue, adding, 'They've got to know you now.' He suggested we should include some community hymn-singing and perhaps 'a few testimonies'. He thought this should commence at about 10 pm and conclude 'somewhere around 11 pm'. Then he added, 'Do remember they're on holiday!' (We did commence at about 10 pm but finished nearer midnight!)

On the Tuesday afternoon a group of home league ladies did a spoof on *Mary Poppins* which went so well that Colonel Fred Griffin (the Camp Director) thought the men officers could do a copy of this in the evening show. It must be hard to imagine what we looked like as we danced on to the stage! At one point during the week Commissioner Cooper, sitting on the side of the stage, was laughing so much that he fell off his chair!

No one can know what good was accumulated during those years or how many people were won for the Kingdom but we do know that a number of those who came became officers and not a few others found their lifetime partners at Butlin's.

The event was so popular that by the next year the attendance had trebled! Needless to say, Commissioner Cooper was delighted but he realised that the entertainment would be too much for the Bearcrofts alone and so he enlisted Major and Mrs Brindley Boon to look after the entertainment in a second theatre. The effect of the increased population meant that the 'shows' had to be done twice every night in order to accommodate everyone. This also meant that the 'campers' could see two shows every night, one at 6 pm and a different one at 8:30 pm.

One day the commissioner came to find me and said, 'Captain Bearcroft, you are now Major Bearcroft. Go and tell your wife!'

An overseas appointment meant that I was absent from Butlin's for the next seven years, by which time the numbers of attendees had grown to more than 6,000! The venue was now Butlin's in Bognor Regis, where a band and an entertainments team had been established.

Chapter 7

WESTWARD HO!

The Land Of The Maple Leaf

A letter dated 14 May 1968 stated that the Chief of the Staff had appointed me as the Territorial Music Secretary and Head of the Music Department in the Canada Territory (following Brigadier Kenneth Rawlins, whom I had met when touring Canada with Tottenham Citadel Band some years before) and that I was to be succeeded as National Bandmaster in the British Territory by Captain Leslie Condon.

Commissioner William Cooper (whom I had last seen in a Butlin's swimming pool when we both should have been in a meeting) sent a telegram which we received on board a ship bound for Montreal, Canada, which read: 'Bon voyage and God's blessing.'

Jill and I, with our three sons, had said goodbye to our families in England and were now on the high seas bound for a new land. Jill and my youngest son Mark were fine but Bram, my eldest son, and Norman (Norrie) his brother – along with me – proved to be very poor sailors and were constantly sick – so much so that the three of us had to see the medical officer who administered an injection in the hope that we would recover sufficiently to enjoy the rest of the journey.

It was while on board that Jill and I discussed the fact that the Canadian Staff Band had been lost when, back in 1914, the boat on which the bandsmen were travelling was in collision with a Norwegian tanker and most of the passengers perished in the mouth of the St Lawrence River. We wondered why another Staff Band had not been formed and wondered if it might be for us to do so.

On arrival at Montreal we were told that the dockworkers were on strike and that there would be a delay in our disembarkation. As we looked over the side of the ship, we could see a Salvation Army officer on the dockside waiting to welcome us to Canada. It was the Divisional Commander, Lieut-Colonel Cyril Fisher, who so very kindly waited some six or seven hours before we could come ashore. He took us for a meal, then to the railway station en route to the city of Toronto. Once on the overnight train, our three boys were shown which bunks they would occupy. Jill was shown to a small sleeping compartment and I was shown to one directly opposite. In each compartment was a small single bed which one had to pull down before closing the door. Alas! I had already closed the door on my compartment and, having pulled down the bed, could not move! My banging on the door brought an attendant who said, 'Surely you knew to pull the bed down before you closed the door!'

Arriving in Toronto, we were met by Commissioner Clarence Wiseman (then Territorial Commander for Canada) and a few other officers who had gathered to welcome us to this new land. Soon we were at our new quarters (in those days in the north end of the city) and were greeted by Captain Shirley Frayn, who introduced herself as my new secretary. As she was showing us round the house we noticed what seemed to us to be an over-large refrigerator. We were then told that she had complained to headquarters that it was nothing like big enough for a family of five and I was assured that a larger one would be delivered next day!

Newfoundland

A couple of days later I made my appearance at Territorial Headquarters and was duly given a warm welcome. Captain Frayn showed me around and produced some letters, one of which was inviting me to lead a weekend retreat at Corner Brook Temple in Newfoundland the very next weekend! The invitation said that if I had any problem with booking flights, a plane belonging to a Salvationist could pick me up somewhere near Montreal. Well, a plane was available from Toronto Airport and, arriving in Corner Brook, I was driven to the Army's camp, which was called Silver Birches.

The Provincial Commander, Lieut-Colonel Arthur Pitcher, was the Camp Director and he and I shared a caravan for sleeping. Saturday morning included band and vocal rehearsals and a lively discussion period on the topic, 'How can our band be more effective in presenting the gospel?' This produced specific conclusions which, I heard a couple of months later, were being acted upon. On my return to Toronto I received a letter from George Rideout (one of those at the retreat) containing the following paragraph:

'We wish to inform you that you have a standing invitation to come again at any time, with your wife and family if possible, and to again partake of our Newfoundland hospitality. Our one request is that, the next time, stay much longer. Your tolerance of the way we managed to barbarize your music, made all us "Blokes" feel that you should very soon return to us.'

Newfoundland is a beautiful, even magnificent island to visit and The Salvation Army has a very special place in the hearts of the Newfoundland people. Many were educated in Salvation Army schools and all show the greatest respect for the work of the Army. At one time, almost every town and village had an Army corps, a fact I discovered a few months later when leading six or seven councils for bandsmen and songsters in different towns or villages in one week! As I entered what was called a village, there would only be four or five houses plus an Army hall, which would be full at each centre with never less than 60 bandsmen or songsters present.

Commissioner Wiseman, himself a Newfoundlander, was delighted with the report I was able to give him when he welcomed me to headquarters. He then told me that, although headquarters officers visiting corps were expected to travel by train or car, if I was visiting corps at some distance I was free to travel by air. Considering the vast areas to be covered, this proved to be a blessing. I used to think it was a long way from London to Glasgow but now had to get used to thinking in terms of thousands rather than hundreds of miles.

Canadian Staff Band

A month after being welcomed to Canada, I approached Commissioner Wiseman on the subject of forming a new Staff Band. I did express the opinion that it was time to stop grieving about the band that was lost so many years ago and to look forward with a new band. He was very interested in my suggestion and asked how I would go about such an idea. I told him that I already knew a number of players and had seen a few others in the rehearsals I had conducted in and around Toronto. The commissioner asked how I thought a band might work and what would be demanded of the players. Knowing what the International Staff Band did in regard to rehearsals and 'specialing', I was able to come up with a programme that would justify the inauguration and value of such a band. On the question of finance, I pointed out that we would need an outlay of money for instruments and music and that we would aim to pay the money back to headquarters in two or three years. The commissioner was convinced that to have a Staff Band would be a good thing for the territory and agreed that I could commence work on the project. He also agreed that an announcement could be made both in the Army's press and in the national newspapers. On leaving the commissioner's office, I went to a Toronto newspaper office – they published the news the very next day!

Obviously, the next thing to do was to find the bandsmen. I knew a number of fine players now living in the Toronto area and spent a few weeks seeking other players who would meet both the spiritual and musical demands of such a band. A letter to each of the possible bandsmen asked them to come to the Music Department at headquarters for a private meeting with me.

None of them knew what the meeting was about, but each of them left the office delighted with the news and promising not to reveal the reason for the visit. The meeting had made clear what the demands of an appointment to the band would mean and a clear and full acceptance of the demands had to be indicated before the men could be commissioned as bandsmen of the new Staff Band.

The first rehearsal was interesting in that the bandsmen were not aware who else would be in the band or where, in their particular section of the band, they would be sitting. Following a welcome cup of tea or coffee, I introduced each bandsman and prayed that God would use us to his glory and the salvation of sinners. Prior to the meeting, I had been in the room where we were to rehearse and placed the name of each bandsman on the chair he was to occupy for the first few rehearsals.

I felt that the men needed to know that we were not going to copy the style of any other band that they may have been in and that our own style would become evident through a few weeks of rehearsal.

I did feel that although our practice room was small and noisy (it was in the basement and close to heating and cooling appliances) we would need to put up with it for a few weeks but, when I discovered that Toronto Temple belonged to headquarters, we swiftly made a move to use the platform in this beautiful hall with such excellent acoustics.

The breaking of the news that a Staff Band had now been formed caused some opposition to the idea, but the territory has long since proved that the decision to have a Staff Band in the Canada Territory was the right one.

Jill and I were in a headquarters meeting when we heard an elderly colonel making some very critical remarks about the new Staff Band and 'these folk from England'. Jill, unable to contain herself, said, 'Look here, colonel, we were sent here to do a job and we shall do our best to complete it whether you like it or not.' All went very quiet and next morning a large bouquet arrived at our house with a note of apology from the said colonel. He became one of our staunchest supporters! Commissioner Wiseman publicly commissioned the band on Saturday 18 January 1969 in Bramwell Booth Temple in the city of Toronto.

The personnel of the band was as follows:

Soprano Cornet:	Ian Watkinson
Solo Cornet:	Deryck Diffey, Warren Nicholl, Douglas Court and Brian Burditt
First Cornet:	Norman Cuthbert, George Swaddling
Second Cornet:	Bramwell Bearcroft, Murray Whitehead

Flugelhorn:	Cyril Robinson
Solo Horn:	Bramwell Allington, James Brennan
First Horn:	Russell De'Ath, Linden Musgrove
Second Horn:	Major Kenneth Evenden
First Baritone:	Ernest Vickerman, Gert Volz
Second Baritone:	George Cuthbert
First Trombone:	Robert Merritt, Robert Young
Second Trombone:	Captain David Hammond
Bass Trombone:	Douglas Burden
Euphonium:	Major William Brown, Stanley Dean
Bass E flat:	Major Eric Kitchen, Edwin Kimmins
Bass B flat:	William Burditt, William McLelland
Percussion:	Marvin Kitney, James Cooper

During the Inauguration Festival, Commissioner Wiseman dedicated the band flag and the new Canadian Staff Band became a reality.

The first piece the band played in public was Dean Goffin's 'Symphony Of Thanksgiving', which contains the song 'For All The Saints', and the following will explain why this music was chosen.

The previous Staff Band, along with territorial leaders and delegates on their way to the 1914 Congress celebrations in London, England, were on the *Empress Of Ireland*, when it was in collision with another vessel in the mouth of the St Lawrence River. Most of the Salvationists were lost in the icy waters of that great river.

Fifty-five years later, following the announcement that a new Staff Band was to be formed, a small number of men of the first Staff Band (who had been unable to go to the London Congress) came to see me with the request that they would like to purchase the flag for the new band and that Lieut-Colonel Ernest Green (who actually had been with those travelling to London and had managed to swim ashore) should be the one to present the flag to the new band.

Major William Brown was commissioned as the Deputy Bandmaster and I was commissioned as the Bandmaster.

Mrs Frances Jerrett, a songster at one of the Toronto corps, became a great friend to the band and, during the festival, presented a number of new instruments – including a BB flat bass, a bass drum and a bass trombone – in memory of her husband Jack.

Halfway through the Inauguration Festival, a character dressed as the early-day Salvationist Captain James Bateman (known as the King's Minstrel) appeared and made his way to the front of the hall, saying that he had heard that some of his songs were going to be played on this occasion. Captain Lloyd Eason, of the Special Efforts Department, stepped up to greet him and was somewhat surprised when the character began to eat some jam sandwiches (which he produced from a violin case) as he sat and listened while the band played Ray Steadman-Allen's new piece, 'The King's Minstrel', containing three of James Bateman's songs. (In fact it was Bill Chinnery who, because of his London Cockney accent, was chosen to act the part.)

Bill Chinnery was welcomed at the next rehearsal when he joined the band on second cornet. He proved to be an excellent bandsman and was especially good at giving his testimony in our open-air meetings, where he never failed to draw a crowd of listeners.

In one of the rehearsals prior to the inauguration, I had emphasised the need for the band to be seen on the streets, considering that the work of the new CSB was to reach people with the good news of the gospel of Jesus Christ. In this regard, it was required for the band to march to and from open-air meetings with colours waving and an invitation for all to come to the meetings at the Salvation Army hall. The inauguration weekend was the first opportunity for this to happen, so I announced that a march of witness would be the order for the Sunday morning before the holiness meeting.

Came the time to march away and all the bandsmen were there ready for the challenge. Following the command 'Quick march!' by Bill Burditt (who became our official command giver) the band began to play the Erik Leidzén march 'In The King's Service'. Hardly had the music started when I noticed that the trombone sound was missing. I thought it best not to look round (in case they were trying to tell me something) but to just keep marching. Soon the basses faded out, followed by the horns and baritones and finally the cornets – the drums were all that was left! I had not reckoned with the icy temperatures of the Canadian winters and all the instruments had frozen up! Looking round, I saw the trombone slides were all frozen in an extended position and unable to be moved and I thought, 'Now what do we do?' However, the problem was resolved as the bandsmen all began to whistle a well-known tune and, with accompaniment from the drums, carried on doing so until the band had completed the whole plan of the march – sub-zero temperature or not!

On arrival at the hall, Deryck Diffey grabbed a handful of snow and placed it in the bell of his cornet and then sought out the commissioner to prove what a stout-hearted company formed the new Canadian Staff Band!

In the weeks that followed a couple of changes had to be made. Our flugelhorn player was finding the travelling to be too much so Brian Burditt was transferred to flugelhorn. Seeing that one of the horn players went missing, Tom LeGrow joined us on first horn. One more fairly early move was to bring Major Bill Kerr (who had just come to Territorial Headquarters) on to the second euphonium.

During a visit to Brantford, a new Guards pattern side drum was presented to the Staff Band and, in a weekend visit to Argyle Citadel, a trombone was presented in memory of Band Reservist Cliff Cummins. A few weeks later, the parents of James Cooper (one of the new band's percussionists) presented a set of timpani.

Songs Of Faith

Very early in my Canadian appointment, Colonel Albert Dalziel, then retired and living in Toronto, had the conviction that a Canadian supplement to the Salvation Army song book would serve a very useful purpose and approached me on the subject. He was not happy about the fact that a number of Canadian corps were using songs of a lesser quality, many of which had little or no relation to the Army's message of salvation and holy living.

Albert Dalziel had been closely associated with Albert Orsborn in the early days of their officership and they had written a number of songs together, an early example being 'I Give Thee My Best' and, a little later, the Army classic 'Great And Glorious'. (It was this song that George Marshall used in his much-loved band selection of the same name and, even as I write, I can hear this majestic melody appearing as the centrepiece of the selection.)

Colonel Dalziel had spoken to Commissioner Wiseman about the need for such a book and had received his approval for the project. The colonel had already chosen a number of songs and we soon got to work finding others. We decided that 100 songs would be sufficient for a good collection. We agreed that the first one in the book should be 'Joyful, Joyful We Adore Thee' (words by Henry van Dyke to music from Beethoven's Ninth Symphony) and the last one should be 'O Canada!' (the Canadian national anthem). Eleven songs by Sidney Cox, three songs from the Gowans and Larsson musicals, Oliver Cook's 'I Know A Fount', Albert Orsborn's 'Sacred Hands Of Jesus' and songs by three Canadian Salvationists – Arnold Brown ('I Believe'), John Wells ('His Saving Power') and Douglas Court ('Win The World For God') – were included.

I felt the matter of pitch was important. In my opinion, songs pitched too low produce poor congregational singing. The idea that the highest note should be an E flat (top space of the musical stave) is a dismal one. It requires a bit more energy and effort to sing above this level and the result, found in the power of a song so pitched for a congregation, is quite remarkable.

I really discovered this fact when conducting large choruses at the big festivals in the Royal Albert Hall. I would sometimes turn round to the congregation and, with a sweep of the hand, invite the audience to join in a final chorus and they always would heartily rise to the challenge and sing the higher notes with real abandon.

The next job for the *Songs Of Faith* was to arrange and score the music for the bands. I decided that the English *Triumph Series* scoring would be the most useful and Colonel Dalziel found a man who could print the music for both the vocal and the band parts, the only problem being he could not read music! He said he would copy exactly what was given to him in manuscript form even though he would not understand it. We decided to give him a trial and he proved to be excellent. Additional checks of the proofs were done by taking them to the Staff Band rehearsals and playing the songs through. The bandsmen were asked to bring pencils and mark anything sounding wrong. We would play through six or seven songs each week and the pencils didn't get much use!

My fondness for high euphonium parts caused me to ask Major Bill Brown (our excellent euphonium soloist) if the euphonium parts were too difficult. He replied, 'If you can't play them, you shouldn't be on euphonium!'

The *Songs Of Faith* book was purchased by most English-speaking countries and many thousands of copies were sold. A number of songs from *Songs Of Faith* were included in a book called *Keep Singing!* (published in London in 1976) and the 1986 edition of *The Song Book of The Salvation Army* contains no fewer than 69 songs from *Songs Of Faith*.

One day, my wife met Mrs Commissioner Wiseman who, after some conversation, said that she was about to go home and lay the table for supper, to which Jill replied, 'I wish I could do the same.' To Mrs Wiseman's inquiry as to why she couldn't do the same, Jill replied that her dining-room table was covered with manuscript and proofs of the new *Songs Of Faith* that could not be moved as they had to be kept in a special order for the printer. Mrs Wiseman went on to ask if there was an office at home and Jill's answer was, 'No!' The very next morning, the Property Secretary came to see me with the news that I was to go with him to see a new house that did have an office – we moved to it a week later!

Every year the Staff Band gave a programme at the Harbour Light (a centre for people with drug and alcohol problems) and during one of these programmes the officer-in-charge, Major Ossie Millar, asked Jill if she could spare a few hours to do some office work for him. Jill was delighted with the request and became a regular visitor to the centre. Major Millar was very happy to tell me that, on the second day she was at the centre, the men came to dinner wearing ties! Jill, our three boys and I would go every Christmas to Harbour Light and present a programme while the men and a few women were having

National Bandmaster, British Territory

Composers Conference held at SP&S, then at Judd Street, London (1961)

All London Bandsmen's Councils held at Clapton Congress Hall (1963)

Canadian Staff Band

Lieut-Colonel Ernest Green, a survivor of the *Empress Of Ireland* disaster, presenting a flag to Commissioner Clarence Wiseman for the new Canadian Staff Band (18 January 1969)

Festival of Gospel Song

The sergeant-major of the Six Nations North American Indian Reserve

Western Canada Tour

The Canadian Staff Band with Commissioner Wiseman at the Parliament
Building in Ottawa

Erik Leidzén

Canadian and New York Staff Bands in New York Temple
for an Erik Leidzén festival (1973)

Cobham Hall

The A Band at Cobham Hall in 1982 (Mark is on flugel horn)

Willing Helpers

Major John Mott as
Bandmaster of the
Household Troops Band

dinner. I was very pleased to hear that the Staff Band still make the yearly visit to the Harbour Light.

We also used to visit a home for women, similar to Harbour Light but where women could stay for long periods of time. Here there was a lady who, every year, wanted to sing 'O Holy Night' with me accompanying her at the piano. As she sang, she would move into various keys throughout the verses, but always got to the home key for the final few bars. The applause which followed was like a 'booking' for the next year!

One day I received a letter from Sidney Cox saying that he was coming to Ontario to conduct a series of meetings and wondered if I would be available to play the piano for him. (We had had contact before concerning a band selection I had written containing three of his songs, 'You Can Tell Out The Sweet Story', 'O What A Hiding Place' and 'By The Pathway Of Duty'. The original manuscript had the title 'Songs Of Sidney Cox' but the Music Board changed it to 'Songs Of Testimony'.)

It was a delight to meet him and to hear him speak about many of his songs. I last met him when he was living in retirement in a home in Detroit, just across the river from Windsor in Canada. From his conversation I could tell that, although he was announced as the Reverend Sidney Cox, he was still a Salvationist through and through.

Festival of Gospel Song

I very much wanted to copy the Festivals of Gospel Song in which I had been so involved in London and, after a few weeks of intensive rehearsal with a number of songster brigades in Greater Toronto and surrounding divisions, I felt we were ready to go!

The Festival Chorus was formed by songsters from the following corps: Belleville, Brantford, Bloor Central, Earlscourt, East Toronto, Etobicoke, Galt, Hamilton Argyle, Kitchener, Mount Dennis, North Toronto, Oakville, Oshawa, St Catherines, Scarborough, Toronto Temple, West Toronto, Woodstock and Wychwood.

The Massey Hall in Toronto, Canada, has much in common with the Royal Albert Hall in London. While smaller than the famous

London venue, it has been used by the Army for the commissioning of cadets, congress meetings, music festivals and (like the Royal Albert Hall) it has witnessed the presence of the Lord in great glory, power and joy as his people have opened their hearts to him. The hall has a large seating capacity and a splendid stage capable of accommodating a 500-voice chorus and a 30-piece band.

The first Festival of Gospel Song was presented by a 500-voice Chorus and the Staff Band on 26 April 1969 in a packed Massey Hall. The festival commenced with 'O for a thousand tongues to sing my great Redeemer's praise' to a new setting of the tune 'Richmond'. Other songs were 'Bound For The Promised Land', 'Songs Of The Soldier' (Charles Skinner's rousing selection), 'Storm The Forts Of Darkness', 'A Song Of Praise' (Catherine Baird and Leslie Condon) and Mendelssohn's 'How Lovely Are The Messengers'. Mrs Captain Alexander sang 'Water's Edge' and the girls from the music camp sang Michael Kenyon's 'The Lamb' and Charles Wesley's 'Love Divine, All Loves Excelling' to Mozart's 'Ave Verum'.

> Love divine, all loves excelling,
> Joy of Heaven, to earth come down,
> Fix in us thy humble dwelling,
> All thy faithful mercies crown.
> Jesus, thou art all compassion,
> Pure, unbounded love thou art;
> Visit us with thy salvation,
> Enter every longing heart.

Charles Baker (a young man from Montclair Corps in New Jersey, USA) gave a great performance of Ray Steadman-Allen's trombone solo 'Immortal Theme' and an obbligato to the male chorus singing 'What Will You Do With Jesus?'

The programme concluded with Erik Leidzén's 'The Cross', with the songsters singing the songs included in this work, with its ending being a setting of the old gospel song:

Jesus, keep me near the cross;
There a precious fountain,
Free to all, a healing stream,
Flows from Calvary's mountain.

In the cross, in the cross, be my glory ever;
Till my raptured soul shall find rest beyond the river.

The lovely acoustic properties of the Massey Hall plus the devotion of the singers to their task and the accompaniment of the newly formed Canadian Staff Band made for a memorable evening. So much so that the Festival of Gospel Song has been an annual feature ever since.

I well remember the occasion when Jill and I received an invitation to conduct some meetings in the Six Nations North American Indian Reserve, 40 miles from Toronto, where the meetings were held in a disused Quaker hut with just an earthen floor. As we gathered around a pot-bellied stove I was delighted to hear the efforts of a newly formed young people's band playing 'Onward, Christian Soldiers'. At the close of the meeting I invited the band to come to the next Festival of Gospel Song to be held in the Massey Hall, adding that they should come wearing their traditional dress.

The band came, with the young people dressed as requested, and gave a rendition of 'Onward, Christian Soldiers' to the delight of all present for the occasion. Following their presentation, Commissioner Wiseman announced that a new hall was to be built on the reserve in place of the old wooden building. On hearing this news, the sergeant-major of the corps, dressed in traditional clothing with a glorious feather headdress, broke into what I can only describe as a war dance accompanied by loud applause from the audience. Some months later, the Canadian Staff Band was present on the reserve for the opening of the new hall.

A letter from Major Harding Beckett, the officer responsible for the work on the Six Nations reserve, expressed the following:

How do I say thank you for last Saturday night? Needless to say, I am sure it was the last push, which made 'the powers' decide to build a hall and appoint an officer. Our kids were scared out of their wits. You and Jill will always have a special place with the Indians.

The first anniversary of the Staff Band was held on 17 January 1970 at Toronto Temple and the following report, by Mrs Major David Hammond, appeared in the Canadian *Musician*:

Flanked by the combined songster brigades of Galt, Kitchener, North Toronto, West Toronto and Woodstock, the Canadian Staff Band celebrated their first birthday with an appropriate gift of music. Glancing down the programme, it was obvious that Bandmaster Major Norman Bearcroft had tried to please everybody – surely one of the world's impossible tasks! Listening to 'Songs Of The Morning' written by Eric Ball in 1937, and 'Song Of Courage' by the same composer some thirty years later, provided an interesting study in contrasts for the musicologists present. One came away with the feeling that our bands are going to be playing Eric Ball's music for many birthdays yet to come.

Included in the Festival Chorus's offerings were a rollicking sea-shanty – 'Homeward Bound' (Leidzén) – and a very pleasing arrangement of 'Down From His Glory'.

Perhaps in honour of our musical elder statesman, Divisional Bandmaster Jack Green OF of Belleville, who had opened the meeting with prayer, the Band and Chorus presented 'Land Of Song', a march Norman had written for the Welsh School of Music.

Major Ray Steadman-Allen's 'Melodies Of Dvořák' (for many the musical highlight of the evening, and revealing the Staff Band at the height of its efficiency in showing a fine sense of ensemble playing alternating between dainty pianissimos and stimulating fortissimos) made the audience feel as if the Slav dancing girls would come swirling down the aisle in their colourful dirndl skirts at any moment.

The Salvation Army's answer to Rodgers and Hammerstein, Gowans and Larsson of *Take-over Bid* fame, were well represented by Bandsman Douglas Court in his vocal rendition of 'A Different Man'. The devotees of the virtuoso school were surely well pleased with the musical offerings of the two instrumental soloists. With his customary aplomb and artistry, Major William Brown conquered the intricacies of 'Harbour Light', then an unpublished euphonium solo written by the Staff Bandmaster. Robert Merritt, playing brilliantly, probably caused some of the more conservative eyebrows in the audience to be raised in Leslie Condon's trombone solo 'Song Of Exuberance'. Featuring Latin-American rhythms, it would seem to be music strictly for the non-square under-thirties. Perhaps this is to be the sound of the seventies.

The other revolutionary offering of the evening was 'Just Like John' – an often-humorous musical description of an old-time 'how-do-you-do' testimony meeting. As Staff Bandsman Douglas Burden said in his testimony, 'If that is what it used to be like in the Army, they must have had a swinging time.'

The evening concluded on a more conventional note with the playing and singing of Erik Leidzén's selection 'On The Way Home'.

Western Canada Tour

The first major tour of the band was in 1970 to Western Canada, from 9 to 18 October, the cities visited being Regina, Vancouver, Victoria, Edmonton, Calgary and Winnipeg.

The repertoire for the tour included the following: 'Praise' (Heaton), 'Celebration' (Condon), 'On The King's Highway' (Leidzén), 'To The Front' (Bowen), 'Song Of Courage' (Ball), 'Symphony Of Thanksgiving' (Goffin), 'The Call Of The Righteous' (Condon), 'None Other Name' (Leidzén), 'The King's Minstrel' (Steadman-Allen), 'Melodies of Dvořák' (Steadman-Allen), 'Just Like John' (Bearcroft) and 'My Treasure' (Heaton).

Solo items were: 'Wondrous Day' (Leidzén) – cornet soloist Deryck Diffey, 'Rhapsody On Negro Spirituals' (Steadman-Allen) – trombone soloist Robert Merritt, 'Song Of Exuberance' (Condon) and 'Song Of

Triumph' (Bowes) – euphonium soloist Major William Brown, 'A Different Man' (Gowans and Larsson) and 'We're Going To Win The World For God' (Court) – vocal soloist Douglas Court. Other items included a horn ensemble, 'On The Sunny Side' (Bearcroft), and a trombone ensemble, 'Wonders Begin When The Lord Comes In' (Steadman-Allen).

Colonel Arthur Moulton became the band's first Executive Officer in October 1971. The colonel was always proud to announce that he was a Newfoundlander by birth, a fact that was made very obvious in the second major tour of the band, which was to Eastern Canada and Newfoundland.

This tour began on Friday 8 October 1971 in Halifax, Novia Scotia, followed by five days in Newfoundland, commencing at St John's for three days before going on to Grand Falls and Corner Brook. Thursday 14 October found us at Saint John, New Brunswick, then it was on to Ottawa with the final weekend in Montreal.

Colonel Arthur Moulton was very much at home on this tour, for which I had composed a new suite entitled 'Songs Of Newfoundland' (songs I got from a book which Arthur Moulton had lent me), which included 'We'll Rant And We'll Roar', 'Jack Was Every Inch A Sailor', 'Let Me Fish Off Cape St Mary's', 'I'se The B'y' ('I'm The Boy') and concluded with 'The Ode To Newfoundland'. The playing of this suite of their own melodies so delighted the listeners that we had to play it again! Tears certainly flowed as, for the second time, they stood for 'The Ode To Newfoundland', their own national anthem.

We were joined in Ottawa by Commissioner Wiseman for the remainder of the tour, first at the Parliament buildings (where a short concert was given to the Members of Parliament) and then in the auditorium of the High School of Commerce, where the evening festival was held. The final weekend of the tour was spent in Montreal, where the opening march just had to be Norman Audoire's 'Montreal Citadel'. It was noted that every day of the tour saw the band on the march!

The 1971 Canadian version of *The Musician* gave a review of the three years' service of the Canadian Staff Band as follows:

Another birthday of the Canadian Staff Band gives the opportunity to look back on three years of useful activity. Campaigning with music has taken the band to every province in Canada as well as to a number of large cities in the United States.

Engagements have found the band not only in concert but fulfilling the traditional role of The Salvation Army, presenting an evangelical thrust on the march and in open-air meetings. The scene of seekers at the mercy seat repeated in many centres visited has been evidence of the impact made through the musical ministry of the band.

In 1971, the Staff Band travelled literally thousands of miles and was equally at home in the cloistered setting of an Anglican cathedral or in a grim maximum security prison, in a sophisticated arts and culture centre or in a crowded marketplace, at the city hospital or at a Harbour Light centre, in the majestic Houses of Parliament or in the multi-varied types of Salvation Army buildings.

During the past three years the band has received encouraging interest from all parts of the territory and a growing acceptance of it as a truly all-Canada Staff Band or, as the bandmaster of a leading band many miles from Toronto said, 'We feel the Canadian Staff Band belongs to us.'

Expression of goodwill and appreciation of the band has been shown in the practical support received and the gratifying fact that the band is now debt-free. Through gifts, donations, the sale of records and the careful budgeting of campaign expenses the capital indebtedness, which was in the form of a loan from territorial headquarters, has now been repaid.

To mark its birthday the Third Anniversary Festival will be presented in the Bramwell Booth Temple, Saturday, January 15. The Territorial Commander, Commissioner C. D. Wiseman, will preside and, with Mrs Wiseman, will be guest leader of the weekend meetings.

July 1972 was when Eric Ball and his wife Olive were celebrated in a festival at Toronto Temple. Eric conducted six of his compositions ranging from 'King Of Kings' (1931) to 'The Kingdom Triumphant' (1963). Eric played the pianoforte accompaniment for two vocal solos, 'The Door Sergeant' (1935), the soloist being Douglas Court, and 'True Life' (1932) with Mrs George Watson as soloist.

The piano that Eric was playing was a very good, full-size grand but, sadly, it had lost a leg when the men moving it up on to the platform dropped it. A couple of wooden crates were 'standing in' for the missing leg! As a matter of fact, this was not the only accident in the preparation for Eric's visit.

The first one occurred when Major Bill Hosty (second cornet player in the Canadian Staff Band) pressed the button which opened the huge platform curtains that had been drawn for a meeting which did not need the platform. Foolishly, someone had pinned a large, heavy item on to the front of the curtains where they met at the middle. The button Bill pressed started the motor that opened the curtains, tearing them badly as it did so.

The third disaster concerned the platform lights that were suspended on a bar from the ceiling. Bill had been complaining that the lights above the second cornet stand were not operating and asked me to go into the room which housed the handle which was used to lower or raise the lamp bar. I found the handle and the bar came down easily enough but when Bill, having fitted new lamp bulbs, signalled for me to raise the bar again, the handle became hard to move, causing Bill to order me to try harder. This I did and the wire which was attached to the handle I was winding snapped and the bank of lights fell to the floor with an almighty crash!

So there we were – curtains torn, the lighting bar crashed on the floor and the piano minus one leg! The next morning the electricians came and repaired the lights and we were able to keep the curtains open until they could be repaired. The operation on the piano leg had to wait for a few more weeks!

Colonel Arthur Moulton, knowing I needed a piano at home, offered me one from a corps that had moved to a new building. I went to see it and, although its appearance left much to be desired, it had a good sound and I was very pleased to have it. Seeing its colour was white, my son Norrie, a very good artist, decided to paint pictures of corps happenings all over it. There was one of the corps officer playing his piano accordion and one of the hall keeper, a very little man who, having great strength, could move the very heavy risers on the platform with seeming little effort. Other aspects of the corps activity had to be removed when seen by Norrie's mother!

The Canadian Staff Band's fourth anniversary was again held at Toronto Temple and featured Major William Brown and Major William Kerr in a euphonium duet especially written for them entitled 'Timepiece'. This was based on the old song 'Grandfather's Clock', to which Salvationists used to sing 'On, On, No Surrender'. Deryck Diffey and Arthur Dean were heard in Ray Steadman-Allen's duet 'Happy In The Fight'. Leslie Condon's tone poem 'The Present Age' concluded the programme.

Seeing that we were playing a lot of manuscript music, I asked the men, if and when a wrong note should appear, not to take time in the rehearsal talking about it, but simply to mark the spot and to let me see it after the rehearsal. This all went very well until we had a new solo cornet player join us. On his very first rehearsal, he raised his hand and said, 'This bar does not have enough notes in it.' All went very quiet until Tom LeGrow, in a very slow manner, said, 'You shouldn't have said that!'

General Erik Wickberg came to Toronto to lead the 90th Anniversary of the Army in Canada Congress. As in all these events, music played a large part both in accompanying the singing and in solo items. A 500-voice chorus was at the Massey Hall for a Festival of Gospel Song and the Chorus, Staff Band and fanfare trumpets presented songs typical of salvation warfare through the years, including 'Nothing But Thy Blood Can Save Me' and 'Storm The Forts Of Darkness'.

Storm the forts of darkness,
Bring them down, bring them down!
Storm the forts of darkness,
Bring them down, bring them down!

Pull down the devil's kingdom,
Where'er he holds dominion;
Storm the forts of darkness, bring them down!

The song is number 698 in *The Song Book Of The Salvation Army* –
look it up, it will do you good and will remind you of the real purpose
of The Salvation Army.

The final meeting on the Sunday night ended in a Hallelujah
Wind-Up, which caused General Wickberg to write me a personal note
which concluded with:

> 'One of the memories we shall carry with us for a very long time
> is that of the Canadian Staff Band leading the march round at the
> close on Sunday night!'

Canadian Staff Band goes to the USA

The band made a visit to New York in March 1973 for Bandsmen's and
Songsters' Councils for the USA Eastern Territory, led by Lieut-
Commissioner and Mrs Bramwell Tripp. Major Stanley Ditmer led a
vocal clinic and I did a technical session with the Canadian Staff Band
and became the after-dinner speaker. A report in the British *Musician*
included the following:

> The 'star' attraction for the USA Eastern Territorial Bandsmen's
> and Songsters' Councils, attended by more than 1,000 delegates, was
> the visit of the Canadian Staff Band, formed only four years ago.
>
> Composed of 30 players, who travel up to 100 miles to attend
> their weekly practice, their music, engaging fellowship and glowing
> Salvationism made their presence as well as their performance a
> unique and unforgettable experience for the hundreds who packed
> the Centennial Memorial Temple, in New York, for the major
> festivals... Other groups present who participated in the Saturday
> afternoon festival... were the New York Staff Band, Buffalo Citadel
> Band, Montclair Band, Hartford Songster Brigade, the Cadets'
> Chorus, Manchester YP Band and Hoboken YP Singing Company,

whose captivating, bi-lingual performance 'brought the house down'...

The glorious music, the spirit of elation and celebration which seemed to characterise this festival, also provided insights into the serious purpose of Army music and led, naturally, toward the beautiful and moving experience of the Sunday morning holiness meeting when God became very real in music, witness and in the prayers and message of Lieut-Commissioner Bramwell Tripp. The simple testimony of Commissioner Leslie Rusher, and the moving singing of the united delegates' chorus, led by Major Bearcroft, of 'Jesus, See Me At Thy Feet' brought moments of quiet reflection leading to decision and commitment when, at the close of the meeting, many knelt to renew their vows and rededicate their lives to God.

On the Sunday afternoon, we joined with the New York Staff Band (Bandmaster Derek Smith) in giving a festival in honour of the life and music of Erik Leidzén.

Hard though it is to believe, most of the band made the journey to and from New York in an old DC3 aircraft. (This kind of aircraft was very popular during the Second World War and it was a real surprise to discover that one could be hired for short journeys.) The crew consisted of a pilot and a hostess, who was there to make tea or coffee. She told us that she was really a singer and was just doing this job between engagements. At our request, she sang a song for us in a very pleasing manner – so pleasing that Major Bill Brown (our deputy bandmaster) wanted to sing a duet with her and so, while one of our bandsmen, Jim Brennan, made and served the tea and coffee, the hostess and Bill Brown sang a number of duets amid the loud noise of the old aircraft and even louder cheers from the bandsmen!

An invitation for the Canadian Staff Band to spend a Sunday in Pittsburgh, USA, proved to be very interesting. The Anglican church was the venue for the morning worship service, in which Colonel Arthur Moulton brought the message and the band played several suitable pieces.

The afternoon found us in a maximum-security prison to give a band concert. On arrival we were told that there had been a riot in the prison a couple of days before our visit and that the inmates had attempted to set fire to the place. The very large building in which we were to play still had the smell of smoke about it and some temporary lighting had been installed for our visit. Prisoners had the choice of coming to hear the band or just walking round the nearby exercise yard. About 50 were in the hall when we started but, on hearing the band, prisoners soon filled the place to capacity. Guards carrying semi-automatic weapons surrounded the hall.

It was a very strange feeling in that the lighting, being so poor, made it difficult to see the faces of our audience. Deryck Diffey stood to play a cornet solo called 'Rhapsody On Negro Spirituals' and as the piece became more involved I could hear some shouting from the audience. I was hoping it would soon stop, but it increased in volume and I could now make out what was being shouted. It was, 'Go man, go! Go man, go!' accompanied by loud clapping.

At the conclusion of the solo, there were loud cheers as Deryck took a bow. I discovered that the man doing all the shouting was a huge black man sitting right on the front row. The odd thing was that, seeing the lighting was so poor, he was still wearing sunglasses! He stood, shouting, 'More, more! We want to hear that guy play his solo again.' Remembering the regulation forbidding encores, and then considering the size of the man, I said, 'Well, we will have to give Deryck a little rest before he plays it again and, meanwhile, perhaps you and I can have a little chat.' 'Good idea!' he said and then went on to say, 'We have a band here in the prison.' 'Oh,' I said, 'and what do you play?' 'Baritone,' he replied and then added, 'I'll tell you what, we could do with this guy Deryck in our band,' to which Deryck himself replied, 'What do I have to do to get in?' He then played the whole solo again and the response was even noisier than the first time!

A few weeks later, I wrote a new solo for Deryck called 'Golden Slippers', based on the old spiritual of the same name.

The 1930 Salvation Army song book had a 'converted' version of the song, the first verse being as follows:

Oh, the blessed Lord!
He has saved my soul
From the world and the devil, and
He's made me whole;
And my heart is kept
So white and clean
For to ride up in the chariot in the morn.

Deryck, a unique player of spectacular ability and able to play 'lip trills' at a very high range, really stirred me to write a solo only playable by a soloist of his standard. He would never say a phrase or section was too difficult. In the first manuscript version of 'Golden Slippers' I had written a series of lip trills in a range that climbed higher and higher, so much so that, following one rehearsal, Jill said that I would need to make some changes or he would kill himself! (In this version the trills went a third higher than the printed one.) Reluctantly, Deryck accepted my revised version and, in the many times he played the solo, always gave a spectacular performance, much to the great delight of the listeners.

Chapter 8

LOCOMOTION

On Tour In Australia

Commissioner Harry Warren had been on the training staff during our session at the International Training College. He was now Territorial Commander of the Australia Southern Territory and he wrote a letter inviting me to visit his territory. A similar letter from Colonel Richard Holz invited me to the Australia Eastern Territory. Dean Goffin (then a divisional commander and the Territorial Music Secretary in New Zealand) also wrote to me asking why I was not going to New Zealand, seeing that he had heard that I would be 'reasonably near'. I replied that I had not received an invitation from New Zealand but would be happy to call in on the way to Australia. Dean replied saying my news was good and that he had arranged Divisional Councils for bandsmen and songsters in Auckland on the day I arrived, followed by a festival in the evening! He added that this should work out all right seeing I could sleep on the aircraft, in which I would have been for many hours!

It was great to see Dean again as I stepped off the plane and, after a cup of tea at the airport, we made for the venue for the councils. The New Zealand *War Cry* contained the following report:

> Major Bearcroft was introduced by Lieut-Colonel Dean Goffin, who drew on personal experiences to give humorous and fascinating insights into men and music. Dean and Norman had worked together for a number of years in the British Territory and on the International Music Board.
>
> During the festival, Major Bearcroft demonstrated the interpretation of music with the Newton Band and Congress Hall

Songster Brigade. The songster brigade's singing of 'O for a thousand tongues to sing' was a fitting conclusion to the evening.

Following this, Dean and I went to Bandmaster Tom Rive's home for the night's billet and it was a great joy to meet Tom and Mrs Rive again. Needless to say, I was almost asleep by the time we finished supper but managed to keep awake long enough to get into bed. Then Dean (who was sharing the same room) wanted to talk about the old days! Dean was still talking as I stirred a couple of times! Next morning Tom suggested that I might like to go and pick a grapefruit from a tree in his garden for my breakfast. This was the first time I had picked a grapefruit from a tree and it was lovely!

Tom (with his great skill as a composer) wrote a very appealing setting of the old song 'Be In Time' (*The Musical Salvationist*, January 1982). This song, included in the Army's first song book, may now seem a little quaint, but it is the same message Jesus gave as recorded in Matthew's Gospel, Chapter 24, where he speaks of the urgent need to be ready to meet God. Two of the verses of the song are as follows:

> The voice of wisdom cries
> Be in time, be in time,
> The voice of wisdom cries
> Be in time.
> To give up every sin
> In earnest now begin,
> The night will soon set in,
> Be in time.
>
> Backslider, dost thou hear?
> Be in time, be in time;
> Backslider, dost thou hear?
> Be in time;
> Thy sinful course forsake,

Thyself to prayer betake;
Thy deathless soul's at stake,
Be in time.

Incidentally, when studying ancient music at the Vatican in Rome, Tom would always arrive in his Salvation Army uniform – and it was a red tunic!

My first stop in Australia was at Perth where the corps is known as Perth Fortress, thus giving way to the realisation that this was a corps with a long and glorious history. Musicians Councils (following a festival on Saturday night) were held on Sunday morning and afternoon with a public salvation meeting in the evening. I will long remember the march from the Sunday night open-air meeting, for the very colourful counter-marching which, on arrival, took place right outside the hall. The next stop was at Adelaide, which included a meal with the bandmasters and songster leaders, followed by a festival and a billet with some old friends, Don and Mrs Haines.

The next three days were spent at an adult music school at the Victor Harbour Holiday Centre. The opening date (11 September) was the date my Jill and I had been married 25 years previously. I was a bit surprised when I made my way to the rehearsal room to find a lady in a wedding dress waiting for me at the door. She said that she was 'standing in' for Jill on this our silver wedding day. When we entered the room, a band played 'Here Comes The Bride'. A wedding cake was cut and shared around the assembled musicians. Another welcome surprise was to hear a recording of my Jill's voice wishing me a 'happy anniversary'.

On to Melbourne for a Friday rehearsal and festival with the Melbourne Staff Band, in which it was a great pleasure to conduct some of my numbers and to end the programme with Dean Goffin's 'Symphony Of Thanksgiving'.

Music Leaders Councils were held on the Saturday night, with Bands and Songsters Councils on the Sunday. A music festival in Launceston was followed by a band and songster festival the next day before a flight to Canberra.

Arthur Gullidge

While I was in Canberra I visited the National War Cemetery in the hope of finding a memorial to Bandmaster Arthur Gullidge who, with the military band of which he was the bandmaster, was captured by the Japanese. They were being taken somewhere by ship when it was torpedoed by an allied vessel and all on board were lost. I went to the office to get some information and the person who saw me wanted to know what was so special about Arthur Gullidge seeing that, almost every week, someone makes the same inquiry. I was able to tell him what Arthur Gullidge had meant to The Salvation Army and that our bands still play his great marches, as well as his devotional selection 'Divine Communion'. I was taken to a commemorative site where his name appears. The person showing me the site joined in a prayer of thanksgiving for the life and influence of Arthur Gullidge. I found myself whistling his splendid march 'Victorious' as I left. It features this song:

> *Ever is the war cry,*
> *Victory, victory!*
> *Ever is the war cry,*
> *Victory!*
> *Write it on your banners,*
> *Get it on your knees,*
> *Victory, victory, victory!*

The next series of meetings, rehearsals and festivals was in the Australia Eastern Territory. It was here that I was met by Colonel Richard Holz (then the Chief Secretary), who accompanied me to some of the venues for this part of the tour. A Spring Festival was held in Sydney (it seemed strange to me having a 'spring' festival in September!) with councils the next day. On the Tuesday, Major Terracini (the Australia Eastern Music Secretary) and I were at Wollongong for an evening with their band and songsters. A similar evening was spent at Orange and Newcastle before the final weekend in Brisbane.

It was during one of these days that Colonel Holz (who told me to call him Dick) informed me that a lady known as Mrs Mussel, who used to look after our children when we lived in Fordingbridge back in 1952 and who was now living in Australia, just wondered if there was a chance of seeing me while I was over there. Dick invited her to the evening meeting but she explained that she had to work and, although she had asked for the time off, had been refused. Dick told her that she would still see me and that we would meet in the park near to where she lived. I was delighted when he told me this and the next day we set off to see this lady.

Although it had been a number of years since I had seen her, I recognised her straight away. Dick then told her that, seeing she could not come to the meeting where Norman was to be, we had now come to have a meeting together where she could be. With that, we sang a verse of a song together, Dick prayed and read some Scripture, then invited me to have a few words before a closing song, which Dick asked her to choose. The whole incident proved to me what a true caring Christian Richard Holz was. He could have just arranged a telephone call or said he would tell me about her inquiry, but no! This was the real Richard Holz and I will never forget his kindness and care for this little lady he had never even heard of before! I remembered my mother saying, 'Actions speak louder than words!'

I was due to fly back to Canada on the following evening only to discover that there was a strike at the airport. The flight should have been to New Zealand, on to Los Angeles and then to Toronto. The New Zealand air company arranged for me and the other passengers to stay at a hotel in the airport and said that there would be no flights out in the near future. My problem was that I was due to lead a big festival at the Massey Hall in Toronto on the coming Saturday with a full dress rehearsal on the Thursday evening. I got into bed feeling a little frustrated when a man came to the door with the news that a flight was leaving for a French island just east of Australia, from where there was a connecting flight to the USA. He then asked if I wanted the one available seat. Did I want it! I was up and dressed in seconds and on my way to the airport. I encountered a little problem on arrival at the French island in that the *gendarme* wanted to see my permit for being there! Seeing I was due to leave in just a few minutes they said they would overlook my carelessness this time! I eventually arrived in Toronto on the afternoon of the Thursday night rehearsal.

Chapter 9

THE SOUND OF BRITAIN

Canadian Staff Band Tour of Britain (31 May to 17 June 1974)

At six o'clock in the morning on Friday 31 May 1974, the National Bandmaster (Captain Trevor Davis) was at London Airport to meet us and we were soon on the bus to Brighton Congress Hall and a very welcome breakfast. Very few had managed to sleep on the flight and so were glad to spend the rest of the morning in various parts of the hall in the hope of some sleep, before a march through the streets of Brighton and a civic reception at the Royal Pavilion.

The evening festival was held in Brighton Congress Hall and it was a particular joy, on marching into the hall, to see retired General Wilfred Kitching and his brother-in-law, Commissioner Edgar Grinsted, sitting on a platform near to the band. (We were to give our performance in the body of the hall with the congregation sitting all round us.) At the interval, I asked the General if he would conduct the band in his selection 'Christ, My Companion', but he felt the excitement of the occasion would be just too much for him. However, he did stand to take our greeting and thanks after we had played his music.

The next night being the occasion of the Songster Leaders Councils Festival at the Royal Albert Hall, we were featured in the programme, which was presided over by General Jarl Wahlström and the Chief of the Staff, Commissioner Arnold Brown. It was very evident that Commissioner Brown wanted his own countrymen to do well!

The International Staff Band struck up Leslie Condon's march 'Celebration' and the Canadian Staff Bandsmen made their entrance, led by the Army flag carried by Staff Bandsman Gert Volz and followed by Staff Bandsman Tom LeGrow with the Canadian flag with the maple leaf at its centre. You can perhaps imagine my feelings as I followed the band down the steps and across the hall in which I had worked so often in previous festivals of this kind. I was brought back down to earth and had to smile when, marching past an elderly colonel I had known back in my Southall days, he shouted in a very loud voice, 'Good old Norman!'

Major Leslie Condon, the producer of the programme, wanted the Canadian Staff Band to play some of the music which I had written especially for the band during my time in Canada, and so the programme included 'The Sound Of Britain' (written for this tour), 'Golden Slippers' (cornet soloist Deryck Diffey) and 'Word Of Grace' (also written for this tour and played by trombone soloist Robert Merritt). Then Douglas Court sang 'A Different Man' (from one of the Gowans and Larsson musicals). The Canadian Staff Band united with the International Staff Band to play my nephew Brian Bowen's 'My Comfort And Strength' and the march 'Motondo', by my old friend from the Southall days, Donald Osgood.

The next day being Sunday, we were the very busy guests of Regent Hall Corps (known to all as 'the Rink'), which gave us the joy of being on the march three times and in the three meetings in the packed hall.

It was while we were at Regent Hall that we marched to an open-air stand in a road that came out on to Oxford Street (one of the busiest roads in London and the road on which Regent Hall is situated). A crowd quickly gathered to hear and see the band and were delighted when Bandsman Bill Chinnery (who was short in stature) climbed a lamppost, which was only just in Oxford Street, and gave his testimony of the Lord's leading in his life. When he had finished, and the crowd were clapping in appreciation, Colonel Arthur Moulton (our Executive Officer) shouted, 'Zacchaeus, you come down, we're going to the corps for tea!' – reminiscent of the Sunday school chorus:

Zacchaeus was a very little man
And a very little man was he.
He climbed up into a sycamore tree

For he wanted the Lord to see.
And as the Saviour passed that way
He looked up in the tree and said:
'Zacchaeus, you come down!
I'm coming to your house to tea!'

I remember it from my days in the primary class!

An article on the front of *The Musician* dated 22 June 1974 was as follows:

After a cloudy morning, the sun came out to enhance the auspicious occasion of the first-ever visit of a Canadian Staff Band to Buckingham Palace. Wide and straight, and lined on either side by majestic plane trees in full foliage, The Mall was a near perfect setting as the band marched from the palace with a precision worthy of the Grenadier Guards. As the band passed by the statue of Queen Victoria, which stands in the middle of the road immediately in front of Buckingham Palace, a light wind wafted the three flags – Canadian, British and Salvation Army – and Army music filled the air. It was a sight to stir the heart of every Salvationist – and many were among the crowds of tourists and holidaymakers who enjoyed an hour's programme by the band in the palace forecourt. This privilege, accorded to very few bands, will be among the highlights of the band's visit to the United Kingdom, and by its deportment and playing ability it made a real contribution toward the image of The Salvation Army in Canada and Britain.

It was while the Canadian Staff Band was playing in the Palace forecourt that Captain Trevor Davis, standing next to the flag, heard a very loudly whispered 'Trevor!' coming from the other side of the railings, but he did not look round to see who was wanting him. Again he heard 'Trevor!' and, not wanting this to continue, turned to see who was calling his name. As he turned, a lady who had been at the Salvation Army week at Butlin's where Trevor had been in the entertainments team gave a thumbs-up sign as she shouted, in a loud voice, 'BUTLIN'S!'

Jill was there at the Palace with her mother and mine and she took a photograph of them both standing at the Palace gates as the band marched out – they were both looking very pleased with it all!

The British tour included visits to the following centres: Brighton Congress Hall, Regent Hall (London), Chatham, Southsea, Paignton, Bristol, Swansea, Birmingham, Liverpool, Glasgow, Edinburgh, Newcastle upon Tyne, Nottingham, Norwich Citadel and Southall Citadel.

Incidentally, we had taken a good number of our recordings with us in the hope that the income would help us in some expenses. For some reason, we did not offer these for sale until we did a programme in a bandstand in Bournemouth. Jill, who was looking after them, was very pleased to announce that every record we had brought with us was sold before the concert had ended!

Commissioner Arnold Brown returns to Canada

Commissioner Arnold Brown succeeded Commissioner Clarence Wiseman as Territorial Commander for Canada in September 1974, and the Canadian Staff Band gave a welcome home programme for him. In September 1975, Commissioner Arnold Brown presided over a programme given by the Central Band of the Canadian Armed Forces and the Canadian Staff Band in Ottawa. Both bands were seated on the stage and played alternate pieces from their repertoire. The concert began with the combined bands playing a march, 'Fame And Glory', conducted by the Director of the Forces band, and I was invited to conduct the final combined item, 'Finlandia'.

Also in 1975, Colonel Ernest Parr, a great lover of bands and a very accomplished soprano cornet soloist, succeeded Colonel Arthur Moulton as Executive Officer of the Staff Band. Most weeks Colonel Parr would arrive at the rehearsal with enough copies for everyone of a printed verse of a song or a poem which he thought would be an encouragement to the band members. He remained the Executive Officer for the remainder of the time I was with the band.

An invitation came for Jill and me to be the guests at the New York Staff Band retreat in 1975. This gave me the opportunity to spend some time with their bandmaster, Derek Smith, with whom I had spent some years together in the Guards regiments. Derek was in the Horse Guards Band and I was in the Life Guards Band. The duties of these two bands were almost identical, with one band stationed in the Knightsbridge Barracks and the other in the Windsor Barracks. Every so often the bands would change places so that each band would have the specific duties of either venue. There was a period when the two bands were stationed in Windsor with the band rooms being in the old Etonian Club rooms on the banks of the River Thames. Derek lived in Ealing and I lived in Southall. The train from Ealing to Windsor had to come through Southall and I would be waiting for him there so we could journey together to our rehearsal rooms.

It so happened that, during that period, there was a flood in Windsor where the River Thames had burst its banks and the surrounding roads were under water. One morning during the flood, as we were walking to our rehearsal rooms, we saw lots of sheets of military band music floating on the River Thames and we were so happy to think that the flood might mean that we would have some new music to play! The good news was that rehearsals had to be cancelled until the place could be dried out and the bad news was that in a day or so the old music would be replaced.

January 1976 saw the seventh anniversary of the Canadian Staff Band and this was celebrated at Toronto Temple. William Brown excelled in his playing of 'Glorious Fountain' and the festival concluded with Erik Leidzén's 'Pressing Onward'. By this time a number of recordings of the band were available, including 'The Gospel Train', 'Golden Slippers' and 'The Sound Of Britain'.

As stated earlier, I always felt that, in weekend visits to corps, the band should be active in the streets, which meant marching to and from open-air meetings. Commissioner Will Pratt, writing in his book *A Funny Thing Happened On... THE WAY* gives the following report from his visit to Canada:

Lieut-Colonel Norman Bearcroft, composer, conductor and organizer of major musical events, certainly relishes marches and meetings on the streets. That was evident to me when, in the 1970s, I called on him during a visit to Canada where for seven years he was head of the music department and had formed the Canadian Staff Band.

I was immediately invited to accompany the staff band for a weekend of events at Orillia, Ontario. When I first heard the town's name I thought it would be spelled like the name of the tune to which we sing the hymn 'From Greenland's Icy Mountains', as well it might have been since the snow was piled six feet high on either side of the roads.

But the sun shone brightly from an azure sky on Sunday morning, enough to convince Bandmaster Bearcroft that the band could march (or glide) to play to the patients at a local hospital. It meant playing non-stop to prevent valves and slides from freezing in the sub-zero temperature.

Open-air meetings are not held regularly on Sunday mornings in Canada, there being a fine system of adult Bible classes held in Sunday school. But Norman argued that open-air meetings were a requirement of International Orders and Regulations, a favourite argument he used effectively about several matters. Since he was a top man from London and therefore should know, his bandsmen acquiesced. Besides, they liked him.

As a visitor, I was accorded a place behind the Flag Sergeant for the return march from the hospital, flanked by Norman and the band's Executive Officer. The double tap of the drum to signal the commencement of the march had scarcely sounded when a mongrel dog positioned itself in front of me immediately behind the Flag Sergeant. Its nose hovered over the Flag Sergeant's shoes, as though he had cleaned them with meat paste instead of shoe polish. Its tail drooped and he did not seem to be a happy dog. No amount of shooing or shouting affected the dog... he just kept following the flag.

But as we approached the T-junction road ahead, it suddenly darted forward and turned to face the band, placing itself centrally with paws astride, as though controlling the traffic. When the band had marched past, it scurried back to take up its position behind the Flag Sergeant again. Nose to his shoes and tail still drooping, there was no display of pride in its achievement.

As the next turning came in sight, we wondered what our faithful hound would do. To our delight, it repeated its performance exactly and did so yet once more, at the last turning before we arrived back at the citadel. Thirty Canadian Staff Bandsmen can testify to the accuracy of my tale!

I have never given any credence to the idea of reincarnation. It's ridiculous to imagine that any former Salvation Army Corps Sergeant-Major's traffic-controlling spirit had taken up residence in a four-footed friend... though haven't I seen that haunting, hang-dog look on the faces of burdened local officers at some corps?

National Music Camp

It was in our first year in Canada that we held the first National Music Camp, which attracted young Salvationists from all parts of Canada – from Newfoundland in the east to Vancouver in the west. The staff members were: Mrs Major Hammond, Mrs Winnie Watson, Major William Brown and Major Ken Evenden. Other visitors included Mrs Major Burrows, Robert Merritt and Deryck Diffey. Captain Shirley Frayn was the school secretary. The venture was successful and the music camp is now a permanent fixture in the Canadian calendar.

The second year of the camp saw Tom LeGrow as the camp sergeant-major and, one evening, Tom saw a gang of youths about to enter the camp looking for girls. Tom, having a large Alsatian dog, went over to them while holding the dog on a short leash. As Tom neared the threatening youths he said, 'I can't hold this dog on this short leash any longer,' at which the youths made a run for it. When saying to Tom how good it was that he had the dog he replied, 'If I had let the leash go, the dog would have just wagged his tail and rubbed round their legs!'

Toronto Temple Corps

Jill, my three sons and I served as soldiers of Toronto Temple Corps for the time we were in Canada. The Temple building itself was a superb auditorium in downtown Toronto which attracted all kinds of people to the meetings held there. Major and Mrs George Clark, a most interesting and gifted couple, were the corps officers. George was a good accordion player who had the knack of being able to play the final note of a song and have the accordion back on the floor in a fraction of a second.

One Sunday, Major George Clark, announcing that the 85th anniversary of Toronto Temple would be in a few weeks' time, said, 'All sorts of things will be happening, among which Norman is going to write a march called "Temple 85" to mark the occasion and it will contain the chorus we sing every Sunday, "He's the Christ of yesterday, today, forever".' This was the first I had heard about it but, knowing it was useless to argue with George, I just went home and wrote the march.

A lasting memory of Toronto Temple Corps was the Sunday night a lady sitting on the front row listening to Major Clark's sermon opened up her handbag and took out a live dove which, after stroking it, she let fly. The bird went high up to the ceiling and, after circling the gallery for a few moments, came back to the lady who put it back in her handbag. George just continued with his sermon as if nothing had happened. A few minutes later, she opened the bag again and took the bird out, at which point Major Clark, in a somewhat reproachful voice, said, 'You really must not let that bird fly around in this hall.' Her response to that was, 'Look here, if you had been shut up in this handbag as long as this bird, you would be glad to stretch your wings, or maybe in your case, your legs.' Away went the bird for a second flight. By then George, knowing he had lost the congregation, suggested, 'Let's all sing about the birds upon the tree-tops.' We then sang the chorus a couple of times, and the meeting was over.

There was more than a touch of the pioneer spirit in the corps and it was not unusual to have someone under the influence of alcohol interrupting the meeting. We had one or two kindly sergeants who would sit with them should they get too noisy. It was very encouraging to see new folk at the mercy seat, often people of faiths other than Christianity perhaps just visiting Toronto, coming face to face with gospel of Jesus.

Major and Mrs Clark farewelled from the corps and were succeeded by Major and Mrs Edwin Hiscock, two Newfoundlanders. On the way home from their welcome meeting Jill suggested that perhaps the new officers did not feel at home in the corps. Now it is well known in the Canada Territory that the Newfoundland officers like plenty of drum in the meetings and we came to the conclusion that the loss of our drummer, just two weeks before our new officers arrived, was the cause of the problem.

'You need to get a new drummer before tonight's meeting,' said Jill (this was because I was leading the Temple Band at that time). As we were about to sing the opening song of the next meeting, I addressed the major, asking if he would like to have a drum playing with the band. 'Yes! Oh yes, a hundred times yes!' he replied. 'I've been wondering what's missing here at the famous Toronto Temple.' I replied, 'My wife will play the drum for you!' While Jill was getting over the shock of my suggestion, the band sergeant fetched the drum and, after setting it ceremoniously on its stool, handed her a couple of drumsticks, saying she might want to 'do a roll on the ends of the songs'.

'Now we are in business!' exclaimed the major, and so we were. I later discovered during a rehearsal that our new drummer was not always willing to obey the bandmaster's instructions!

Well, if ever the song 'Come, join our Army, to battle we go' was particularly applicable to a corps, that corps was Toronto Temple. It was certainly at war with the devil and we were glad to be counted among its troops.

This was the first and only time my complete family were in a band all together – Bram on solo cornet, Mark on second cornet, Norrie on first trombone, Jill on the drum and me in the middle!

In 1976, orders from International Headquarters stated that we were to return to London and back to the British Territory as I was to be the National Secretary for Bands and Songster Brigades.

A farewell salute, presided over by Commissioner Arnold Brown, was given to us on Wednesday 16 June 1976. We felt sad in leaving Canada and the Canadian Staff Band, whose members had given me such wonderful support during our years in the Land of the Maple Leaf.

The final number on the programme was a setting I had done for the band to use at the close of a weekend visit. The words are:

Blest be the tie that binds
Our hearts in Christian love;
The fellowship of kindred minds
Is like to that above.

Actually, this was not the end of my leadership of the band because, a couple of days following this festival, I went with the band to Newfoundland for a short tour, concluding with a congress in St John's, led by Commissioner Arnold Brown. The thought of leaving the band, with which I had had such exciting and challenging times, was hard to take but such is life as a Salvation Army officer for when one has to go, one has to salute and go!

Chapter 10

VANGUARD

National Secretary for Bands and Songster Brigades

A very warm welcome awaited us on our return to National Headquarters in London. I was pleased to discover that Major June Kitchen was still the departmental secretary and Major Joy Webb (who was now also responsible for the Arts and Drama section) was still in the same office. Brindley Boon, now a colonel, had been transferred to International Headquarters to be the officer responsible for all the arrangements for the International Congress to be held in 1978.

Song Book Council

I felt very privileged in being appointed a member of the Song Book Council that was convened to produce the present 1986 *Song Book Of The Salvation Army*. On arrival at the council I met the other appointed members, Commissioner Kathleen Kendrick (Chair), Major Will Davies, Colonel Brindley Boon, Colonel Stanley Hunt, Lieut-Colonel Ray Bowes, Brigadier Doris Saunders, Mrs Commissioner Norman Marshall and Major Ray Holdstock.

The first task was to decide which songs from the 1953 song book should be withdrawn in order to make space for other songs suggested for inclusion in the new book. This proved to be a very difficult task in that some of the songs proposed for deletion would have very special meaning for someone, somewhere. The council members were free to voice opinions and this led to discussions on the value of each song for salvation warfare. Voting was not a part of the solution but it became obvious which songs were going, even though every person did not agree with every decision.

The song book prior to the 1953 version was the 1930 edition, which included an instruction from William Booth (Founder of The Salvation Army), found in the original *Penny Song Book* as follows:

'Sing the simple old truths in the simple old hearty way that God has already blessed so widely to the salvation of souls and the making and training of red hot soldiers.'

It was a timely instruction for those of us who were about to revise the 1953 edition.

Sixty-nine songs from the Canadian *Songs Of Faith* book were accepted for the new song book, a number of these having been included in the *Keep Singing!* supplement, from which other songs were also selected.

A strange quietness would come over the council when one of the great holiness songs was read and the names of the writers became very dear to us. When dealing with an Army war song, the group would get quite animated and very few of these were discarded.

Lots of letters asked that the Founder's song, 'O Boundless Salvation', should be number one in the new book but most, if not all, of the council members thought that its place was in the 'Gospel – Response' section.

I very much enjoyed the council meetings and the need to dig and delve deeply into every song. I have continued my study of the song book and have come to the conclusion that, for me, the Salvation Army song book is second only to the Bible as a means of grace. We all realised what a sacred task was ours!

Final Tylney Hall Music School

Our return to England in June 1976 did not allow much time to prepare for the National School of Music to be held at Tylney Hall a month later. A new school for boys up to the age of 15 had been started at Sunbury Court, and the age group for Tylney Hall was now changed to include those aged between 16 and 25 years. We then discovered that the Tylney Hall authorities were stating conditions that made it hard for us to operate and so 1976 became the last of the very happy days of Tylney Hall. Incidentally, it was during this week that a young euphonium player, Derick Kane, went for an audition for a place in the International Staff Band. The years have certainly proved the worth of that visit!

Alf Springate had been at most, if not all, of the schools of music, from the very first one held at Hadleigh up to this year at Tylney Hall. The boys wanted to mark this anniversary and, noticing that his briefcase (which he always brought with him for the morning prayers followed by announcements) was very old and very worn, they clubbed together to buy him a new briefcase. Alf was quite moved when the presentation was made and, the next morning, he came in carrying the new briefcase, much to the pleasure of the boys. On arrival at the stage, he very carefully opened his new case, from which he took out the old case containing his notes!

Cobham Hall

An announcement in the 11 December 1976 edition of *The Musician* stated, 'National School of Music to go "Co-Ed" next year', and that the venue was to be Cobham Hall, in Kent.

The idea of going co-ed had been considered some years before when Denis Hunter took me to Tylney Hall to see if there would be any objections to a visit from the girls of the Sunbury music school coming to Tylney (see Chapter 4). Many now married couples can thank the music schools for their meeting each other in this way.

Major John Larsson, in his capacity as National Youth Secretary, was the leader of the school and I was the school's director of music.

We understood that the total accommodation of Cobham Hall was about 200 and quite a lot more than 200 applications arrived at headquarters. It was decided that any persons over the 200 could come providing they brought their own bedding and would be happy to sleep in the corridors. The corridors were filled to overflowing!

A lovely room with a fine grand piano was available for the girls' singing rehearsals. Known officially as the Gilt Room because of its golden decor, it was referred to by our students as 'the Guilt Room'!

117

A long, narrow room, one floor up, sufficed for all the united gatherings and for the massed band rehearsals. Unfortunately, this room was acoustically very lively, causing the massed bands to seem extra loud. In order to conduct an hour-long rehearsal with massed bands in this room I needed (much to the merriment of the boys and girls) to wear cotton wool earplugs!

It was reported that a ghost could be seen at night at the entrance to the main hall, where an old horse-drawn gilt coach stood. On her nightly visit to the girls' room, my wife discovered there was some real concern about a ghost, which, it was reported, appeared near the coach late at night. Jill therefore told the girls she would sit in the gilt coach from 11.45 pm until 12.15 am. To my shame, I confess I did not share the vigil with her but was very pleased when she returned to our room at 12.30 am, unscathed and unbowed. She commented that the ghost must have been as scared as her husband, owing to the fact that it didn't show up!

The final festival was held in the Fairfield Halls in Croydon with a capacity crowd attending. An abridged version of the report in *The Musician* is as follows:

Those who mourned the passing of the former Tylney Hall and Sunbury Court National Schools of Music need not have worried. The first festival to emerge from the new 'co-ed' school held at Cobham Hall, Kent, and presented in the Fairfield Halls, Croydon, possessed just as much jubilant Salvationism expressed in music as before, and the standards attained were almost beyond belief. It was the kind of programme which allowed members of the audience to settle back and permit the music to envelop and transport them to the rarefied heights of inspiration and ecstasy.

Incidentally, this festival marked the 30th anniversary of music schools in Great Britain. The fact that General Arnold Brown, fresh from his election to that high office, was the guest for the evening brought that special something which only he could give.

The three bands, which had come together at the beginning of the week, were known as the Trevor Davis Band – which played 'The Warrior Psalm' – the Bram Williams Band – 'The King's Minstrel' – and the Norman Bearcroft Band – 'Treasures From Tchaikovsky'.

Later, a selection of players from each band – which caused the General to wonder if this was to be *his* band (humour which the capacity crowd was quick to appreciate!) – came together as the A Band. I conducted instead of the General, and it played Leslie Condon's great march 'Celebration', which has the chorus 'We'll keep the old flag flying' as its trio. Forty-seven cornetists brought a touch of pageantry to the programme as they appeared in a double semicircle on the elevation of the stage and, without music copies, presented a skilful rendition of 'The King's Trumpeters'.

The General, referring to the vocal students as 'the Army's own Royal Choral Society', invited Bandmaster Don Osgood to conduct their first item, 'To Be A Pilgrim', and, during the evening, they sang a further 12 songs. Songster Mrs Mary Miller and Songster Leader Fred Crowhurst shared the conducting and brought out the entrancing beauty of the girls' voices. Songster Dorothy Brown (now the International Staff Songster Leader) sang, as the only vocal soloist of the evening, an arrangement of 'Healing Waters'.

An interlude preceded what only General Arnold Brown could describe as 'the pièce de résistance – the climactic and exciting musical magic carpet of "The Sound Of Britain" by the massed bands', which deservedly received tremendous and sustained applause. In utter contrast, the emotive 'Lessons From Nature' – with which the programme concluded and which featured the entire school – produced, as the final notes died away, not wild acclaim as might have been expected, but a deep, reverent hush. In the ensuing dramatic silence the General's voice, lifted in prayer, thanked God for the 'art of Heaven which has been brought to earth'.

Thus ended an impressive, almost overwhelming evening of music at its soulful best and, if there were a few tears being shed behind the scenes as young people took leave of one another, perhaps they found some comfort in the knowledge that next year's festival had already been booked for 2 September 1978.

One year, on one special Wednesday morning the A Band gave the first reading of 'Romans 8' – a new work written by Ray Steadman-Allen for the National School of Music. The National Youth Secretary, Major Norman Howe, was taking the book of Romans as a basis for our daily worship and had asked Ray to write some music for this special week. The result was an amazing work with references to 'A Mighty Fortress Is Our God' (Luther's hymn), 'This Joyful Eastertide' (look it up in the song book, it's number 153 – another to do you good!), one of Ray's own choruses 'We Are Born Of The Spirit' and finally the tune 'Cross Of Jesus', which has the words:

> In the cross of Christ I glory,
> Towering o'er the wrecks of time;
> All the light of sacred story
> Gathers round its head sublime.

As the work came to a close, absent was the good-natured banter that usually follows a number played by the A Band at music school, and all present were aware that the Lord was there, standing with us. Nothing more was said or sung as, one by one, the students quietly left what had become for all a holy place.

It is interesting that the last but one meeting that General Arnold Brown led, prior to his retirement, was again at the Fairfield Halls with the National School of Music. Again he was the compère and was obviously very much at home with the students and congregation.

To mark the occasion I had written a march called 'Cobham Hall', containing two melodies, 'Able To Save' – a chorus (now number one in the chorus section of the song book) which the General had previously asked me to write for a series of campaigns he was to lead in many parts of the world – and his own song 'I Believe' (number 222 in the song book). Just prior to the first performance of the march, the General asked me, 'What tunes are in the piece?' Wanting it to be a surprise, I looked a bit vacant and tapped my head so he would think I was trying hard to remember. He then turned to my wife Jill and said, 'Your husband is a strange fellow, he has written a march but doesn't know what's in it.' Jill replied that she had heard me writing something, then added, 'But it could have been anything.'

The General rose to his feet and, addressing the crowd said, 'Well, we are now going to listen to a new march conducted by its composer, who has no idea what is in it!' Then he added, 'Let's hope *we* shall know by the time it has been played!' I began to conduct the band and, after the first section was concluded, signalled to the vocal students to rise and sing with the band, 'Able to save, able to keep, yes, my Lord is able.' I looked over to the General and his face was a picture as he nodded approval. The singers sat down until we reached the trio of the march, when I again brought the singers to their feet and they sang his song:

> On God's word relying,
> Every doubt defying,
> Faith is heard replying;
> Praise God, I believe!

At this point, he was quite overcome and asked me to introduce the next item.

In later years, in a festival given by the International Staff Band in the town of Bournemouth, where Jill and I had by then retired, the Staff Bandmaster, Stephen Cobb, asked all those in the Staff Band who had been students at either Tylney Hall or Cobham Hall Music Schools to stand. All but a couple of the bandsmen stood and Stephen presented a large bouquet of flowers to Jill.

Back to Butlin's

No sooner was the National Music Camp over than, again, I was responsible for the entertainment at the Holiday-plus-Fellowship week at Butlin's. The number of people expected that year was about five or six thousand.

Major Norman Howe, then corps officer at Boscombe Corps in Bournemouth, invited Jill and me to his quarters to discuss the coming week at Butlin's. I was very glad when he said that an entertainments team was already in place which included Captain and Mrs Peter Dalziel, Captain June Kitchen, George and Lily Crookes, Major Joy Webb, Captain Trevor Davis, himself and Mrs Howe. I was also very glad when he added that most things were all ready in place.

For the following year a new entertainments team had to be established. It included Captain and Mrs John Mott, Major Joy Webb and Songster Stella Gambling (actresses and set designers), Captain and Mrs Peter Mylechreest, Kevin Ashman, Captain Rob Garrad and Captain Diane Lillicrap. Derek Grinter came as the organist, Richard Carroll was stage manager and lighting and sound were under the control of Mark Bearcroft. Once a year, Colonel William Snape was brought into the team to be the chairman for the Old Time Music Hall. He was tailor-made for the job!

Since Butlin's first began, the band has been a major part of the programme and was on duty for the Sunday meetings, open-air meetings, the yearly march with all the folk who had come for the week and the twice-nightly variety show in the Gaiety Theatre. The band met every morning for rehearsal and certainly had a very busy time. Bram Williams followed Roy Burton (whose health prevented him from continuing as the bandmaster) and Bram was just the right man for the job. His sense of humour, his personality and very experienced musical ability attracted players from all over the country who just had to be in the band. Bram's wife, Mary, always came with him and often found herself conscripted for a part in one of the evening shows. I can remember one evening when Mary and my wife Jill had to be two very tiny people (the part called for Munchkins) and, in order to appear very small, they came on to the stage on their knees. They were laughing so much that, when it came to speaking their lines, they were quite unable to make any audible contribution!

One year, when Major George Whittingham was there with the SP&S Trade Department, we needed a five-minute spot filled and

George volunteered to help us. He was to enter the stage as a window cleaner with a ladder, prop it against some screens and wash the windows which had been painted on the screens. Then he was to keep dropping things and having to keep descending and climbing the ladder, singing all the time – which is what a happy window cleaner does.

George was busy doing all this when the screens against which his ladder was placed gave way and, with an almighty crash, George landed on the floor with his bucket of water now all over him. The crowd, roaring with laughter, kept clapping hoping for more of the same. As George left the stage, he came to apologise for ruining the act. I replied, 'You are on again in the next house. Do exactly the same again.' The fact that he got a few bruises and was very wet was beside the point!

Each of the Butlin's venues had a Gaiety Theatre and a Showboat as well as many other smaller halls. All were served by many dedicated and talented leaders as well as artistes and musicians. Strange though it may seem, people were won for the Kingdom and, as I said earlier, we do know that a number of those became officers in The Salvation Army and not a few others found their lifetime partners at Butlin's.

Just imagine 6,000 people on the final Friday march around the grounds, with the commissioner taking the salute. This was led by Major Malcolm Snell (who was such a great help to us in so many ways) – carrying the Army flag – and the band, which was required to keep playing with just a few drumbeats between the pieces they played. All occupants of wheelchairs (I had commissioned them as the Mounted Brigade) were included in the march, with willing folk happy to push them, and all were singing along with the music of the band. Flags were there in abundance and a very happy time was had by all.

The years have seen the great success of the Army week at Butlin's, with many thousands of people taking their holidays first at Clacton, then at Bognor Regis (for which Major Leslie Condon wrote a splendid march of the same name) and then, quite a few years later, at

Skegness. When one thinks of all the welfare officers, as well as the great number of gifted people who helped to make the Butlin's week such a success, we can see Commissioner William Cooper's vision of Holiday-plus-Fellowship well and truly realised.

Incidentally, on one occasion on the other side of the world at an open-air meeting in Perth, Australia, a lady tapped me on the shoulder and said, 'See you at Butlin's.' What a greeting!

Chapter 11

IN GOOD COMPANY

Willing Helpers

From 1976 until retirement I had great help, in turn, from three very gifted National Bandmasters. The first was Captain Trevor Davis (who had first served in this capacity with Major Leslie Condon), then there was Captain John Mott and, finally, Captain Howard Evans. Each one was quite different in style and temperament but each possessed a real creative ability so much needed in this kind of work.

Captain Trevor Davis (a fine musician and a good pianist) had been the National Bandmaster during my time in Canada and had returned to corps work before my coming back to London. With a congress coming on, I needed some help and Trevor came back as the National Bandmaster. We made many long journeys together, with Trevor doing most of the driving. I remember one occasion when the traffic, being so heavy, caused us to arrive at the hall just a few moments before the rehearsal was due to start. Trevor suggested that I go and start the rehearsal while he found somewhere to park the car. As I walked into the hall, I received loud applause from the several hundred singers. We had a prayer and were soon into the first song. Trevor arrived a few moments later and (not knowing that we had already had a prayer) was soon up on the podium ready to do the next song. First he looked round at me with a questioning look on his face, then, turning back to the songsters, said, 'I think we should have a word of prayer before we go any further.' There was a little subdued laughter as Trevor had a further word with the Lord. Trevor has written a number of songs and band selections now published for general use. Trevor went back to corps work, became a divisional commander and, later, the Executive Officer of the International Staff Band.

Captain John Mott was the next National Bandmaster. I had known John for some years and was well aware of his gifts and his creative energy. His aptitude for writing and performing at the Butlin's week singled him out as a man who wants to get on with the job! John was always looking for new ways of getting the work done and was never happier than when in front of a group of players or singers. On his tours he would seek out and visit bandsmen or songsters who were sick or in hospital. I remember one occasion when an officer, with us for Musicians Councils and obviously not wanting to be there, spoke to his wife in French, saying what a dull weekend this was to be. Not knowing that John spoke French, he was a bit red-faced when John said, 'No, this will be one of the best weekends of your life!'

It was at a National Music School that John suggested that it would be a good idea to take the A Band for a tour when the school came to an end. I agreed and the band went with John and had a wonderful time. This was the beginning of the present Household Troops Band which has had such a remarkable and exciting career over the many years since. The band has made a number of excellent recordings and just to see them on the march is a great experience!

Captain Howard Evans followed Captain Mott, joining us just before the 1990 International Congress. A little time before this, I had conducted his marriage to Heather. Howard is a fine musician and an excellent pianist. He also wrote some music for the massive Congress Chorus and some of it is now published for songsters. He also has a number of compositions for bands, ranging from hymn settings to advanced festival music. The Congress Sunday saw him at the Royal Albert Hall leading the Congress Chorus, while I was at Wembley doing the same thing. Subsequently Howard, though no longer an officer, became the bandmaster of the Amsterdam Staff Band and the Music Secretary for The Netherlands Territory. At the time of writing he is back in England and is the bandmaster of Boscombe Band in Bournemouth.

Other very willing helpers include the following:

Ray Steadman-Allen, always a great support, each year at my request would produce a big choral work for the Royal Albert Hall festival. In about September I would give him a call and suggest that he might write something for the following June festival. He always replied, 'What sort of thing do you want?' I would always reply, 'I'll leave that to you.' He never failed!

One year, during the time that Ray and his wife Joy were serving in Australia (and a few weeks after I had issued my usual invitation for some music), I received an excited telephone call from him at about three o'clock in the morning (he had forgotten about the time difference between England and Australia) with the news that he had an idea for a piece. I must have sounded very sleepy at the other end of the line as he went on to describe the contents of his idea and even more dozy when, after he had sung me a few bars, he waited for my response! I was about to say that I hoped it would sound better than the way he was singing it when, mercifully, the line went dead.

A few weeks later the music arrived and proved to be all that I had hoped for and just what we needed to inspire the singers and stir up the audience. When the sound of the great chorus filled the Royal Albert Hall I wondered, 'Can this be the same piece that Ray sang on the telephone?'

Ray Bowes (Bandmaster of the Staff Band during the years I was responsible for these events) was always his helpful self. If the band was accompanying a visiting soloist, Ray would seek to put everyone at ease and was always willing to accept whatever tempo or style the soloist required.

On one occasion I was to lead the Royal Albert Hall congregation in an opening song and, on the spur of the moment, asked Ray to get the band to play the opening few bars. He must have misunderstood my request and played the whole tune (which was quite a long one) and included the chorus for good measure. The congregation seemed to enjoy the fact that I had a 'What on earth are you doing?' look on my face and they broke into applause as the band neared the end of the chorus.

Ray used to say to anyone who questioned him about me, 'I don't know why, but we have been friends for years!'

It was just before a headquarters Christmas gathering that General Arnold Brown suggested that, with the Staff Songsters, I might be able to make the programme a little more cheerful than it had been the previous year, adding, 'In one of your songs.' So, in accordance with the request, the Staff Songsters began singing 'Ding dong merrily on high', in which I had written a few bars of 'Soldier, soldier, won't you marry me with your musket, fife and drum', which goes on to explain that he cannot marry because he has no coat, hat, shoes or whatever to put on. I stopped the songsters and said, 'We actually need a real live soldier who likes to dress up, in order to make the song come alive.' By now, Ray, realising that something was afoot, slid down low in his chair. 'Ray Bowes,' I said, 'just the man we are looking for!' Some of the women songsters had brought garments of one sort and another and had placed them in a barrel. As each verse came to its climax, Ray was obliged to put on the given garments – much to the delight of the congregation. Yes, the meeting became very cheerful and the General said, 'We will have the same again next year'! Ray said something quite different!

Howard Parris, a superb pianoforte accompanist, travelled with me on a number of occasions, including two performances of Handel's *Messiah*, and was also the first pianist for the International Staff Songsters. He always seemed to know exactly what I wanted without me having to make specific requests. He always claimed that he was an 'accompanist' and not a 'soloist'. One would never believe this when hearing him playing the required 'solo spot' in one of our festivals!

Richard Phillips, who followed Howard Parris as pianist for the International Staff Songsters, also had that great gift of just knowing exactly what the conductor wanted, both in rehearsal and performance. I never once had to ask him to play something differently in accordance to my wishes. This uncanny gift made him such a treasure and a delight to work with. I can remember the occasion when, on arriving at the large hall in which we were about to give a programme, he discovered that the piano was of the electric variety! Undaunted, he went ahead as if he were playing the finest 'concert grand'. On another occasion, the piano was standing on some rather high blocks, so that the keyboard was as high as Richard's shoulders. This made Richard look as if he were dusting a shelf, rather than playing a piano! I think that Richard would consider himself an 'all-rounder' as a pianist but, to me, he is first and foremost of the classical variety. He also has a number of compositions for band and songsters published by The Salvation Army.

Michael Kenyon was a real unassuming helper and the composer of almost 70 band pieces. He also wrote and arranged many vocal numbers, including a beautiful setting of William Blake's 'The Lamb' (inspired by Saint John's description of Jesus, as found in the first chapter of his Gospel): 'Behold the Lamb of God who takes away the sin of the world!' Michael's setting is sheer beauty! He was also the excellent pianoforte accompanist for several other performances I conducted of Handel's *Messiah*.

Michael Clack, a superb organist and musician, was always willing and able to play whatever was required in meetings and festivals at the Royal Albert Hall. He never seemed to be worried about the various manuscripts that he would receive at the last minute and, in his own quiet, unassuming manner, would always produce exactly what was required. With his back to the conductor (which is how the organ is situated at the Royal Albert Hall) and with a band between him and the conductor, he would follow the requirements of the conductor by the use of a mirror just above his head without any problems – well, that's how it always appeared!

Bram Williams, for a good many years the bandmaster of Birmingham Citadel Band, was a great help to me at the National Schools of Music. On the retirement of Bandmaster Alf Springate, Bram assisted me in the running of these schools. He later took on the leadership of the extremely large band during the Army week at Butlin's, where his sense of humour and willing spirit got the best out of musicians there on holiday.

Demand and Response
The 'It'll be all right on the night' theory is not one to be used when making music to the glory of God. The kind of music that calls for no real effort to perform is better not performed. There must be a real

challenge to master, one that will not only be to do with the range (highs and lows) but also the need for real spiritual and physical exertion to meet the demands of the music. In other words, it really does have to cost something to produce and present a piece of music to the Lord and to those who have come to listen.

When I have been faced with producing a choir or band which will overcome the technical difficulties of singing or playing strong music, I have thought of the words of David in the Old Testament who, when he was given the opportunity to build an altar for worship on some ground that had been offered to him free of charge said, 'I will not offer to God that which cost me nothing' (see 2 Samuel 24:24). It might be a good idea to include this reference on the printed commission received by all bandsmen and songsters!

Bands and songsters invited to take part in one of these festivals received their invitation well before Christmas and any specially commissioned music would be in the hands of the participants early in the new year.

The festival chorus was usually about 700 or 800 strong and chosen from three different areas in the North, the Midlands and the South of England. This meant that each area would bring about 250 singers. Each area would have at least three united rehearsals before coming to the festival in London and the rehearsals were always occasions for fun and laughter as well as real hard work.

This procedure meant that those of us conducting the music at the London venue had to take at least nine or ten separate area rehearsals before the event, which was when singers and band or ensemble came all together for the first time.

If the upcoming occasion was an international congress with a 600-voice chorus for the Royal Albert Hall and a 1,000-voice chorus at Wembley during the first weekend and two such choirs for the second weekend, plus a couple of events during the week, then the number of rehearsals would rise to 60 or more. Yes, making music is a costly business. One might say on the above scale, a very costly one! Don't try it if you want to avoid hard work, long hours and long late-night journeys.

I was always amazed at the love and devotion shown by our bandsmen and songsters who came (at their own expense) to take part in these meetings and festivals. They had to meet the cost of travelling to area rehearsals as well as to London, which always meant the use of a bus. If it were for a congress weekend, they would have to find their own accommodation, usually for two nights, and in addition they would have to bring or buy their own meals.

Through it all, no one ever grumbled! It was always a great sight when, following a gruelling rehearsal at the Royal Albert Hall, some 800 songsters could be seen having one great picnic on the steps of the Albert Memorial opposite. Someone always packed an extra lunch or tea in case someone else forgot to bring theirs and the fun and laughter enjoyed by all had to be seen and heard to be believed.

On their arrival at the Royal Albert Hall they would be shown where to sit. Some found themselves on the lower part of the stage while others were perched up in the highest extremities of that stage where, it is no exaggeration to say, they would need opera glasses to see who was sitting on the opposite side of the stage. Yet, far or near, once they rose to their feet to sing they were all part of the chorus and no one was more important than anyone else.

Talk about the angels singing! Here they were from all walks of life, all with their own joys and sorrows, and many having journeyed hundreds of miles. Even though it would be the early hours of the next morning before they got home, for the next few hours they would be singing about their Saviour, Jesus Christ, and nothing can exceed the joy of doing that!

We often had several bands on the stage at the same time because it is possible to have three bands on the apron of the stage and two others on the first risers immediately behind the apron. This meant we would have to be at the Royal Albert Hall early in the morning, prior to the bands arriving for their rehearsal, in order to set out the seating as required. Invariably, the first band to arrive would push their seats out a bit further, robbing the other bands of a little space in order to get a bit more comfort in which to perform. The next band would do exactly the same thing and this would go on until the end of the rehearsals. When the bandsmen had finally left the stage we would rearrange the seating exactly as we had done in the morning and, as the bands came to the stage for the performance, no one ever seemed to know that the seats had been changed back to their original positions and everybody was happy!

The smaller bands of the territory have been featured in these festivals. On one occasion the bandmaster led his small band while having to play the E flat bass himself. They got the best reception of the night!

I was always grateful for the presence of the International Staff Band at these events. Whatever was asked of them they would do in great style.

Chapter 12

TRAVELLING HOME

Cars And Musicians

My father-in-law Arthur Lister, who was an expert mechanic and worked on buses for London Transport, helped me to have some understanding of what happened under the bonnet of motorcars. This proved very useful in the days before the provision of cars for officers was approved and it certainly helped me with my musical friends, as the following will reveal.

Ray Bowes, then the Bandmaster of the International Staff Band, had just finished a lunchtime rehearsal. He came to my office to see if I could explain what was wrong with the electrical system of his car. I followed him to the parking place under headquarters and asked him to show me what was causing concern. When he pressed the horn button the lights went on and when he switched on the windscreen wipers the traffic indicators went into action. He assured me that he had not touched anything and thought that something had 'just come loose'. Looking under the bonnet, I found maze of wires, some of which were just hanging down. After some serious adjustments, all was well. Ray, in thanking me, said that 'Something must have come loose when I was washing the car!'

Ray Steadman-Allen liked the small 1934 Austin Seven car which I had and which would go many miles on a gallon of petrol. Another good thing was it was a very simple car without any additions that could go wrong. In fact, it was just what he wanted. He had seen an advert for such a car and asked if I would go with him to see it. Having told him to 'let me do the talking', we set off to find the car on which his heart was set. He seemed very happy as we turned into the appointed road and there, 100 yards ahead, was the car. We drove

133

slowly towards it, then quickened up as we got nearer. 'You didn't stop,' said Ray. 'No,' I replied, 'it was just a rusty mess and would need more money to renew than the car cost in the first place!' Ray was a very quiet passenger on the journey home in my very good, sparkling – Austin Seven!

Dean Goffin, whose New Zealand driving licence had expired, needed a licence to drive in England, so went with me for a few practice outings. Came the day for his test and, in my car, we went to the examination centre to prove his ability to drive in England. The examiner got in the car with him and they drove off at what I thought was a very fast speed. A short time later, my car reappeared and came to a very sharp halt with the back left-hand wheel on the pavement. It seemed a long time before the examiner left the car and, after a couple more minutes, Dean got out and said to me, 'You won't believe it, but that stupid man has failed me!' Then, after a few minutes, he said, 'I think it was your car that caused me to fail!' I took him back to my house where Jill made some coffee in an attempt to soothe the troubled brow.

Some time later, Dean, having now passed his test in an examination centre's car, bought a brand new car for himself. This was delivered to his house the day before we were going to conduct a music weekend in the North of England. Calling me to his office, he said that he thought he should take an early train and that I should drive the new car, bringing Cissie Skinner, whom he had invited to come and present the Bible reading on the Sunday morning. I collected his car and, with Cissie, set off to meet up with Dean in the appointed city. No sooner had we started than it began to snow. All went well for the first 100 miles, then the car began to make some strange noises. When I slowed down, it stopped altogether. A telephone call brought a man in a tow truck and we were towed, in Dean's brand new car, to a garage. (Oh, the shame of it!) After some examination, the garage man told me that the snow had got into some electrical apparatus that was poorly covered and that now, having dried the offending part, he had put sufficient masking tape on to keep it dry for the time being. He then said that new cars should not need this kind of attention. We arrived too late for me to rehearse the music I was to conduct, and Dean was very silent about his new car!

During my days in Canada, Bill Chinnery (second cornet player in the Canadian Staff Band), who owned a car body repair shop, had taken my car in for a respray and lent me a courtesy car to use while the work was being done. On the day I was to collect my car, I left home in the courtesy car for the body shop. I had to stop at the traffic lights but when the lights went green and I tried to go the car would only go backwards! A policeman came and asked what the problem was and just smiled when I told him what was happening. 'Get out and let me try,' he said. Having given the correct signals and made sure that the gear was in the right place he began to move – backwards! Looking puzzled, he asked where I lived. I pointed out the street, just a short distance from our present position, and he said, 'I will hold the traffic while you back up to your house.' This he did, much to the amusement of the crowd which had now gathered! Bill Chinnery's only remark was to say, 'Trust in the Lord and be good!'

In the early days of the Second World War, Phil Catelinet, then a tuba player in one of the London orchestras, would occasionally pick me up in his car and take me with him to an orchestral rehearsal. The car was old and a bit battered but got him to and from his orchestral duties. One night, as we were travelling home, one of his headlights fell off! 'Phil,' I said in an urgent voice, 'one of your headlights has fallen off!' 'Don't worry,' he said in a quiet, unexcited tone, 'There is still one left!'

Jill and I, being invited back to Toronto, Canada, for a Canadian Staff Band anniversary weekend, were staying with our long-time friends Tom and Joyce LeGrow. Tom, thinking that we should have a car for the few days we were there, got one for us. One night, arriving home with Tom in his car and about to get out, I said, 'Tom, you have forgotten to lock the car.' 'Lock the car?' he said – in a somewhat cynical tone. 'This isn't England. You don't need to lock cars here!' I then said, 'What about the other two cars here?' (One belonged to Joyce and the other one was the car he had hired for us.) I was about to give him a lecture on safety, but thought better of it. At 6.30 next morning, he banged on our bedroom door and said in a very loud voice, 'OK, what have you done with the cars?' All three had been stolen! Thinking I had played a trick on him, he was very dismayed when I denied all knowledge of their disappearance.

When Tom told me that the police had been informed, I just had to say, 'Well of course, in England we always lock cars.' Some time later, the police found the cars and said to Tom, 'It's always a good idea to lock your car!'

I need to confess that, when I took my driving test in the city of Portsmouth, I went straight past a traffic control policeman who had his hand up in the 'Stop' position. The examiner must have dozed off for a moment or two because he added words of congratulation when telling me that I had passed the test!

Chapter 13

HIGH FIDELITY

Councils For Bandmasters And Songster Leaders

The annual councils for bandmasters and songster leaders are for their own spiritual welfare and encouragement and the value of such councils is beyond question. To see the Assembly Hall at the William Booth College completely full of these music leaders is an inspiration. The morning and evening sessions are both devotional and, in my day, were always led by the General (a tradition initiated by General Bramwell Booth). It has always been a time of heart-searching and music leaders have returned to their corps renewed in heart and mind for the task they have to fulfil, week by week.

The afternoon session is usually more of a technical one with advice and instruction in the various aspects of Salvation Army music. It has also been the custom for the Staff Band and (later) the Staff Songsters to sing or play a few numbers in the intervals between the meetings, thus giving the delegates the opportunity to hear new (and as yet unpublished) music.

The first Bandmasters and Songster Leaders Councils weekend, for which I was now responsible, commenced on Saturday 4 June 1977. It so happened that 1977 was the year of the Royal Silver Jubilee, so our festival was called the Royal Silver Jubilee Festival and was, as always, held in the Royal Albert Hall. I decided that, for this year, we would have an all-male chorus of 600 voices, for which we had drawn men from no fewer than 35 bands.

The Musician headed its report of the festival as follows:

HAPPY AND GLORIOUS
Royal Albert Hall jubilee festival fit 'to set before a queen'

Flag-bedecked London's jubilee celebrations really got under way on the Saturday prior to the commencement of official proceedings. The occasion was, of course, that of the sparkling jubilee festival held in the Royal Albert Hall in connection with the biennial bandmasters councils. It was an event which would have been worthy of 'setting before a queen' had such a royal patronage been possible.

At my request, Ray Steadman-Allen wrote an arrangement of the National Anthem for the Male Chorus, fanfare trumpets, Staff Band and congregation, with the second verse leading into the opening song:

> O worship the King, all glorious above;
> O gratefully sing his power and his love;
> Our shield and defender, the Ancient of days,
> Pavilioned in splendour and girded with praise.

It certainly set the standard for the evening.

Other bands taking part were Bristol Easton and Enfield. The youthful Connah's Quay Timbrelists gave a dashing display to the march 'Praise' and soprano singer Delia Jones collaborated with Major John Gowans in an item entitled 'Jonah-Man Jazz'. Major John Gowans also gave a moving and dramatic Scripture recital leading to the Male Chorus singing Albert Orsborn's heart-warming song 'The Calvary Track' (song book number 59).

> I know thee who thou art,
> And what thy healing name;
> For when my fainting heart
> The burden nigh o'ercame,
> I saw thy footprints on my road
> Where lately passed the Son of God.

No one was more surprised than Eric Ball when, being called to the platform and amid a standing congregation, he was presented with an illuminated scroll by the Chief of the Staff for 'Fifty years of dedicated service to the music of The Salvation Army'. As Eric was about to leave the stage, I handed him the baton with the request that he now conduct the united bands and singers in his selection 'Constant Trust'. I had to tell him that the Chorus, who were already standing, would be joining the band in the various songs included in his selection, and the result was as if the angels had joined us. When, on the way home, I said this to Jill, she replied, 'Well that's exactly what happened.'

The next day saw 400 bandmasters and deputy bandmasters at the International Training College for the annual Bandmasters Councils led this year, in the absence of the General, by the Chief of the Staff, Commissioner Arthur Carr. Other speakers for the day included Bandmaster William Himes of Flint, Michigan, Bandmaster Roy Burton from Woking, Commissioner Harry Williams (then Chairman of the International Music Board), Bandmaster Richard Gilmore of Derby Central Corps and Captain Trevor Davis, the National Bandmaster. Bandmaster Michael Clack was the pianist for the day, which concluded with a song with words by Will Brand, who had gone to be with his Lord only a few days earlier:

> *By the love that never ceased to hold me,*
> *By the blood which thou didst shed for me,*
> *Whilst thy presence and thy power enfold me,*
> *I renew my covenant with thee.*

Sunbury Court was the venue for a Bandmasters Refresher Course when, the next day, 50 bandmasters came together for a week of inspiration and fellowship. Our chief guests were retired General and Mrs Coutts, who led the daily Bible study. The General took lessons from the parables as his topic, which he entitled A Slice Of Life. Other very welcome guests were Eric and Mrs Ball. Eric worked with the delegates' band in a daily period of band training, taking as his main piece his own tone poem 'Exodus'.

Among other guests who came for brief periods were Lieut-Colonel Ray Steadman-Allen, who spoke about the production of music for bands, Major George Whittingham, who talked about the Trade Department, and Captain Joe Burlison, who gave graphic accounts of his experience in coping with serious emergencies. We were privileged to have three bands coming on successive evenings, these being the International Staff Band with Major Ray Bowes, Staines Band with Bandmaster Brian Bowen and Portsmouth Band with Bandmaster Harold Nobes. General Coutts and Eric Ball shared the chairmanship on each occasion.

Fun and laughter abounded during the cricket matches in which no one agreed to being 'out!' We all left Sunbury in very high spirits.

General and Mrs Arnold Brown were officially welcomed to London on Tuesday 19 July 1977 in the Westminster Central Hall. The music items were from the International Staff Band and the students from the National School of Music, who sang three songs: 'On The Way To Heaven', 'Come Join Our Army' and 'Sing We The King'.

No sooner were these engagements over than it was time to start preparing for Butlin's!

I had received an invitation to go to Switzerland where songsters and string band members had waited 21 years for a national music congress to be organised to meet their special needs. Well, Butlin's concluded on the Friday night and I had to be in Switzerland the following morning! A very convenient aircraft got me to Berne in time for the Saturday afternoon rehearsals, followed by the evening festival and other gatherings after that. On the Sunday morning, having had such little sleep, I found it difficult to keep awake during the sermon. It was at this point that an interpreter, whispering in my ear what was being said, sent me right off to sleep!

My several visits to The Netherlands in connection with councils for bandsmen and songsters were interesting. It was here I first met Captain William Palstra, the Music Secretary for that territory. William was also the bandmaster of a band comprised of men working at headquarters. He told me that, during my visit, this band was to become the Amsterdam Staff Band. I then had the privilege of conducting the band for the first half of the Saturday evening programme, before handing the baton to William Palstra for the actual commissioning and the remainder of the programme.

My next engagement with the band was for a bandsmen's councils weekend when Major Maurice Cooper was the Staff Bandmaster and Music Secretary for that territory. I was quite surprised when Maurice said that he would translate for me when I gave a talk about Salvation Army music and composers. As far as I know, he did excellently!

In April of 1979, Maurice took the Amsterdam Staff Band to England for a ten-day tour, accompanied by Lieut-Colonel H. Pauwels and Captain Trevor Davis.

My long-time friend and colleague Don Jenkins later became the bandmaster of the Amsterdam Staff Band. Don, an excellent trombonist, was also the bandmaster of Bristol Easton Band. (I well remember him conducting this band in an excellent performance of 'Fantasia On Three Spirituals' at the Royal Albert Hall.) Don also served as an instructor at the National School of Music held at Cobham Hall.

Chapter 14

SONG OF EXULTATION

The 1978 International Congress

The 1978 Congress (for which I had the responsibility of organising and rehearsing a very large part of the required music) was upon us. With the Congress Chorus of 1,000 voices now gathered in the vast auditorium at Wembley, we awaited the arrival of the Prince of Wales. As the tumultuous applause which welcomed His Royal Highness faded, and following the opening song, I led the Congress Chorus in the anthem 'Break Forth Into Joy', which seemed to me to be a fitting welcome to the thousands who had gathered. As an introduction to General Arnold Brown's message we sang, at his request, Evangeline Booth's song 'The Wounds Of Christ Are Open' (*SASB* 237).

> *The wounds of Christ are open,*
> *Sinner, they were made for thee;*
> *The wounds of Christ are open,*
> *There for refuge flee.*

The evening meeting had the pageantry of the Army's beginning. The musical history of the Army was represented by a reference to the Fry family of Salisbury (who formed the first Army band) and was brought into the 20th century by the Staff Band playing 'The Triumph Of Peace' (Eric Ball).

General Brown had commissioned Ray Steadman-Allen to set the 11 Doctrines of The Salvation Army to music, a mammoth task considering the length and varying styles of each of the doctrines. Ray produced a splendid work, which by its very nature took at least 25 minutes to sing and hundreds of hours to rehearse. Considering the principal belief and message of Salvationists – 'We believe that the Lord Jesus Christ has by his suffering and death made an atonement for the whole world so that whosoever will may be saved' – the whole congregation were requested to join the Congress Chorus in the singing of this statement of faith, without which there could not be a Salvation Army.

An exhilarating evening of music at Wembley, celebrating a century of music in the Army, was presented simultaneously in the Royal Albert Hall, with each venue having a Congress Chorus. Can you imagine how much work had to go into this? A 1,000-voice Chorus at Wembley and a 600-voice Chorus at the Royal Albert Hall! While the solo band items differed in each venue, the items in which the bands and chorus joined together were the same, and as follows: Leslie Condon's march 'Celebration', in which the Chorus sang 'We'll keep the old flag flying', and Eric Ball's great tone poem 'The King Of Kings', in which all the melodies it contained were sung as well as played.

'Marching Through The Years', a piece I had written for the Congress, contained references to 21 classic Army marches written by composers already in Heaven, as follows: Erik Leidzén – 'Pressing Onward', 'In The King's Service' and 'Excelsior'; Emil Söderström – 'Minneapolis IV'; George Marshall – 'Mighty To Save', 'Stand To Arms' and 'Spirit Of Praise'; Arthur Gullidge – 'Unconquered', 'The Heaven-Bound Throng', 'Victorious' and 'Emblem Of The Army'; Bramwell Coles – 'Victors Acclaimed', 'In The Firing Line', 'The Flag Of Freedom' and 'Under Two Flags'; Henry Goffin – 'The Red Shield'; Norman Audoire – 'Montreal Citadel'; William Broughton – 'Divine Love' and 'The Roll Call'; Harold Scotney – 'The Quest'; and James Merritt – 'The Canadian'.

In his editorial comments on 'Marching Through The Years' (appearing in the front of the published score), Captain Maurice Ozanne thanked me for 'marshalling and dovetailing together themes from the past into one nostalgic whole, truly a mammoth task'. The captain went on to say, 'This work constitutes a limited Roll of Honour of those who have contributed so much to the Army tradition.' I must

144

say how much I enjoyed writing this piece and I do realise what stamina is needed to play it!

My son Mark was asked to look after the sound equipment at Wembley, which included working the reel-to-reel tape machine for the timbrel groups who had brought tape recordings of the music they required for their various drills. A problem arose when a timbrel group from Korea said to Mark, 'We want number three on the tape.' When Mark tried it out, all the music was traditional Korean and sounded the same to him. Seeing they had given him their tape just minutes before the programme, he just had to make a guess and – all was well!

Another timbrel group gave him a tape which began with a drum tap followed by five seconds' silence before the music started. He was told that the drum tap was the sign for them to raise their timbrels high until the music actually started. Came the time for the item and the group marched smartly to the stage to await the drum tap. It came loud and clear, at which point all timbrels were high and lifted up, but following the five-second delay no music was forthcoming! The tape had broken and it took Mark the best part of one minute to stick it back together while the timbrels remained in the high position until the music began. Some of the assembled audience thought that the opening of the item was 'Just a bit too long!'

Another problem arose when almost every programmed speaker got to one of the four microphones placed across the stage and felt the need to tap it with their fingers before commencing to speak. An engineer, whose job it was to switch on whichever microphone was needed, complained that the tapping of the same by most of the speakers was causing a problem. The problem was made worse when, after tapping a microphone and not hearing any response, the said speaker would walk to the next nearest microphone and give it a tap! At one point Mark, in an attempt to calm the troubled waters, told the engineers that this could be the first time that some had ever seen a microphone!

Prior to one of the Congress music festivals, General Brown told me that he wanted all the commissioners to be on the stage at the Royal Albert Hall for this occasion. I explained that every inch would be occupied by a musician with a brass instrument and that the commissioners would not want to be sitting with a trombone so close to their ears. The General left me, repeating that he wanted the commissioners on the stage, adding, 'I know you will do your best!' Much as I wanted to adhere to the General's request, I knew I would have to find a way round it. Even as I was standing there, an idea came to my mind.

Enlisting the aid of a few very charming songsters, I asked them to be at the stage door through which the commissioners would be entering, and to say, 'Do you want to sit on the crowded stage among all the bandsmen or would you like to sit in the Royal Box where the Queen sits?' I added, 'Don't tell them that the Queen will be sitting there and there's no need to tell them that she won't.' All but three of the commissioners said they would much rather be in the Royal Box than squeezed on the crowded stage. Following the programme, the General asked me what had happened to the commissioners. When I told him that they all said they would like to be in the Royal Box he muttered, 'Hmm, how interesting!'

One musical event, for which I was not responsible, was the Symphony Of Praise, given by three Staff Bands: Melbourne, New York and the ISB. This was the one time I could sit in the congregation and just enjoy what was given by these three splendid bands.

The International Staff Band opened the proceedings with the 'Fanfare For A Dignified Occasion', during which the other two bands made their entry with their national flags. General Arnold Brown greeted each of the bands before they played 'The Banner Of Liberty', written by Arthur Goldsmith and published way back in 1921.

Lambert Bittinger and Ronald Waiksnoris, cornetists from the New York Staff Band, played a very interesting and busy duet, 'To Set The People Free', written by Bruce Broughton, followed by the Melbourne Staff Band playing 'Quintessence', a new work from Robert Redhead. The bands then stood to sing an arrangement of 'Wonderful Words Of Life', arranged by Ray Bowes.

The ISB's euphonium soloist, Derick Kane, played a new solo which I had just written for him, called 'Better World' – a very demanding piece and one in which he gave (and still does) a flawless performance. (It is a strange feeling to be sitting among a crowd of listeners when one of your own pieces of music is being played – you are not sure if you should clap at its conclusion!)

The New York Staff Band then played a new piece, 'Thy King Cometh' by Leslie Condon. It was interesting to watch Leslie as the music unfolded and to notice that at no point did he look troubled, but very happy!

The second half of the programme began with the cornets and trombones from each band, arranged in a semicircle and playing 'Bells Of Heaven', theme and variations on the Spiritual 'Peter, Go Ring Them Bells', written for this occasion. They certainly made the bells ring!

The united male chorus stood to sing 'God's Voice' (words by Alfred Gilliard), to the tune which appears in Sibelius's *Finlandia*, and this was followed by a trombone solo, 'New Horizons', written by Robert Redhead and played by Ken McClimont with the Melbourne Staff Band.

'The Holy War' by Ray Steadman-Allen was the International Staff Band's offering and was presented with all the drama contained in this great work.

Colonel Stanley Ditmer's reading from the Bible created the right atmosphere for a new work by Ray Steadman-Allen entitled 'Daystar'.

If I had to choose one piece by Ray for my 'desert island' sojourn, this would be the one. The magnificent arrangements of 'Fairest Lord Jesus, Lord Of All Nature', which appear several times in the work, are, to me, so moving that words cannot express the emotion I feel as the music unfolds. This was the final piece of a festival I will never forget:

> Fairest Lord Jesus,
> Lord of all nature,
> O thou of God and man the Son;
> Thee will I cherish,
> Thee will I honour,
> Thou my soul's glory, joy and crown.

147

A sell-out event of the Congress was the Meet The Composers Festival on Saturday 8 July 1978 at Wembley, when 14 Army composers were present to conduct their own music.

The festival opened with Albert Jakeway conducting the five bands in his march 'Onward To Conquer', with its inspiring declaration, 'Salvation Army, Army of God, onward to conquer the world with fire and blood.'

Erik Silfverberg, from Denmark, took the Congress Chorus through his 'Jesus, The Name High Over All', a melody which Ray Steadman-Allen suggested 'leapt to the top ten'. I would think that this was the first time Erik had conducted this song with 1,000 singers!

Leslie Condon conducted Govan Band in his 'The Call Of The Righteous', a composition which has captivated both players and listeners the world over.

Stanley Piper (songster leader in the days he was at Southall Citadel) provided the pianoforte accompaniment for Mrs Major Mingay, who sang his song 'My Desire'.

Herbert Mountain, at my request, conducted the massed bands in his inspiring march 'Sheffield Citadel'. (This was the march I had played with Ilford Band while marching back to the hall through the rubble of the bombing back in the early 1940s.)

Stanley Ditmer, from the USA, conducted the Congress Chorus in his song 'I'm In His Hands'. (I remembered him conducting his song at the Congress when I later stood with just a few people and sang, on his promotion to Glory, this much-loved song.)

Ray Steadman-Allen came and conducted Upper Norwood Band in his 'Lord Of The Sea', with its seafaring melodies, particularly the one which commences with 'Jesus walked by the seaside'.

Ernest Rance was the next composer and, because of his great gift of several exquisite songs for congregational singing, he led the whole assembly in his setting of 'Would You Know Why I Love Jesus' to his beautiful melody which he called 'The Reason'.

Brian Bowen (my nephew!) conducted Manchester Citadel Band in his march 'The Southern Cross', which, with its particular style, is called a Festival March owing to its difficulty and required stamina.

148

Canadian Staff Band Tour of Britain

The Canadian Staff Band at the Royal Albert Hall (1974)

The Canadian Staff Band leaving Buckingham Palace

Staff Bandsman Bill Chinnery testifying in Soho, London

Staff Bandsman Tom
LeGrow with the
Canadian flag in Oxford
Street, London

Star Lake USA

Star Lake Music Camp with Director Major Tom Mack (1978)

The Royal Albert Hall

Bandmasters Councils Festival at the Royal Albert Hall (1980s)

Camp Victory, Ukraine

Camp Victory

Camp Victory Band

Brindley Boon, born in Willesden, Middlesex, on 11 August 1913 (I knew this because I worked with him for a few years in the Bands Department) and the Executive Officer for this Congress, was next and conducted the Congress Chorus in an extended composition entitled 'Into The Presence Of The King'.

Two composers were featured in the next piece (a cornet solo entitled 'Rhapsody For Cornet And Band') – Ray Bowes, who wrote the music and conducted the Staff Band, and Terry Camsey, who was the soloist. The solo contains a lovely melody written by Terry and beautifully scored by Ray.

Donald Osgood (whom I knew so well in the Southall days) conducted the Congress Chorus in his setting of the old song which has the lines 'I'm off for a trip in the gospel ship, to Canaan's happy shore', which we used to sing as, 'I'm off for a trip in the gospel ship and I'm not coming back any more!' Don's setting became very popular with songster brigades.

It was my turn next and the music chosen was 'Just Like John' with Enfield Band playing. The music is written around the idea of the old-fashioned how-do-you-do meeting, when it was the custom for the person giving his or her testimony to call on someone else to do the same and he or she, in turn, would call upon another. Some of the testimonies would be simple and others may have a touch of pomposity, while a deaf person may think he or she was called upon more than once! The melody is an old Spiritual, 'Walk In Jerusalem Just Like John'.

In complete contrast, Michael Kenyon (for many years a member of the Music Editorial Department) conducted the Congress Chorus in his setting of Muriel Mole's 'He Careth For You'.

Eric Ball was the composer of the final work of the evening, 'The Kingdom Triumphant'. Eric was very happy that I had scored in the main melodies for the Congress Chorus and a glorious sound came from the 1,200 musicians as Eric conducted his masterpiece. The effect of the final triumphant verse was breathtaking as the 1,000-voice chorus, accompanied by the five bands, sang:

149

Yea, amen, let all adore thee
High on thy eternal throne;
Saviour, take the power and glory,
Claim the Kingdom for thine own;
Hallelujah! Hallelujah! Hallelujah!
Everlasting God, come down!

And so ended a night to be remembered – a night never to be forgotten.

'Begin the day with God,' sang the 1,000-voice Congress Chorus in the massive hall in Wembley at the start of the Day of Salvation meetings, led by General Arnold Brown and the Chief of the Staff, Commissioner Stanley Cottrill, on the final Sunday of the 1978 International Congress. The day concluded as many hundreds of Salvationists made their way to make their covenant with God at an improvised mercy seat which, at times, was six rows deep across the arena.

Among other music featured in this meeting was an arrangement of an old song by William Baugh (1852-1942), the inspired words of the second and last verses being:

Sin will abound till grace comes in,
Then grace shall triumph over sin;
Just now, dear Saviour, let it be,
Now give me perfect victory.

'Tis true I have no room to boast;
When most I'm saved I'm humbled most;
Kept low by grace, and not by sin,
My soul shall make her boast in him.

There's victory for me! There's victory for me!
Through the blood of the Lamb there is victory for me;
He came to set his people free
And give them perfect victory.

Jacqui Proctor sang 'I Have Not Much To Give Thee, Lord', accompanied by June Collin at the pianoforte.

In the afternoon meeting, Captain Trevor Davis took the congregation 'Down Memory Lane' in his own arrangement of songs under this title. *The Musician* correspondent wrote, 'This popular piece is obviously not going to be put away and forgotten after the Congress.'

The New York Staff Band, in great style, played 'The Good Old Way' and the Congress Chorus rounded the meeting off with 'We're Sure Of Victory', by Erik Leidzén.

The music of the final meeting included Howard Davies's 'The Wonder Of His Grace', played by the Melbourne Staff Band, and 'Jesus, See Me At Thy Feet' – sung by Olive Hodgetts (a soldier of Waltham Abbey Corps, where Jill and I had been the corps officers back in 1956). The Founder's Song, 'O Boundless Salvation', brought the 1978 Congress to an end.

Knowing how things can go wrong at such events, Jill always arrived with a bag full of bits and pieces 'which might come in useful'. The bag would include, among many other things, needles and cotton (red, white and black), buttons of various sizes and a supply of safety pins.

Feeling the need for a little exercise, Jill set off for a walk around the corridors of the Wembley Arena and, in doing so, came across an officer whom she thought was from the Far East, looking very agitated and distressed. In faltering English, he told Jill that the flag, which he had been instructed to carry in the opening ceremony as the representative of his country, was still in its wrappings. He had obviously expected the rings which attach the flag to its pole to be sewn on and ready for use but this had not been done. Here he was, wanting to show the flag representing his country, with no way of getting it ready.

Jill was in her element! The bag (which I so disliked carrying) contained the answer to this delegate's need! A few words of reassurance, which she realised the man did not understand, and the needle and cotton were being worked at breakneck speed.

As she finished and handed him his flag, his thanks were overwhelming as he hugged and kissed this angel who had just appeared from nowhere at his moment of great need. Who he was, or where he was from, Jill never discovered but, as she watched him carrying his yellow, red and blue symbol of God's love for the whole world, she found new meaning in the words of the song:

> *Just where he needs me, my Lord has placed me,*
> *Just where he needs me, there would I be!*
> *And since he found me, by love he's bound me*
> *To serve him joyfully.*

On the way home I asked her why she had not come and taken her place with me on the platform. 'I couldn't,' she replied. 'I forgot to bring my black shoes!'

Star Lake USA

Although I had received a number of invitations to be the guest at the Star Lake music camp in New Jersey, USA, the summer of 1969 was the first opportunity I had to accept.

For once, the Americans can go back in history further than the British, a fact Jill and I discovered at the Star Lake reunion night, when some of the visitors could remember when they were 'campers' way back in the early 1930s!

My first impression was of the enormous size of the place. In The Salvation Army's camp grounds known as Star Lake there are several individual camps used for various activities – including youth and senior citizens work, alcoholics rehabilitation programmes, and so on. The music week for the national camp (also used for divisional music camps) attracted over 180 students, and this year included some 30 young Salvationists from Sweden, Britain and Canada. (I do know Canada is not overseas when you live in the USA.)

We were greeted by Captain Tom Mack (the composer of a number of songs, including the very popular 'He Leadeth Me'), who was then the Territorial Music Director for the USA Eastern Territory, and Captain

Lawrence Moretz, Territorial Youth Secretary (now a commissioner and Territorial Commander of the USA Eastern Territory), who, with their wives and a fine team of helpers, looked after the students.

The age group was from 13 upwards, so there was a wide range of youth. My particular task was to conduct the Star Lake Band and Star Lake Chorus, both of these groups being selected from the top-grade players and singers. Bandmasters Lambert Bittinger, Charles Hansen and Ivor Bosanko conducted the three other bands. The three chorus groups were directed by Bandmasters Ronald Holz and Terry Camsey and Jeanette Bosanko.

Music played by my group included 'Melodies From Dvořák' and 'On Ratcliff Highway'. The latter number, a slice of Army history, caused much interest, and I took the opportunity of playing various snippets in order to get the programme of the work over to the players before giving a concert performance.

There were approximately 30 young people in the Star Lake Chorus, many of whom were very fine singers and we enjoyed music ranging from 'All Will Be Well' to Ron Tremain's 'Praise'.

The days were full of band and chorus rehearsals, theory classes – ranging from elementary theory to composing and arranging – individual and group classes for instruments and voices and even calligraphy classes for those interested in copying music. Very useful!

Halfway through camp, a telephone message arrived from Major John Bate, Private Secretary to General Arnold Brown, saying, 'The General wants to see you as soon as you get back to London.' Our first thought was, 'Is it Australia?' (This thought came because we knew there had been some talk of this before we went to Canada.) Well, owing to the fact that we were going to Labor Day meetings at Camp Wonderland in Massachusetts, we could only speculate as to why the General needed to see us so urgently.

The days at Star Lake flew past, spent in such good company, and we felt that the Army in America was rich in its young people and looked well for the future.

The Labor Day Weekend camp meetings, led by Colonel and Mrs Rightmire (territorial leaders in Japan), were very different to anything we had previously known. The meetings could best be regarded as old-fashioned revival meetings. The singing was full of life, the testimonies enthusiastic and every meeting was full to overflowing. In the dining room, I discovered that Mrs Rightmire shared my love of honey and it was almost a competition to see who would eat the most!

Chapter 15

I'M GOING TO SING

The International Staff Songsters

Back at International Headquarters, with Major John Bate saying, 'The General will be pleased to see you,' I was ushered into General Arnold Brown's office and greeted with a smiling face. After an inquiry about our trip to the USA, the General said, 'Well, I suppose you want to know why I need to see you.' Then, a little more seriously, he said, 'Norman, I want you to bring into being the International Staff Songsters.' Having no immediate reply from me, he went on to say, 'You have had experience in forming the Canadian Staff Band and now I want you to form the Staff Songsters!' How do you reply to such a request? I thought it best just to say, 'OK,' and I then added, 'What are you expecting and when do you want it to happen?' He replied, 'I have booked the 8th of March for the inauguration at the Fairfield Halls in Croydon so now you had better get on with it.' Then he added, 'Norman, I have just one request regarding this new section. It is my hope and desire that you revive the "heart songs" of the Army.'

He could not have asked for anything better so far as I was concerned. I love to read and sing those songs – songs which are the very essence of the Army. We have a treasury full and overflowing with wonderful words and melodies, which I doubt can be exceeded by the angels themselves. We have songs from the pens of Herbert Booth, Albert Orsborn and many, many others, including some who have only written one song, but whose immeasurable gift to God and the Army has resulted in many thousands coming to the cross and finding salvation.

Before I left he prayed that God would bless this new endeavour and, as I left, he added, 'You can come and see me at any time should you encounter any problems.' I went straight back to my office and sat very quietly for a few moments. The telephone ringing brought me back to reality and it was Jill, asking, 'Where are we going?'

As with the Canadian Staff Band, the first thing to do was to find the personnel. Having met so many songsters in councils, festivals and in corps visits, I did know a few singers and set about contacting them.

Jacqui Proctor, Yvonne Seddon, Deryn Edwards and Irene Debonnaire I knew were good sopranos and Isobel Skinner and Stella Gambling were good altos. Dennis Anderson was the only tenor I knew and David Sewell was the only bass I knew. Word got round and I was soon getting applications from would-be Staff Songsters. Fortunately, I knew an excellent pianist in the person of Howard Parris – known to me as Frank, he was the husband of my niece Joan – who agreed to join and, together in audition, we listened to and accepted those already listed.

The audition was to test the range and quality of the voice and the ability to sight-read music, as well as their Salvationism, their general demeanour and their willingness to accept the demands which they would have to meet.

Auditions – how I hate auditions! My feeling is, if they are good Salvationists and have the courage and desire to come and sing for me, I would like to accept them all. But I would then end up with a group of 200 or more songsters (a little more than the General wanted)!

The final accepted list of singers for the new Staff Songsters was as follows:

Sopranos:	Jacqui Proctor, Yvonne Seddon, Margaret Sanders, Janice Bristow, Margaret Smith, Deryn Edwards and Irene Debonnaire
Altos:	Sheila Turton, Isobel Skinner, Ruth Flett, Ruth Atkinson, Stella Gambling, Audrey Willis, Shirley Hutchinson and Pauline Mercer
Tenors:	Dennis Anderson, Graham Caudle, Stewart Bristow, Kevin Sandford and Gerald Boniface

Basses:	David Sewell, Wycliff Rutherford, Martyn Lawson, Paul Fensom and Martin Collett
Pianist:	Howard Parris
String Bass:	David Bareham

Colonel Ken Bridge, a New Zealander serving at headquarters, was appointed as our Executive Officer and it was he who welcomed the singers to our first rehearsal. Ken, a fine musician, proved to be an excellent compère in the many programmes we did and was inspirational in his conducting of the devotional meetings. The request he made concerning the ending of our meetings and programmes was for the songsters to leave the stage or platform and spread themselves in the aisles among the people to sing the Benediction. This was always the song 'When Jesus Looked O'er Galilee'. The beautiful words by Catherine Baird were perfectly matched by the beautiful music of Ernest Fewster. As you read it or, even better, sing it, you will realise our reason in closing a gathering with this song.

When Jesus looked o'er Galilee,
So blue and calm and fair,
Upon her bosom, could he see
A cross reflected there?

When sunrise dyed the lovely deeps,
And sparkled in his hair,
O did the light rays seem to say:
A crown of thorns he'll wear?

When in the hush of eventide,
Cool waters touched his feet,
Was it a hymn of Calvary's road
He heard the waves repeat?

But when the winds triumphantly
Swept from the open plain,
The Master surely heard the song:
The Lord shall live again!

This first rehearsal was held in the Bramwell Booth Hall at International Headquarters, when everybody met everybody else, some for the first time. I had set out the seating and placed their names on the seats in the order that they would be singing – sopranos (highest on the back row), altos, tenors and basses.

Realising that we did not have a library of music, Major George Whittingham, then working at the Trade Department, supplied us with a set of *Gems For Songsters* – a collection of songs taken from *The Musical Salvationist* (a bimonthly production of new songs) – and, after a few words of welcome and details about what would be expected from everyone, we began to sing. I was delighted with the way they sang the first song straight through and we were into the next one in minutes, which again they sang through with little need for comment. This went on for some time and, thinking it may be near the time to close, I discovered we still had an hour to go! I knew then that we certainly needed some new and more demanding music – music more akin to the *Festival Series* available to bands.

By the next rehearsal, remembering the General's request for 'heart songs', I had completed an arrangement of 'The Well Is Deep' (*SASB* 351), Albert Orsborn's words to the secular melody 'A Voice In The Old Village Choir', and also took as much as I had written of a new number for the inauguration of the Staff Songsters, 'Jesus, The Very Thought Of Thee' (*SASB* 61).

My wife Jill expressed her opinion that, after the songsters had been singing for an hour-and-a-half, a cup of tea or coffee would be welcome and would give them a chance to rest their voices. This became a regular feature but, with the talking which accompanied the break, I wasn't sure about the 'resting the voice' reason!

I discovered that the more I challenged them, the more they were able to produce. It became accepted that the final item of a demanding programme would be something like 'Worthy Is The Lamb' with the 'Amen' Chorus from Handel's *Messiah*.

In a packed Fairfield Halls in Croydon, the inauguration of the International Staff Songsters, led by General Arnold Brown with the

158

Chief of the Staff, Commissioner Stanley Cottrill, took place on 8 March 1980 – a fact I am always glad to see noted in the *Year Book*!

The Songsters marched into the hall to Leslie Condon's great march 'Celebration', played by the International Staff Band, followed by the well-chosen song 'Shout Aloud Salvation, And We'll Have Another Song'. British Commissioner John Needham (a great supporter) led the assembled host in prayer followed by the ISB playing 'Abundant Joy' by Dudley Bright.

Then, in cadets' commissioning style, the Songsters came forward as their names were called by the Chief of the Staff, saluted the General and received their commissions.

The first music heard from the new Songsters was a new setting I had written for the occasion. It must have been an ordeal for Jacqui Proctor, the next voice to be heard, as she began singing in solo voice:

> Jesus, the very thought of thee
> With sweetness fills my breast;
> But sweeter far thy face to see,
> And in thy presence rest.

This was followed by the four-part male voices singing:

> Nor voice can sing, nor heart can frame,
> Nor can the memory find
> A sweeter sound than thy blest name,
> O Saviour of mankind.

Then, heard for the first time in public, the complete group sang:

> O hope of every contrite heart!
> O joy of all the meek!
> To those who fall, how kind thou art,
> How good to those who seek!

Back to the men only:

159

But what to those who find? Ah! this
Nor tongue nor pen can show;
The love of Jesus, what it is
None but his loved ones know.

The final verse was sung by the full brigade:

Jesus, our only joy be thou,
As thou our prize wilt be;
Jesus, be thou our glory now
And through eternity.

Following the hush that fell at the end of the song, General Brown said, 'I hope none of us will forget that the very first word sung by the International Staff Songsters was the word "Jesus".' This thought was echoed several times during the evening, leaving the congregation in no doubt as to the expressed spiritual and evangelistic priorities of this new group of singers.

More than 50 'heart songs' of the Army were arranged and used during the years I led the Staff Songsters and many were included in recordings we made.

As well as pianoforte accompaniment to many of the songs, I chose to use the string bass, which proved very useful in rhythmic type songs as well as extending the range available to bass voices. (To me the sound of the electric bass guitar belongs more to the pop group style of singing.) The first couple of programmes we did included the use of some percussion but this was soon abandoned for the same reason.

Ray Steadman-Allen provided us with some very exciting music, including 'Praise The Lord, O Heavens' and 'My New Day', both of which were difficult both for the singers and the pianist but brought a new sound to Army music and a challenge to the singers.

Regardless of how far we were away from home, weekend visits in Britain would include a Saturday evening programme and a Sunday morning open-air meeting or a visit to a hospital followed by the holiness meeting. There would be another programme in the afternoon, followed by an open-air meeting and a salvation meeting at night.

Being in the Staff Songsters was not an easy number but stamina, plus grace and being well-saved, kept us happy, glad and ready to work!

By the second year, we had been joined by Captain Diane Lillicrap (soprano), Susan Turner (alto), Malcolm Debonnaire and Ron Willis (tenor), Colin High (bass) and, later, Jane Brill (soprano) and Jonathan Forrest and Mark Bearcroft (bass).

The Staff Songsters were required to be at all events like A Day With God, the annual Christmas event at Westminster or any national events led by the General.

Applications for the Songsters to visit corps came from all parts of Britain, as well as some from overseas – including Sweden, France, Holland, Canada, Norway and the USA.

The personnel for the 1986 tour of the USA was as follows:

SOPRANOS
Jacqui Proctor
Anne Whitehead
Valerie Ashton
Jackie Faulks
Irene Debonnaire
Helen Parker
Veronica Mitchell
Ira Burton

TENORS
Dennis Anderson
Kevin Sandford
Gerald Boniface
Andre Price
Brian Huke
Malcolm Debonnaire

ALTOS
Susan Turner
Christine Thomas
Carol Gray
Ruth Atkinson
Andrea Hazell
Sheila Turton
Stella Gambling
Pauline Mercer

BASSES
Wycliff Rutherford
David Sewell
Colin High
Mark Bearcroft
Jonathan Byfield
Timothy Bareham

Executive Officer: Colonel William Clark
Pianist: Richard Phillips

Other songsters who sang in the ISS during my leadership include: Sue Blyth, Teresa Bramwell-Davis, Howard Faulks, Margaret Hynd, Shirley Rubery, Major Robert Garrad, Tracy Bearcroft, Dean Pallant, Major Royston Bartlett, Mel Gunn, Carol Johnson, Joan Spencer and Alec Mitchell. Colonel Bill Rivers and Lieut-Colonel Ivor Rich both served as Executive Officers.

A number of recordings were made at the EMI Studios on the then long-play system and later on compact disc.

It was always a challenge to write music for the Songsters and, although once or twice I was informed that I was asking too much of them, they always met the challenge.

Open-air meetings were always a joy to the Songsters and me and we would always sing on the march back to the hall. It was for this that I arranged Bramwell Coles's march 'The Flag Of Freedom'. It can be heard on a recording entitled 'Be Of Good Cheer'.

Marching As To War

In 1988 a letter arrived informing me that I was to be the Musical Director for a seven-week television series that Anglia Television Company wanted to produce about The Salvation Army. I then discovered that Canon Ivan Bailey had devised and written the script and Felicity Maton was the director and producer, both of whom came to my house for a day to discuss the production and the music required. Music was to be a major part in the series and, having heard about the Staff Songsters, they both hoped that they would be willing and available for many of the scenes.

The series was called *Marching As To War* and the leaflet supplied by the television company conveyed the following information:

Anglia Television's seven-part series *Marching As To War* draws on the great musical and organisational resources of The Salvation Army to tell its story using a combination of documentary, archive material and dramatised events. The programme sets out to project the heady flavour of the crusading early years and examine the role and relevance of Salvationism in today's society.

The presenter is Roy Castle, who believes the Army embodies the real meaning of Christianity – helping people in trouble. 'As Jesus said, "What you do for them, you do for me",' says Roy, who then adds, 'I reckon they've cracked it. They've got the real message of what life is all about. I've yet to meet a Salvationist who's miserable. They believe in letting your life go along the way God wants – be happy and content while at the same time always trying your best.'

To me, Roy seemed to be just the man we needed to present this series and the weekly programme proved him to be the right choice. The seven episodes were as follows:

1. Why Should The Devil Have All The Best Tunes?
Although I was not of the opinion that the Devil had all the best tunes, I went along with the idea for the sake of the series. Roy Castle traced the origins of The Salvation Army, beginning at William Booth's birthplace in Nottingham, then outside the Blind Beggar public house in London's Whitechapel. He recalled Booth's meeting in 1865 with a group of street evangelists, which marked the launch of the East London Christian Mission, out of which The Salvation Army was to grow. Booth hired music halls for his meetings and some of their popular songs were adapted to promote the Army's message.

It was great fun for me to arrange the tune 'Champagne Charlie' for Roy and the Staff Songsters with some brass and woodwind accompaniment. Here are our words to this tune:

> Bless his name, he sets me free,
> Bless his name, he sets me free,
> O the blood, the precious blood,
> I'm trusting in the cleansing flood.
> Bless his name, he sets me free,
> Bless his name he sets me free,
> I know my sins are washed away,
> And now in Jesus I am free.

163

2. The Birth Of The Band

This episode told the story of The Salvation Army undergoing persecution and how the first band was formed in Salisbury, when Charles Fry and his three sons went to form a bodyguard for Booth's followers and took their brass instruments to help with the singing.

For this segment, I enlisted the help of Kevin Ashman with his cornet, Howard Evans with his trombone and Carl Woodman with his bass for a scene which was filmed in the actual house where the Fry family had lived. Roy, with his cornet, acted the part of Charles Fry and the other three acted as the sons.

The film shows them rehearsing a piece in which the father is having some trouble in getting one of the sons to play the right notes. Another scene is outside the Town Hall in Salisbury where three Army lassies are holding an open-air meeting. One of the lassies was my wife Jill, another was Howard Evans's wife Heather and the third was Kevin Ashman's wife Andrea. They caused quite a stir as they made their way through the streets of Salisbury in their old-style uniforms. Actually Roy, hoping that the players would be good enough for the task, discovered that he had a job keeping up with them!

3. A Woman's Place Is In The Pulpit

This episode was about the courtship of William Booth and Catherine Mumford, their marriage, Catherine's place in the pulpit and the equality of men and women in the preaching of the gospel. Tracy Bearcroft (my daughter-in-law, who later joined the Staff Songsters) sang 'Blessed Assurance, Jesus Is Mine' to Stephen Foster's tune 'Beautiful Dreamer'.

4. Soup, Soap And Salvation

Roy Castle went with the soup run from Regent Hall Corps, and the work at Hadleigh Farm Colony was featured. Hadleigh Temple Band is seen marching over the colony in a very strong wind, which really made the flags fly!

5. The Army Goes Worldwide

The work of Commissioner Charles Péan on Devil's Island and the spread of the Army around the world are shown in this programme. Roy Castle portrayed the very colourful 'Joe the Turk', a dynamic Armenian Salvationist who went to prison 57 times for fighting for the rights of Salvationists to preach the gospel on the streets of America. A group of Staff Songsters, presuming they had come just to sing, suddenly discovered that they had to be actors in a scene where Joe the Turk invades a tavern, playing his cornet and singing, 'You've got to take the message to the crowd.'

A few of the women Songsters, wondering why I was not cast in a visible part, contacted the producer and asked why this was. The producer replied that the only part not covered was that of the bartender and she was unsure whether I would be happy to act this part. Their reply, 'He would be delighted to be included', found me being made up as the barman. The producer assured me that, with the make-up and beard, no one would recognise me. It so happened that the following week, while at the Music School, a film arrived for me to see the completed scene, so I thought it would be nice for the students to have a preview. Remembering that the producer had said that no one would recognise me, I was a bit surprised when, at my very first appearance, they all shouted, 'Look, there's Norm!'

6. The Right Side Of The Law

This was about the exposure of the sexual slave trade in London, when the prominent newspaperman William Stead and Bramwell Booth set about persuading Parliament to raise the age of consent. It also looks at the work of Lieut-Colonel Alida Bosshardt in the red-light district in Amsterdam.

7. A Modern Army General

General Eva Burrows was interviewed in this episode and gave an up-to-date statement on the Army and its work all round the world. When Roy Castle asked General Burrows what William Booth would say to her were he able to return today, she replied that his prime objective would still be to bring everyone to a personal knowledge of Jesus Christ – and to that end would say, 'Go on, girl. Go to it!'

The television producers wanted to highlight the work of the Army with the armed forces in two world wars and latched on to the Gowans and Larsson song 'There's Nothing Like An Army Cup Of Tea'. Roy Castle played the part of a soldier and two of our Staff Songsters, Valerie Ashton and Jane Brill, were the Army girls giving out tea. It so happened that a picture of Roy between Valerie and Jane marked all the publicity posters for the series. All three were in costume and holding Army cups of tea.

8. William Booth

The final scene of the series was shot at the Royal Albert Hall during a Bandmasters Councils Festival, and was a tribute to our Founder, William Booth. The television producers engaged a professional actor, Philip Latham, for the part of William Booth. He had a striking likeness to the person he was portraying as he gave the Founder's final speech, thought to be spoken in this very same hall on 9 May 1912:

'While women weep, as they do now, I'll fight; while little children go hungry, as they do now, I'll fight; while men go to prison, in and out, in and out, as they do now, I'll fight; while there is a drunkard left, while there is a poor lost girl upon the streets, while there remains one dark soul without the light of God, I'll fight – I'll fight to the very end!'

Under massive spotlights provided by Anglia Television, the 800-voice chorus which packed the Royal Albert Hall stage was accompanied by the International Staff Band in the singing of Dean Goffin's arrangement of the Founder's Song, 'O Boundless Salvation', with the whole audience joining for the final verse:

And now, hallelujah! the rest of my days
Shall gladly be spent in promoting his praise

166

Who opened his bosom to pour out this sea
Of boundless salvation for you and for me.

Philip Latham waited to see me and to say that he felt very moved as he spoke those lines of William Booth's final message, then concluded by saying, 'What a man he must have been!' As he shook my hand, he said, 'And you are still marching as to war!'

Chapter 16

SPIRIT OF THE ARMY

The 1990 Congress

Considering how important music is to a Congress, I was a little surprised to learn that most of the arrangements for the one to be held in 1990 (just ten months ahead) were now almost complete. I made some inquiries only to be told that this was not going to be a 'musical' Congress.

It so happened that Jill and I were away on holiday in our caravan in the New Forest when I received a message that some headquarters officers were coming the next day for a meeting in our caravan. They duly arrived and had come to talk about the coming Congress. Again it was expressed that music was not going to be so important and, on hearing this, Jill – making tea for the visitors – began to whistle the tune 'I've heard that song before', which caused one of them to say, 'No, no, you have it all wrong!' The smile on her face said it all! One of the officers then went on to say that music would not be as *prevalent* as it had been in previous congresses.

I then asked what would be required from us and was then told, a Brass International Festival with a 500-voice male chorus at the Royal Albert Hall for the first Saturday; a 1,000-voice Congress Chorus for the Sunday at Wembley; a 1,000-voice chorus with five bands and three songster brigades for the Composers Festival on the second Friday at Wembley; a 600-voice chorus and three songster brigades for the Festival of Salvation Song at the Royal Albert Hall on the second Saturday; and a 1,000-voice chorus at Wembley for the second Sunday. Having heard all this, Jill, pouring a second cup of tea, said, 'Oh, I see what you mean about music not being so important this time!' A word of prayer, and they were gone.

Very early on the first Sunday morning of the Congress, the 1,000-voice chorus were at Wembley for the first united rehearsal. I had met them all several times in regional rehearsals, but this was the first time we were all together as we rehearsed the music for the day.

The next few days did not require large groups of musicians but visiting bands and groups were required for the various meetings.

A Composers Festival was held at Wembley on the second Friday and featured the music of Dudley Bright in 'Assignment', with the massed bands and Congress Chorus; John Larsson in 'Wonders Begin' with the Congress Chorus; Ray Bowes in 'Sunshine Mountain', with Birmingham Citadel Band; Trevor Davis in 'Joy Because Of You', with Brisbane City Temple Songsters; James Curnow in 'A Psalm Of Praise', with the USA Southern Territorial Band; Joy Webb in 'Share My Yoke', with the Congress Chorus; Peter Ayling in 'Singing Praise', with the Congress Chorus; Brian Bowen in 'My Comfort And Strength', with Boscombe Band; Stephen Bulla in 'When We Cannot See Our Way', with the International Staff Songsters; Albert Jakeway in 'Rosehill', with the massed bands; Ivor Bosanko in 'I Bring Them To Jesus', with the Melbourne Staff Songsters; Keith Griffin in 'All Creatures Of Our God And King', with the Congress Chorus; Terry Camsey in 'Sing A Happy Song', with the Congress Chorus; Robert Redhead in 'Shout Salvation', with the International Staff Band; Brindley Boon in 'I Dedicate Myself To Thee', with the Brisbane City Temple Songsters; Michael Kenyon in 'The Lamb', with the International Staff Songsters; Peter Graham in 'The Ambassadors', with Montclair Band; and Ray Steadman-Allen in 'Logos', with the massed bands and Congress Chorus. My own offering was 'Reflections' sung by the International Staff Songsters.

There was an intense interest in this festival with the opportunity to see the composer conducting his own work and contemplating just how many hours of writing and rewriting had gone on before these presentations.

I have a letter from Michael Kenyon in which he said, 'I think that the moments I had conducting the Staff Songsters in my setting of William Blake's "The Lamb" were the most satisfying experience in the whole of my musical life.' (There are a number of settings of this poem but, for me, Michael's is the best.)

It was in the final meeting of the Congress and during the appeal following the General's address that my son Mark and his wife Tracy went forward to respond to the call of officership, which led them to the training college in 1991.

And so, another great Congress came to an end. All the hard work, all the hours spent in travelling, arranging music and rehearsals (and a thousand and one other things) were certainly worthwhile.

My wife Jill missed the first Sunday morning meeting of the Congress owing to the fact that she was at Ely Cathedral, where our son Bramwell was being ordained as a priest in the Church of England. The bishop officiating at the ordination saw Jill, in her Salvation Army uniform, sitting in the congregation and, at the part of the service when people are invited to welcome each other, he made his way to Jill. When he arrived he said, 'I presume you are Bramwell's mother so I have to tell you, Bramwell is not leaving The Salvation Army – he is bringing The Salvation Army into the Church!' To say she was deeply moved is to put it mildly.

One of the hymns sung in the service was:

> O thou who camest from above
> The pure celestial fire to impart,
> Kindle a flame of sacred love
> On the mean altar of my heart.

> There let it for thy glory burn
> With inextinguishable blaze,
> And trembling to its source return
> In humble prayer and fervent praise.

> Jesus, confirm my heart's desire
> To work and speak and think for thee;
> Still let me guard the holy fire,
> And still stir up thy gift in me.

Ready for all thy perfect will,
My acts of faith and love repeat,
Till death thy endless mercies seal,
And make the sacrifice complete.

How strange that I first heard this hymn by Charles Wesley when Commissioner Denis Hunter – then the British Commissioner – speaking at a bandmasters councils, used it as the basis of his messages. In the morning session, Denis used the first two verses as a challenge to service and the final two as a confirmation of God's call. It is number 199 in the song book and is sung to the tune of 'Hereford'.

Chapter 17

IN JESUS' STEPS

Women Poets

For me, poems from the minds of women seem to have an ethos all of their own and the five for whom I have had the privilege of writing music to their words, Lily Sampson, Catherine Baird, Olive Holbrook, Ivy Mawby and Marianne Farningham, seem to make my feeling clear.

Lily Sampson

As a very young person I wrote some music to words by Lily Sampson, an Australian officer who worked for a few years in the Editorial Department in London. I am not sure how I got the words but they certainly had that 'something' which made me want to set them to music. The first verse and chorus is as follows:

Is there a place where I may go,
  Bewildered and unsatisfied?
Conscious of faults, I seek to know
  Some better way, some heavenly guide;
Is there a place where God will hear,
  Where even I may find him near?

Just where you are God will find you,
You may his whisper receive;
O let him lead you by infinite grace;
Deep in his mercy you'll find such a place;
Pardoned and cleansed you may there seek his face,
Enter if you can believe.

Catherine Baird

A letter from the International Training College arrived saying that, following their request, Colonel Catherine Baird said she would write the words of a cadets' dedication song if I would write the music. Up until then I had not met the colonel but was delighted to get the invitation and a copy of her words. In a few days I had completed the work and, at her invitation, went to her home to give her the music I had written.

The directions to her home brought me to a road in Balham, South London, where, in her retirement, she lived in an upstairs flat. It was a very rough-looking road and certainly in need of some attention. Greeting me at the door, she said, 'Did you see those lovely trees in our road?' Oh dear! I hadn't seen the trees for looking at the dirt! I now knew that I was in the presence of a very special person. We had a little chat by way of getting to know each other, after which I gave her the music I had written to her beautiful words. She sat and looked at my work for quite some time then said she thought the words and music were made for each other. The final verse and chorus are as follows:

> O may I hear, in every suffering cry,
> The call of him who died for all mankind.
> Help me to share the Shepherd's lonely watch,
> Or climb the rugged steeps his lost to find.
> I dedicate my love to thee
> That love may overflow in me.
>
> *Spirit of truth attend me now,*
> *While I present my solemn vow:*
> *All that I am I pledge to thee,*
> *Spirit of love, abide in me.*

After a cup of tea and some homemade cake, she asked me, 'Do you ever just sit?' When I said, 'You mean, sit and think?' she said, 'Oh no! Just sitting with an empty mind and no thinking.' In reply, I said, 'I would be thinking all the time, "Am I thinking?"' To which she said, 'It is possible – but maybe not for you!'

After a long conversation, and as I was about to leave, I said, 'Well, the next time we meet will be on a Friday in the Royal Albert Hall and the cadets will be singing our song.' 'Oh no,' she replied. 'Friday is the day I take Mrs Williams out in her wheelchair.' When I suggested that someone else could take her out in her wheelchair, she just looked at me and, with a shake of her head, said, 'No!' in such a way that I could tell that nothing whatsoever could interfere with her Friday commitment to this little unknown lady in her wheelchair.

Soon I had read all the books of poems by Catherine Baird that I could find and discovered what a unique place she has in Salvation Army literature. I asked her to come and speak to songster leaders who were attending a week-long conference at Sunbury Court in 1981. Seeing that I was very disappointed at her negative answer, she said she would come, 'but just to answer a few questions that I might like to put to her'. She then added, 'Say, about 20 minutes?' 'Done!' I said, before she could change her mind.

Captain Diane Lillicrap (then working in the Bands Department) brought her by car to Sunbury and my wife was at the door to meet her. This was the first time the two had met, but she made Jill feel as if she had known her all her life. As they entered the door where so much Salvation Army history had been made, she put her arm through Jill's arm and said, 'Can you feel the influence of all the prayers and love that have gone out from this place?' Jill felt as if she had found a soulmate in this extraordinary person.

Catherine (as I was now instructed to call her) had brought Commissioner Kathleen Kendrick, a friend of hers, to read a poem now and then just to give us a break. As the interview progressed, I found it easy to ask her questions with her answers often laced with humour. She told us that her parents, who were Australian officers, were posted to South Africa and it was there that she first came into contact with prostitution. She had seen the girls out on the street and learned what their trade really was. Catherine went on to say that she felt hatred towards these girls to such a degree that words could not express her feelings.

After reading again about the love of Jesus for the sinner, she felt utterly condemned in her own heart about her feelings of resentment towards these girls. Catherine confessed that her sin of hate was far, far worse than that of these poor girls and then realised that love was the greatest of all gifts. 'You may have noticed,' she said, 'that in many of my poems I refer to Jesus as "Love".' We were then all asked to read a verse from two of her songs in which the word 'Love' begins or originally began with a capital letter. The first is Number 874 in the song book:

> With Jesus' name upon their lips,
> The vale of death his servants tread;
> In him they dared believe; in him
> They dare depart; nor sigh, nor dread;
> To *Love* committing all their loves,
> All counted good through peace or strife,
> Content to die believing still
> In Jesus, everlasting life.

Another favourite song of mine and many others is number 449 in our song book:

> O *Love*, revealed on earth in Christ,
> In blindness once I sacrificed
> Thy gifts for dross; I could not see,
> But Jesus brings me sight of thee.
>
> O *Love*, invisible before,
> I see thee now, desire thee more;
> When Jesus speaks thy word is clear;
> I search his face and find thee near.
>
> O *Love*, forever claim my eyes!
> Thy beauty be my chosen prize;
> I cast my load on timeless grace
> That my free soul may run the race.

After we had read the second verse of this song, Catherine asked me to write a new melody for the words. I did so, calling it 'In Jesus' Steps'. (It was published in the January 1991 edition of *The Musical Salvationist*.) The words of the chorus are:

> *I come to thee with quiet mind,*
> *Thyself to know, thy will to find;*
> *In Jesus' steps my steps must be,*
> *I follow him to follow thee.*

The promised 20 minutes stretched into a whole morning of several hours and ended with her requesting that we should all sing her favourite song, Charles Wesley's 'Love Divine, All Loves Excelling', to the Welsh tune 'Blaenwern', after which she took her leave and Diane drove her home. Everyone in the room was so overcome by her presence that it was hard to leave and go for dinner. Songster Leader Burn (from Bedlington Corps) had the foresight to take the words of the whole morning down in shorthand, and much of his work appears in a book about Catherine Baird called *Pen Of Flame* (written by an old friend of mine, Major John Izzard).

Catherine Baird went to Heaven in 1984 and General Frederick Coutts, who had worked closely with her in the days that they were in the Literary Department at International Headquarters, conducted her funeral service in Balham Congress Hall on 8 May 1984. Having to be a fair way north of London the same evening, I sat in the back row so I could make a quick getaway.

As I was sitting there, some rather rough and poorly dressed women joined me. After a few moments, one of them said to me, 'Did you know Cathy?' Before I could answer, she said, 'She was a funny woman.' 'Why do you say that?' I inquired. 'Well,' she said, 'about once a month she would come and knock on my door and say, "I was doing some baking and have made too many cakes and thought you might like some."' 'So why do you say she was a funny woman?' I asked. Her reply was, 'Well, I could understand her making too many cakes the first time, but why did she keep on making too many?'

177

In tribute to Catherine Baird, I wrote some music to three of her poems found in a little book entitled *Reflections*. The music, also called 'Reflections', was published in the January 1986 edition of *The Musical Salvationist* and the poems were these:

(1)   *In every youthful face I see*
The Christ Child smiling down on me;
For once, upon a night of joy,
And clothèd in a little boy
God, in sweet majesty, came near;
His voice was young and passing clear,
Awakening the heart in me
And calling: 'I have need of thee!'

(2)   *Only the lowly and the wise*
Hear victory songs in infant cries!
Proud eyes may swiftly turn away
From Jesus' manger bed of hay,
Yet do the pure, with perfect sight,
See chariots of holy light
And heavenly horsemen, clad in power
Invading time each day and hour.
In silent prayer they venture far
Beyond this world's most distant star,
Encounter God in every place
Where saint and sinner need His grace.

(3)   *I would go silently,*
Lord, when I come to Thee;
Glide as some gallant barque
Into the mighty dark.
Softly and gently ride
O'er the receding tide;
Steer from the shores of time
T'ward an eternal clime.

Lord, on a quiet sea
Let me sail home to Thee.

Olive Holbrook

Mrs Commissioner Olive Holbrook was another lady who, having very special gifts, was invited to come and talk to the delegates at another music leaders conference at Sunbury Court. My first meeting with her was during a lunchtime at headquarters when she told me that she and her husband (now retired) had signed up for a music appreciation course at the London Polytechnic. This prompted me to ask why they had decided to do this. She replied, 'Handel's *Messiah* has come to mean much more to us than we thought possible and Beethoven is more like a friend! It will also help us to understand, and appreciate, the lovely music which our Army composers bring to our bands and songsters.' I was absolutely delighted with her reply.

Mrs Holbrook arrived at Sunbury Court and we took her into a room for a few minutes before going to meet the waiting music leaders. I thought it strange when she asked me to describe the kind of people to whom she would be speaking. When I offered to carry her books, she said she had no books because her sight was almost gone. On arrival in the conference room, and following my introduction, she stood and said to the assembled company, 'I cannot see you, but I can feel the warmth of your love.'

Then, from memory, she quoted the whole book of Paul's letter to the Philippians – four chapters, 104 verses! It was as if the words were hers and she was composing them as we listened to this remarkable lady. Nothing was added and nothing was left out of the Philippian letter. There was something about this occasion that made any comments from me quite superfluous. I think most of us imagined that we must have felt like those early-day Christians when they first read Paul's letter to them.

The silence that followed lasted quite some minutes because applause would have been quite out of place. A request by the delegates for me to interview her following the dinner meal was accepted and another hour of her company was ours to enjoy.

She told us the story of her writing words to the secular melody 'Passing By', which happened like this. In the days that her husband was on the staff at the International Training College, it was her great privilege to share in the Spiritual Days (always a high point in the college curriculum). On one such occasion, for some reason Mrs Holbrook was unable to attend but could still hear the singing of the cadets. When the singing ended, feeling a bit despondent at not being with them, she turned on her radio and heard the melody of 'Passing By' which really captivated her. A few days later, when in a music shop, she was able to purchase a copy of this song, the words of the first and last verses being:

> There is a Lady sweet and kind,
> Was ne'er a face so pleased my mind.
> I did but see her passing by
> Yet will I love her till I die.
>
> Cupid is wingèd and doth range
> Her country, so my heart doth change;
> Yet, change she earth or change she sky
> Yet I will love her till I die.

As she hummed the melody the following words came to her:

> Deep were the scarlet stains of sin,
> Strong were the bonds of fault within;
> But now I stand both pure and free,
> The blood of Jesus cleanses me.
>
> Strong are the foes that round me creep,
> Constant the vigil I must keep;
> But from a secret armoury
> The grace of Jesus strengthens me.
>
> What though the treacherous road may wind,
> Faith in my heart assures my mind;

180

E'en when his face I do not see,
The hand of Jesus reaches me.

This is the lamp to pilgrim given,
This is my passport into Heaven,
Portent of immortality,
That God, through Jesus, dwells in me.

Mrs Holbrook asked if I would make an arrangement of the 'Passing By' melody with her words for our songster brigades. She then made the request that the song be called 'Passport To Heaven'. I did as she requested and the song was published in the October 1986 edition of *The Musical Salvationist*. Lieut-Colonel Ray Bowes, in his comments about this edition, wrote: 'The title may seem strange to some, but Norman Bearcroft, who has made this arrangement, assures us that this was Mrs Holbrook's wish.'

Not long after this extraordinary day, Olive Holbrook had her 'passport to Heaven' stamped by the seal of God's approval on her promotion to Glory. Her song is number 176 in the song book. Look it up! If you have your own song book, you may want to highlight it.

Ivy Mawby

It was back in the days when Muriel Packham (now Muriel Yendell), as the leader of the National Songsters (an all-female group), asked me for a new song for the coming Christmas event in which her songsters would be featured at the Westminster Central Hall. It was only three weeks before the event but Muriel had a way of asking for a new song which one could not refuse. On the way home a melody popped into my mind with the words 'Ding, dong, ding, dong', and although I knew that the same would occur at the beginning of every line, this was all I had. It so happened that Mrs Colonel Ivy Mawby (the writer of many songs) worked on the same headquarters as me and so, next morning, I went to see her. I sang the tune and such words as I had and asked her to write some verses. By three o'clock the same day she brought me the finished song as follows:

Ding, dong, ding, dong, ring out the carillon!
Ding, dong, ding, dong, joy is here.
Ding, dong, ding, dong, let every care be gone.
Ding, dong, ding, dong, Christmas cheer.

In a manger see him lying,
Little Babe so weak and small;
On his mother's care relying,
Cradled in a cattle stall.

See the star so clearly shining
In the darkness of the night;
Wise men of the east 'tis guiding,
By its radiance led aright.

Hear the angel-voices singing,
'Peace on earth, goodwill to men!'
All the bells of Heaven are ringing,
Echoing to earth again.

The song became very popular and, later, I did some variations for cornets and trombones on the tune, calling it 'Joyous Carillon'.

Ivy Mawby had long association with my home corps, Southall, and I have very fond memories of her leading the meetings there. Three of her songs are found in the song book: 675 'Softly The Shadows Fall' (with a beautiful setting by George Marshall), 759 'There Is Strength In Knowing Jesus' (music by Sidney Hubbard) and my favourite, 740 'Like To A Lamb' (music by William Hammond).

Like to a lamb who from the fold has strayed
Far on the mountain, of the dark afraid,
Seeking a shelter from the night's alarm,
Longing for comfort of the shepherd's arm,
So Jesus found me on sin's mountain drear,
Gathered me close and banished all my fear.

Like to a pilgrim in an unknown land
Seeking the comfort of a guiding hand,
Fearing the perils of the winding way,
Pleading for strength sufficient every day,
I met my Lord; and, though the path be dim,
He knows the way and I will walk with him.

Like to a child who, when the night may fall,
Out of the darkness hears his father call,
Far and a-weary though his feet my roam,
Sees in the distance shining lights of home,
So at the last the music of his voice
Will calm my fears and make my heart rejoice.

In the love of Jesus there is all I need,
While I follow closely where my Lord may lead;
By his grace forgiven,
In his presence blest,
In the love of Jesus,
In the love of Jesus, is perfect rest.

I last met Ivy Mawby when she was living in the same Salvation Army officers' retirement home as my mother in Camberwell. In my frequent visits, I would always spend some time with her chatting about her songs and poems. It was on one of those occasions (and for a bit of fun) that I reminded her that, when she was the National Home League Secretary in the British Territory, she made the request that the following ditty should no longer be sung:

Join the Home League! Join the Home League!
If you care to come and risk it, there's a cup of tea and biscuit.
Join the Home League! Join the Home League!
If you cannot join the band, join the Home League!

We then sang it together and had a good laugh!

Marianne Farningham

After hearing the students of the National School of Music sing number 860 in the song book, 'Just As I Am, Thine Own To Be', with a new melody I had written to the words by Marianne Farningham (1834-1909), I decided to use the melody in a solo for the euphonium which I was writing called 'The Great Adventure'. I used this title after reading the second verse of her poem:

> Just as I am, thine own to be,
> Friend of the young who lovest me,
> To consecrate myself to thee,
> O Jesus Christ, I come.
>
> **In the glad morning of my day,**
> **My life to give, my vows to pay,**
> **With no reserve, and no delay,**
> **With all my heart, I come.**
>
> Just as I am, young, strong and free,
> To be the best that I can be
> For truth and righteousness and thee,
> Lord of my life, I come.
>
> With many dreams of fame and gold,
> Success and joy to make me bold;
> But dearer still my faith to hold,
> For my whole life, I come.
>
> And for thy sake to win renown,
> And then to take my victor's crown,
> And at thy feet to cast it down,
> O Master, Lord, I come.

With no reserve, and no delay? Well, there's no other way to come!

Incidentally, and nothing to do with women poets, the secretary for The Salvation Army's over-60 clubs came to see me to discuss a forthcoming over-60 club rally, which was to be held in the Royal Albert Hall in London. He told me that the International Staff Band would be there and wanted the band to accompany the whole audience in singing some well-known secular tunes to which various people in The Salvation Army had put different words. His purpose in seeing me was to ask if I would arrange a number of these for the band, which would then accompany the singing of the thousands of people who would be there.

He had a list of tunes, which included 'It's A Long Way To Tipperary', 'Let's All Go Down The Strand', 'My Bonnie Lies Over The Ocean' and 'Two Lovely Black Eyes'. Came the day of the rally and the Albert Hall was full of very happy people eager to make the event a success. The Over-60 Club Choir had rehearsed the songs with the revised words and song sheets were given to everybody else to have a good sing! When the band struck up with 'Two Lovely Black Eyes', the song sheets were ignored as they all began to sing, 'Two lovely black eyes, Oh what a surprise'. The Over-60 Club Secretary (in a bit of a panic) rushed to the centre of the stage holding up a printed song sheet and pointing to it to remind people to sing the Army words. His action was completely ignored as a very happy audience sang with even greater fervour, 'Two lovely black eyes, Oh what a surprise.' The same happened to the rest of the songs and A GREAT TIME WAS HAD BY ALL!

Chapter 18

WORD OF GRACE

Songster Leaders Councils

It was 23 May 1992 when the last Royal Albert Hall festival for which I was responsible took place. The occasion was the Songster Leaders Councils Festival and the special guests were the New York Staff Band with their bandmaster, Brian Bowen.

The report in the United Kingdom Territory's paper, *Salvationist*, of the festival, written by Colonel William Clark (who for a period was the Executive Officer of the International Staff Songsters) was as follows:

> In the opening prayer of the Songster Leaders Councils festival, held at the Royal Albert Hall in London, Lieut-Colonel Ernest Payton, Executive Officer of the New York Staff Band, said: 'Tonight we want to see Jesus,' and, 'May none of us be left unblessed.'
>
> Both petitions seemed to be amply answered. It *was* a festival in which Jesus was seen and – to judge by the congregation's response – people *were* blessed: not only entertained, amazed and delighted by marvellous music, but also lifted up to Christ.
>
> From the entry of the New York Staff Band, whose members marched to the platform to 'Stars And Stripes For Ever', played by the ISB, to the final united item, 'Give To Jesus Glory', the crowd enjoyed a spiritual and musical feast.
>
> The congregation entered right away into the spirit of the opening song, 'Crown Him With Many Crowns', to Charles Skinner's now celebrated setting. A devotional item by the 600-strong festival chorus then led naturally into prayer.

In his words of welcome, Commissioner John Larsson (TC) asked all musicians present – not just those on the platform – to stand, before expertly guiding the festival through.

It is difficult to describe the atmosphere of so outstanding an occasion. It is not possible, for instance, to describe the impact of the New York Staff Band's excellent first number, 'Come And Get Saved', a new arrangement by Bruce Broughton of the now rarely-used song 'You Never Can Tell When The Lord Will Call You'.

The band also played Eric Ball's lovely music 'Sanctuary' ('In the secret of thy presence') and 'Folk Heroes', written by their conductor, Bandmaster Brian Bowen, the rhapsody recalling heroic personalities in British history.

The ISB excelled. The bandmaster, Major Robert Redhead, has without doubt put his stamp on the band! 'Just Like John' was probably more enjoyable than ever to those who had heard it before. In 'Excerpts From The Finale Of Symphony No 4' there was some quite brilliant playing.

The ISB also accompanied Bandsman Paul Graham in his trombone solo, 'The Word Of Grace', Norman Bearcroft's beautiful meditation on the gospel song 'Christ Receiveth Sinful Men'.

Two solo spots by the ISS showed the section's fine qualities as they sang 'Holy Spirit, Dwell In Me' and 'The City Of God'.

The items rendered by the festival chorus, a combination of 22 corps brigades (13 from Wales), delighted, moved and inspired. Its members produced robust and remarkably controlled singing for so large a group. The foot-tapping 'Let A Little Sunshine In Your Heart' (Philip Coutts/Richard Phillips) was accompanied – as were all the chorus items – by a skilled wind ensemble. 'This song,' remarked the commissioner, 'is going to have a long and useful life.'

The chorus also sang 'A Celebration Of The Risen Lord', the 16th composition for the annual Royal Albert Hall festival provided by Lieut-Colonel Ray Steadman-Allen. It was a masterly arrangement of Passiontide songs to new music.

'A Psalm Of Thanks', a setting of 1 Chronicles 16 by Captain Howard Evans, had a strong Hebrew-music sound that came over very well. It was conducted by the composer, as were other festival chorus numbers.

The final item by the chorus, 'Witness To Christ' (Norman Bearcroft), had a strong gospel content and a touch of nostalgia about it.

Songster Susan Hair, of Gainsborough, was an outstanding vocal soloist. Her beautiful voice ('A fine gift from God,' remarked the commissioner) was heard to excellent effect in 'A Shining Angel', 'I Feel Like Singing All The Time' and 'The Love Of My Lord', a work written years ago by Catherine Baird and Leslie Condon for the National School of Music. The International Staff Songsters provided vocal backing.

Two united items – bands and festival chorus in 'Bournemouth Centennial March' and 'Give To Jesus Glory' – made a thrilling climax to a marvellous evening.

This was the last of the 16 festivals of this kind arranged by Lieut-Colonel Bearcroft, since he and Mrs Bearcroft are soon to enter retirement. The TC paid tribute to the colonel who, with his wife, had made an immense contribution to the life and witness of the Army.

That there was a great deal of Bearcroft music in the programme had been at the request of the commissioner, whose words were enthusiastically endorsed by a prolonged standing ovation.

It had been a great festival, with music not 'over-heavy', but brilliantly enjoyable – Army music-making at its best. Christ had been given the glory, and surely the opening prayer had been answered.

I am not sure how many people present would have caught the humour of the final bars of the 'Bournemouth Centennial March', where a very short reference is made to the song 'Oh I Do Like To Be Beside The Seaside', seeing that our retirement address was to be in Christchurch – beside the sea!

Chapter 19

THE KING'S TRUMPETERS

Victors Acclaimed

Here are my personal recollections of some of the giants of Salvation Army music now in Heaven. These recollections have been taken from the series I wrote some years ago for *Salvationist*. I have revised and enlarged them.

Bramwell Coles

I seem always to have known the name Bramwell Coles. When I was a boy, his was a household name. It appeared on some of the first music I ever played in the young people's band. Bramwell Coles composed some of the Army's finest marches and, as a young man, I eagerly scanned the latest published music to see if there was a new march from his pen. Bramwell Coles was the first Head of the Music Editorial Department I can remember and I will never forget my first meeting with him.

I plucked up the courage (if that's what it was!) to send him my band arrangement of a very popular songster piece. I can't remember what it was now, but eagerly awaited his reaction to my boldness. In due time a letter signed by him (I cut out the signature and pasted it in my mother's autograph album!) arrived inviting me to Salvationist Publishing and Supplies – where the department was then situated – if and when I had written some original music.

Not wanting him to forget me, I commenced work that very day on a march and, in a very short time, had something down on paper which I hoped he might at least look at.

I made my way to SP&S (as it was known by everybody) only to be greeted by a woman receptionist with, 'Do you have an appointment?'

I replied that my letter from Brigadier Coles said to come at any time, so there I was! A telephone call to his office resulted in her saying, 'The brigadier,' she seemed to linger reverently over the 'b' in brigadier, 'will see you now.'

A strange thumping started in my chest as I mounted the two flights of stairs and then made my way through a long, gloomy passage, at the end of which I found myself knocking on a door labelled 'Brigadier Bramwell Coles, Head, Music Editorial'. I suddenly felt I should perhaps have spent a little more time writing the piece I was clutching in my hand. 'Too late now,' I thought, as the door was opened and my hand firmly grasped in his. Even as he gripped my hand I thought, 'This is the hand that wrote "Under Two Flags",' and the opening bars flashed through my mind.

He looked quite like the picture I had seen in *The Musician* (always the same picture!) and straightaway he made me feel welcome. This made me feel a little less worried about the piece I had brought to him.

Just imagine, here I was in the private office of this world-renowned man! There was his pen and inkwell (no ballpoint pens in those days). Everywhere there were new manuscripts. As I sat there I thought, 'This has to be the nearest thing to Heaven!'

Bramwell Coles was a very dignified looking man, tall with grey hair and immaculate in every detail. I wondered, 'How can so dignified a man write such lively marches?' Yet here he was, talking to me! Bramwell Coles, the writer of 'In The Firing Line', 'The Flag Of Freedom' and 'Victors Acclaimed' (even the titles seemed to belie his dignity).

We spent the next hour going over my new piece bar by bar. He kept asking me questions like, 'What were you thinking here?' or, 'Did you really want the euphoniums to be so high?' I tried desperately to give sensible answers, even though, as yet, I had not been so clinical about my compositions.

I got the impression that he was not unhappy with my work though he did offer the suggestion that I try to improve my calligraphy, and showed me some of his own. He was also pleased to hear I was studying *Harmony – Its Theory And Practice* by Ebenezer Prout.

I was very glad to lose a bit of tension when a cup of tea arrived for him, and pleased to see his secretary had brought one for me as well. As we drank, he looked at me long and hard and said, 'We want you to be a useful Army composer.'

Then followed the question, 'Are you going into the training college to become a Salvation Army officer?' Before I could answer (thankfully, because I had not given it a thought), he knelt down and offered a prayer on my behalf. I left his office on cloud nine and really hoped I might be able to live up to the challenge he had given me about writing music for the Army.

Incidentally, the march was published and is called 'To Regions Fair'.

Bramwell Coles did, of course, write music other than marches. My own favourite is his meditation on 'Rock Of Ages'. It has a most inspiring opening, giving a picture of vastness and confidence.

Other works include 'Man Of Sorrows', some variations on 'Good Old Army' and 'The Divine Pursuit'. This number included a movement in 5/4 time, causing some consternation among some bandmasters, since it had not been encountered in Salvation Army music before.

His love for the music of Tchaikovsky is evident in the excellent arrangements he did of some of the Russian master's symphonic works, 'Moments With Tchaikovsky' and 'Treasures From Tchaikovsky'.

As a cadet in the training college, I heard that the International Staff Band was to play the first performance of 'Treasures From Tchaikovsky' at the yearly Rink (Regent Hall) Festival. How fortunate that I was in the Special Service Brigade and on assignment in the West End of London that very night!

I must confess I did not over-struggle against the temptation to slip off to the Rink to hear the final number of the ISB programme, which just happened to be 'Treasures'. My slight fall from grace was all the more relished when Colonel Coles was brought to the platform to acknowledge the response which his thrilling arrangement brought forth from the capacity crowd (including one cadet).

In later years, Colonel Coles returned to Canada for a period and became involved in *The Living Word* radio series, for which he wrote music and arranged many of the songs.

When, some years later, I was appointed to Canada, I found a filing cabinet full of the manuscripts of the songs he had written for the series. Even though these were all one-off productions, each was written with the same care and attention to detail that I had seen in his work all those years before when I first met him in his office in London.

I attended the funeral of Bramwell Coles at Harrow Corps and was both amazed and disappointed that there was no band on duty. However, Donald Osgood (himself a fine composer who had worked with Colonel Coles in the Music Editorial Department) played the piano for the occasion. As the earthly remains of the great man were carried from the hall, Don began to play a section of the Coles festival march 'Departed Heroes', which features the chorus 'Away Over Jordan To Wear A Starry Crown'.

I once heard Erik Leidzén (one of the finest Army composers) say that when Bramwell Coles arrived at the gate of Heaven, John Philip Sousa (the great American march writer of 'Liberty Bell' and 'Washington Post' to name but two) would be waiting to greet him and say, 'Bram, on earth I was called the March King, but now, in Heaven, I must be honest and hand the crown to you!'

Personally, I wouldn't argue with that!

Albert Jakeway

In contrast to Colonel Bramwell Coles, Colonel Albert Jakeway (who became Head of the Music Editorial Department when Bramwell Coles retired) appeared quite blunt in some of his comments. However, as I came to know him, I discovered he was really quite soft-hearted but always on a crusade for Army music and its composers.

My first meeting with him was at Southall Citadel (my home corps) when he came to lead a songster weekend. Stanley Piper (another composer), our songster leader, had written a trumpet part for me to play while the songsters sang a new song called 'God's Trumpet'. Stanley required me to stand a few feet behind the songsters and try not to be seen in order to give the impression that the trumpet sound was coming from the heavens. The item went quite well and received good applause. Colonel Jakeway took quite some time in saying what a splendid song it was and then added, 'It was unfortunate that Norman Bearcroft was practising in the background while the song was being sung!'

Before the weekend was over I received an invitation to call on him at the Music Editorial Department. He then suggested that I should not engage in conversation with the lady-receptionist on the door at Salvationist Publishing and Supplies. He went on to tell me that the Music Editorial Department was not responsible to SP&S, and added, 'If anyone asks you where you are going, just say "Good morning" and walk past.' I found this very hard to do when the receptionist greeted me so warmly. She must have known I had come to see Colonel Jakeway, because she said, 'You'll find the colonel on the second floor.' She then added, with a twinkle in her eye, 'I think he is feeling a little better this morning!'

As I entered Albert Jakeway's office he said, without looking up, 'Take a seat, I won't be a moment.' As he continued to write on some score paper, I noticed he had abandoned his tunic and the sleeves of his collarless shirt (which we all wore in those days beneath our upright tunic collars) were rolled up very high. I also noticed he was wearing braces to keep his trousers up. The braces had a football design on them. (He was very fond of football!)

At last, with a triumphant smile, he laid down his pen and made a great show of putting the lid on his inkpot before handing me his latest work. Quite reverently, I took the score and noted the title was 'The Vision Splendid'.

My first thought was that the title contradicted the composer's appearance: sleeves rolled up, football braces, collarless shirt! Then I thought again. Albert really was a notable vision as there he was, working so hard to produce music that would help on the salvation war.

He told me that the International Staff Band were going to play his 'Vision Splendid' at the Royal Albert Hall in a few weeks' time, and hoped I would be there to hear it. I was there, and delighted when the

Staff Bandmaster, Bernard Adams, invited Albert to conduct its first public performance.

While I was still in Colonel Jakeway's office he passed me another new score, this time an arrangement from one of the great masters. As he handed it to me he said with a wry smile, 'They won't be able to play this piece.' I was about to suggest that perhaps he had then wasted his time, when I remembered my mother's injunction, 'Discretion is the better part of valour,' so I kept quiet.

One day I received a telephone call from Albert Jakeway, asking if I would visit a man who was serving a long sentence in a prison on the Isle of Wight. Albert explained that he had promised to go and see the man, but was unable to do so at this particular time. 'Just go and have a little chat with him,' he said. 'He has been saved while in prison, and has a real interest in band music.'

When I visited the man, I discovered that Albert had led him to the Lord during a routine visit. I also discovered that Albert had made the long journey to visit the man every month and had kept up a regular correspondence with him. The man told me how kind and understanding Albert had been to him, and that they always prayed together before Albert left for London.

When I next saw Albert, I reported on my visit to the man in prison. I commented about his testimony to Albert's kindness and, most of all, that he had led him to the Lord. Albert quickly tried to change the subject but I persisted. At last, he told me it was when he was conducting an Army band programme in the prison that he had first met the man and felt he ought to befriend him. When I suggested that Albert did not want folk to know he had a soft heart, he just grunted something inaudible. But I had discovered a different side to this composer of Salvation Army music! Albert's tone poem 'Where Duty Calls' now has a different meaning for me and, when I hear it, I remember the man in prison.

The tone poem proved to be very popular at a time when bands were coming together again after the war. It was based on the song 'Stand Up For Jesus', and was recorded by Rosehill Band, with Albert as the conductor.

In a meeting with General Wilfred Kitching (himself a composer of many pieces), Dean Goffin – then National Secretary for Bands and Songster Brigades – was discussing a forthcoming All-London Bandsmen's Councils to be held at the historic Clapton Congress Hall. Dean thought it a good idea to invite the Congress Hall Band to be duty band for the day.

Colonel Jakeway (by then retired and acting as a band instructor for the Congress Hall Band) was accepting some conducting appointments with a non-Salvation Army band which, at that time, was not in accord with Army regulations. The General knew this and also knew that Albert was giving rehearsal time to Clapton Congress Hall Band, so his decision was, 'Yes, we will have the Congress Hall Band on duty, but Norman Bearcroft will be the conductor.' I did a couple of rehearsals with the band but imagine my surprise when, on the day and arriving at the Congress Hall, I found Albert already conducting the band in some pre-meeting music. When Dean arrived he told me to inform Albert that the General wanted me to conduct the band. I responded by reminding him that he was the Secretary for Bands and, as such, it was his place to tell the offending colonel. Try as he might, Dean could not get the band to stop playing long enough to get the message to Albert. Reluctantly, the General had to begin the meeting with Albert still conducting.

However, all was not lost! Albert proceeded to deliver 'Hallelujahs!' and loud cries of 'Praise the Lord!' at every possible opportunity. The General warmed to this and, before the meeting concluded, was having a few humorous asides with the colonel before asking him to close the morning session in prayer. I didn't get to conduct the band at all that day!

Albert Jakeway's last appearance in an Army musical event was at the Composers Festival during the 1990 International Congress. I wanted him to conduct his famous march 'Rosehill' in the festival for which I was responsible.

Time being at a premium, I worried that he would take too much time in the rehearsal and, in any case, seeing he was well into his 90s, I thought a rehearsal and a festival would be too much for him on

197

one day. So I told Albert I would do the rehearsal for him and that I would take the march at the very steady pace I knew he liked his marches played.

This I did, and reminded the united bands that Albert was now an older man and to be very careful in their treatment of him. When the time came for him to conduct the massed bands he asked me to stay close to him, help him up the steps to the conductor's rostrum and stay with him during the item. There was a tense hush as he took the baton, looked at the bands, then back to me – he then unleashed the bands at a furious tempo!

As the march neared its end the crowd broke into vociferous applause so that the final bars were lost in the noise. 'What do I do now?' he asked me. 'Give a salute,' I replied. 'Which way do I face?' he continued. 'All the way round,' was my advice. As the crowd continued to applaud, Albert felt for my hand to guide him back to his seat. As we made our way down the steps, above the noise of the crowd, he said, 'Who says I always take my marches slowly?'

Albert was a true Yorkshireman with an indomitable spirit. My favourite march of his is 'Onward To Conquer', which features the words:

> Salvation Army, Army of God,
> Onward to conquer the world with fire and blood.

Colonel Albert Jakeway, who was promoted to Glory in 1992, was all the better for knowing. And I am all the better for having known him.

Erik Leidzén

Among many Salvationists who emigrated to the USA in the late 1920s and early '30s were two remarkable personalities – Erik Leidzén, from Sweden, and Emil Söderström from Denmark. Both were very gifted composers of music and, as such, made a dramatic impact on Salvation Army bandsmen and songsters.

Although both men had much in common, their personalities were quite different. Leidzén, immaculate in appearance, was artistic and refined. Söderström was rough and ready, hale and hearty and happy to shock people.

For me as a teenager onwards, Erik Leidzén was my hero. I found his music fascinating. It had a different sound and he seemed to work magic with the harmonising of simple melodies. He was often heard to say that he wrote music which 'would appeal to the little old lady in the back row'. Personally, I thought his music appealed to the young lady in the front row and everybody in between!

His cornet solos were (and are) beautiful and exciting. 'A Happy Day', 'Tucker' and 'At The Cross Where I First Saw The Light' are but a few of his earlier numbers, and they kept on coming – 'Wondrous Day', 'Songs In The Heart' and so on all bear the same mark of excellence.

Imagine my delight when I was just a lad, when an American *War Cry* arrived in my father's post and, to my great joy, it contained a photograph of Erik Leidzén with the students of the Star Lake Music Camp. How I envied those American kids! I tried to see myself in that band but America was very far off in those days. My father found a picture frame for me, which meant that Erik and his band were now over the mantelpiece in my bedroom.

I was able to gather a few more pictures as the years went by and I noticed that Erik always wore a bow tie! When such a tie arrived in some jumble left on our doorstep (my parents were corps officers) it became my prize possession. Alas, no one seemed very impressed when I was seen wearing it!

Some years later I had the opportunity to meet Erik and his wife Maria when they visited England, staying with Eric and Olive Ball. Southall, where I lived, is but two or three miles away from Ealing, where Eric and Olive lived, and, knowing of my admiration for Erik, Eric Ball arranged for me to meet him after a festival given by the International Staff Band in Ealing Town Hall. It proved to be a thrilling programme, with both Erik Leidzén and Eric Ball conducting their own music.

In later years, after I became National Bandmaster for the British Territory, I wrote to Erik asking him for some information about a piece he had just written called 'A Robe Of White', which had become very popular in a short time. Seeing that I was to give a technical talk (based on this piece) to bandsmen meeting in councils, I thought a few words from Erik himself would add weight to those of mine.

I received a long reply from him telling me how he came to leave The Salvation Army for a number of years and that he had marked his return with a meditation on the tune 'Richmond'. The piece is published in the *Festival Series* and is based on the words 'O for a thousand tongues to sing my great redeemer's praise'. His old skill was evident and his unique scoring quite remarkable.

Erik always sent us a Christmas card and it usually contained a verse of his own, for Erik liked to write verse as well as music.

Some years later, I was invited to be the guest at Star Lake Music Camp and, as I was being given a tour of the complex by the Divisional Commander (Brigadier Charles Southwood), he recounted an incident involving Erik, as follows:

During an open rehearsal, where two ladies were at the back of the room talking, Erik stopped the music and asked the two ladies to leave the room. The ladies smiled back at him hoping he would continue with the rehearsal. He did not continue and in a loud voice said, 'When those two ladies have left, we will resume the music!' (The story was confirmed by Mrs Colonel Southwood, who was one of the two ladies!)

Two days later, Erik arrived for the morning rehearsal with the Star Lake Band and, three minutes later, was lying full length on the floor, still conducting. When someone asked if he was all right, Erik replied, 'If the solo cornet players can sit in a slouched position with legs crossed and still master the intricacies of the work, I can lie on the floor and conduct!'

Quite some time after Erik's death, I had the privilege of taking the Canadian Staff Band to New York for a joint festival with the New York Staff Band in which we were to feature a programme of his music. New York Temple was packed for the occasion and a large picture of Erik Leidzén graced the back of the platform. (I noted that the picture revealed the usual bow tie.) His widow, Maria, was in the congregation and she gave me a wave before we began.

One of the numbers I had chosen for the united male chorus from both bands was Erik's 'Sure Of Victory', a song written in his earlier days for songster brigades. It is a rollicking number in which the singers are required to give a loud shout of 'Where?' in the final bars of each chorus:

> *There where the good old fight is hardest,*
> *There where we bravely meet the foe;*
> *There you will see our colours flying,*
> *Comrades, say are we faint-hearted?*
> *No! No! No!*
> *There where the good old fight is hardest,*
> *There in the midst of sin and woe,*
> *There, there, there,*
> *You will always find us there.*
> *WHERE?*
> *There where the good old fight is hardest.*

After the festival, Mrs Leidzén came to me and was very gracious about the manner in which we had performed her husband's music. Having just played most of Erik's 'big' numbers, I was a bit surprised when she said to me, 'You know, with all the music we have heard this afternoon, the piece he would have enjoyed most was "Sure Of Victory".' She then quoted the words of the first verse:

> Trumpets are blaring, the foe is despairing,
> And we're sure of victory!
> Come, let's be shouting, for no one is doubting
> That we're sure of victory!
> Rally again for a mighty endeavour,
> Christ is our Captain today and forever,
> On to the war, let's attack them once more,
> For we're sure of victory!

201

She looked at me for a moment, then said, 'Erik wrote the words as well as the music and that song just about sums him up!'

I thought to myself, 'What a way to go!'

Emil Söderström

It would be hard to find a character more of a contrast to Erik Leidzén than his old friend Emil Söderström.

Emil was a very gifted man who could write music anywhere and at any time. For many years, he was the staff arranger for one of the major broadcasting companies in the USA, this at a time when music for broadcasting had to have some real substance and not just a few jingles for advertising.

My first meeting with Emil was when Douglas Court – himself a composer of several songs and who was working with me in the Music Department in Toronto – came and told me that Emil Söderström was at the reception desk asking for Norman Bearcroft. Arriving at the desk, I found an unkempt man who greeted me like a long-lost brother.

'I have brought some new music for you to see,' he announced, and proceeded there and then to reach into an old plastic shopping bag for the new score of an organ sonata he had just completed. He obviously wanted me to look at it there and then. No words of personal introduction, no happy greetings from the USA, not even a comment on the weather (obviously he wasn't British!), just, 'Here you are, Norman, look at this!'

The area surrounding the reception desk was hardly the right setting for such an artistic exercise so I ushered him towards a lift and, as we ascended to the seventh floor, he began to apologise for his appearance. He had obviously not shaved for a couple of days and his shirt was a long way from the white it once had been.

He told me he had just arrived from California (he had written a splendid march called 'California') and that he had hitchhiked quite a proportion of the journey. He said he liked the idea of travelling across the USA in different cars and the occasional truck. The last part of his journey had been by Greyhound bus, and then he had made his way straight to me.

When I inquired about his luggage he replied that he always 'travelled light' and that all he really needed was in the plastic shopping bag from which he had produced the organ sonata score.

He seemed a little gruff when I asked him where he was going to stay in Toronto and sharply reminded me that he had come to show me his music and not to talk about where he might lay his head. 'People worry too much about that sort of thing,' he said, in what I thought was a somewhat pious tone of voice. Even so, I asked Doug Court to make a few inquiries. He discovered that a family in Toronto was quite used to Emil's sudden appearances and that he would be welcome there.

Emil spent the next day at our home – and what a day it was! He proved to be a most entertaining person, with a great fund of stories of what had happened to him in the world of music.

When my youngest son Mark came home from school (he was about nine or ten years old) Emil asked him if he was a musician. Mark replied that he was taking piano lessons and that he played second cornet in Toronto Temple Band.

'Are you going to play the piano for us now?' asked Emil.

After a bit of nudging from his mother, Mark began to play a few five-finger exercises. As he played, Emil stood behind him and, extending his huge hands either side of the youthful player, began to add variations. Mark was delighted and moved along the stool so he and Emil could play a duet. Emil took a shine to Mark and I think the feeling was mutual.

Emil asked me if I had ever met Erik Leidzén. When I told him I had, he commented about Erik's intensity during meetings.

He told me that, on one occasion, he was sitting with Erik during the playing of one of Emil's own pieces and Erik appeared quite moved. Emil felt a bit embarrassed about this and thought he would ease the situation with a joke. Tapping Erik on the shoulder he asked, 'Erik, why do firemen wear red braces?'(called suspenders in the USA). 'Oh, I don't know,' said Erik, a bit annoyed with the question. 'Shall I tell you why?' continued Emil. 'If you must,' came the swift reply. 'I'd like to,' continued Emil. By now the music had come to an end and Erik looked at Emil for an answer to this important question. 'Well, if they don't,' said Emil, 'their trousers fall down!' To Emil's delight, Erik burst out laughing. (I know this story to be true because Erik mentioned it to me in one of his letters.)

A short time after Emil's visit to Toronto I was invited to Chicago for a musicians festival and councils. I was delighted to learn that my fellow guest was none other than Emil Söderström.

The Saturday morning and afternoon were taken up with many of the bands of the USA Central Territory playing a piece of their own choice. Each band was to receive a written critique from both Emil and me. I was assured that this was not to be a contest, though we were expected to say which was the best band we heard that day!

I asked the Music Secretary how he wanted us to mark the bands and I was amused to hear that 'excellent' was to be the lowest grade we could give, while 'super' and 'magnificent' were to be reserved for the better bands! When Emil asked about the poorer standard bands, the music secretary replied: 'We have no poor bands.' Emil's face was a picture, but I assured the secretary we would do our best.

The night festival was to include a first performance of the organ sonata, which I had seen emerging from the plastic bag on our first meeting. It was to be accompanied by the Chicago Staff Band and Chorus.

Emil must have misunderstood the reason for him being there because he had told me he was to be the organ soloist. He was quite dismayed when he saw someone else sitting at the keyboard. Emil said, 'They must be going to ask me to conduct the piece.' Alas! Such was not the case and Emil was not a happy man.

He was still muttering loudly as we took our 'seats of honour' in the balcony while the audience stood. As the concert proceeded, Emil became loudly vocal in his opinions, so much so that the people behind began to show their disapproval with some loudly whispered 'shush' sounds.

Feeling very embarrassed and not wanting to tell the surrounding listeners that it was him and not me doing the talking, I suggested to Emil that we should go and have a cup of coffee, seeing we were now into the second ten minutes of the festival! 'Good idea,' said Emil in a very loud voice. As we left, he took the opportunity to shake as many hands of the offended onlookers as he could!

The next day was the musicians councils, and the Territorial Commander led the meeting in a manner designed to encourage his troops. It was a stirring meeting, following which Emil and I were invited to have lunch with the commissioner.

Emil, thinking the atmosphere needed changing, began telling some hilarious stories from his musical encounters. A senior officer thought this not appropriate for the occasion and began to talk about the weekend's events.

As he talked, he noticed that Emil had 'switched off' (he may have been thinking about the next piece he was going to write). Not willing to leave Emil alone he asked, 'You do agree that it was a good meeting, Emil?'

Emil looked a bit bewildered, then, straightening himself up replied, 'I told those people in London to publish my music exactly as I had written it.' I think I was the only one present who knew what he was talking about!

For all his rough exterior, Emil was a man with a very warm heart and, though often misunderstood, he loved the Army. He told me that of all the music he had written (and there was a lot, including a symphony which he lost on a bus in New York!), the music he had given to the Army was his most treasured.

I was in a meeting in which delegates from the International College for Officers were telling of the work in various parts of the world. Appropriately, the band played Emil's 'All Round The World'. In this piece the listener is invited to hear how a well-known Army tune is played in different countries.

As the band played this merry piece, I could once again picture Emil. He was a rough diamond – a very lovable rough diamond – but a real diamond nonetheless!

Eric Ball

As stated earlier, in 1932 my officer-parents, along with their four children (I was the youngest), were appointed to Southall 1 Corps in

205

the West London Division. Strictly speaking, the appointment was for my parents but (like all officers' children) we were certainly caught up in the farewell and marching orders.

Eric Ball, then a captain and a member of the Music Editorial Department, was the corps bandmaster. His wife Olive taught a class in the Sunday school (then known as the juniors).

It's doubtful if any other corps has had so many poets and composers associated with it as did Southall 1, known later as Southall Citadel.

Among the poets (which I will identify by the work which first comes to mind even though most were prolific writers) were: Ivy Mawby ('In The Love Of Jesus'), Joseph Buck ('Love Stands The Test') and May Pike ('Begin The Day With God'). May was Eric's cousin and he set many of her words to music.

Among the composers was Edward (Ted) Hill ('The Southall March'). In 1907 Ted Hill became the Army's first band inspector and Eric told me that if Ted happened to be home in Southall on a band practice night he would attend wearing his carpet slippers, just to let the men know he was off duty that night!

Then there was Cyril Piper, writer of 'Fear Thou Not' (this piece won first prize in an early song-writing competition), Stanley Piper ('The March Of The Soldier), Phil Catelinet ('A Sunbeam'), Donald Osgood ('Motondo') and, of course, Eric Ball, who used to refer to the above as 'so great a cloud of witnesses'.

The intense sorrow we all felt when Eric left the Army's ranks was in direct contrast to our joy on his return. Eric became a soldier of Hanwell Corps, where he and Olive served for many years.

Eric had written 'Resurgam' – a test piece for contesting bands. 'Resurgam' is a deeply spiritual piece, one which he very much wanted the Army to include in its band journals. Eric obtained permission from the publishing company for it to be republished by the Army, and then wrote to headquarters with his request.

I was a member of the International Music Board when his request was presented. The chairman thought the matter should be referred to the General (then Wilfred Kitching) for his decision. The General was delighted and suggested the International Staff Band play the piece at the next bandmasters councils festival. It proved to be of great blessing and an outstanding success.

Eric always showed great interest in our musical events (especially the yearly bandmasters councils festival) and every year wanted to be present for the afternoon rehearsal in the Royal Albert Hall. He preferred to hide away in a box so he could give the music his undivided attention.

One year, without telling Eric (which I now consider to be a bit of a nerve), I decided to add voices to his tone poem 'The Eternal Presence'. It has as its central theme the song by Harriet Beecher Stowe and Ira Sankey, 'Still, Still With Thee'.

There are some parts for solo soprano voice in his score, which are wonderfully suited to an unamplified voice in the Royal Albert Hall, and this gave me the idea of adding the 700- or 800-voice chorus to the work.

We had already started the rehearsal when Eric arrived and, as my wife showed him to his favourite box, we had just reached the solo voice part. Eric asked Jill not to leave him and she saw how visibly moved he was when the massive chorus joined the Staff Band in 'Still, Still With Thee' (*SASB* 632), the first verse being:

> Still, still with thee, when purple morning breaketh,
> When the bird waketh, and the shadows flee;
> Fairer than morning, lovelier than daylight,
> Dawns the sweet consciousness, I am with thee.

Eric's treatment of the last verse is beyond words to express:

> So shall it be at last, in that bright morning,
> When the soul waketh, and life's shadows flee;
> O in that hour, fairer than daylight dawning,
> Shall rise the glorious thought, I am with thee!

During the following tea interval, I was about to seek his forgiveness for adding to his score when he said, 'You can do that to any of my music at any time!' He was delighted, not only that the sound was enlarged, but also that the text of the songs became available to the listener.

I thought it a good idea to invite Eric to the National School of Music (held at Cobham Hall) so that our youthful musicians could have the opportunity of meeting him. 'They won't know who I am,' he said as I escorted him to the hall. He soon discovered otherwise. As he entered, they all stood in awed silence until he reached the platform. Then, as he turned to look at them, the whole place suddenly exploded into a thunderous welcome of clapping, cheering and whistling.

Eric, joining us for a few days, always highlighted conferences with bandmasters and songster leaders at Sunbury Court. The music leaders would sit with rapt attention as he was being questioned by me. I knew what the leaders wanted to know and Eric was always happy to give frank and forthright answers.

Eric loved to recall humorous stories of past days. One concerned the number of afternoons in one week he had been absent from the Music Editorial office. Refusing to give any explanation for his absence, he was told by Colonel F. G. Hawkes that his promotion would be held back.

The following Sunday was the occasion of the Bandmasters Councils, led by General Evangeline Booth. She commenced the day by calling Eric to the platform and promoting him to the rank of major!

What Colonel Hawkes (whom Eric deeply revered) did not know was that General Evangeline had called Eric to her little hut in Sunbury Court three times that very week to look over some songs she had written. She had also instructed Eric not to tell anyone where he had been or what he had been doing!

Eric never retired! In latter years he and Olive (by then living in Poole) would ask Jill and me to call and see them when on holiday in our caravan in the New Forest near Bournemouth.

One afternoon, while sitting in the garden of a favourite retreat of ours, Eric told me of his excursion into the orchestral world. He was invited to conduct one of the famous London orchestras in a series of concerts and, whenever he looked over at the cello players, he would remember his wife Olive playing cello in the Southall 1 Orchestra.

This was made up of three or four violins, two violas, two or three brass instruments, a small portable organ, a clarinet (whose player was predisposed to backslide before a performance) and Olive on the cello. Olive smiled as Eric went on to tell us that she could never master the art of fingering so he had to arrange all the music with the cello playing on the 'open' strings. This meant she could play only four different notes, so his chords had to contain one of those four notes as often as possible.

Following Olive's death, Eric developed an illness and had to enter hospital. It just so happened that Jill and I were on holiday and so were able to call and see him most days. He was obviously far from well so I thought I would make a telephone call to Ray Steadman-Allen, a friend whom Eric admired, to tell him of Eric's state of health.

The very next day, Ray (as I knew he would) arrived to see Eric who, in turn, expressed his delight at such a lovely surprise. For an hour he and Ray talked of days spent in the Music Editorial Department, about Army music and personalities and about what was to be Eric's or Ray's next piece. As they talked, it seemed as if all the years between had dropped away and that it was only yesterday that 'The Old Wells' was written.

Following a fond farewell, Ray and I went to the home of Stan (the bandmaster of Winton Corps) and Mary Randell for a meal together and, in conversation, Mary confirmed that Eric was going to stay with them following his discharge from hospital. This he did, becoming part of a very loving family. (Incidentally, Mary was called to Buckingham Palace in 2007 to be appointed MBE (Member of the British Empire) for her work among the homeless and needy in the Bournemouth area.)

Jill and I last saw Eric when he was again in hospital. Eric knew that his journey to Heaven was almost complete and expressed his desire to give us both his blessing before he left. He asked us to stand on either side of his bed then, taking Jill's hand in his left hand and mine in his right, he lifted them high and said, 'In the name of the Father, and of the Son, and of the Holy Spirit...' a long pause, 'Amen!'

During the pause before the 'Amen', the opening lines of the sessional song 'The Witnesses', for which Eric had written the music to words by Albert Orsborn, flashed through my mind:

> In the name of the Father,
> By the grace of the Son,
> And in the power of the Holy Ghost
> We will be witnesses!

There can be very few days when Eric's witness is not heard somewhere!

Leslie Condon

The traffic lights at a very busy junction en route to International Headquarters had just turned to red as, in my car, I arrived at them, making me the first in the queue to move when the green light appeared. Alas, as the colour changed, the engine of my car cut out! Turn the ignition key and depress the accelerator as I did, nothing would come to life! The symphony of car horns greeting me from behind did little to help me on my way. As the intensity of the irate horns – now accompanied by verbal interjections – grew, I became aware that someone had come to my rescue and that my car was being pushed to the comparative safety of the other side of the junction.

On arrival, I leapt out of the car to express my thanks to the 'angel of mercy' who had come to my rescue. Imagine my surprise when I discovered the angel was none other than Leslie Condon! 'Had I known it was you,' he quipped, 'I wouldn't have bothered!' The truth is that the character of Leslie Condon was such that he would have done the same for anybody. He truly had the spirit of the Good Samaritan, as recipients of his kindness from all over the territory will agree.

We first met when we were welcomed to the International Training College as fellow members of the Ambassadors Session in 1950. We were both assigned to the same work section, for which the instruction read, 'To help in the men's dining room.' This meant dishing out the porridge in the mornings, supplying soup for those who wanted it after the Thursday evening holiness meeting at Camberwell and scrubbing the floor on Friday mornings.

Captain Albert Drury (who wrote the spirited march 'Norwich Citadel'), bandmaster of the cadets' band, asked Les (as he was known to all) to play bass trombone – then known as bass trombone in G. He seemed to be the only one who knew where to place the slide for any given note. Les was heard at his best on the Thursday night march to and from the Camberwell hall. It is hard to believe that the band played not only en route to the Thursday night holiness meeting, but also on the way back to the training college, along a route which took it and 200 cadets through a housing estate where children and others would be sleeping. 'In The King's Service', the march most commonly used, was one in which the bass trombonist (in G!) could really shine. Les was no exception and with a smile on his face would convince his fellow bandsmen that the technical term at the head of the march simply meant, 'Let it rip!'

A few years after training, Les and I accepted the invitation of my friend Dennis Lewis (a one-time dance band leader and, later, the officer at Sudbury Corps in Suffolk) to join him for a day campaigning in his town. The plan was that, with Les playing piano accordion, Dennis playing saxophone and me playing trombone, we should amble up and down the main street interspersing gospel texts with well-known hymn tunes and announcing the evening meeting.

Just in case any of the listening public should miss the spoken invitation, Dennis got the use of a sandwich board (on which he had printed appropriate information) for one of us to wear. I claimed it was impossible to play a trombone while so restricted and Dennis expressed his opinion that, seeing he was the CO and would be seen in the streets the following week, it would be better if someone else undertook to wear the sandwich board.

211

Les offered no excuse so with him 'sandwiched' like a true professional, the three of us set off to rouse the town of Sudbury with our witness. At the end of the day I noticed Les added 'Publicity Officer' to his name when signing for his expenses!

It's doubtful that there was any connection between our musical witness in Sudbury and our future work but, quite soon afterwards, Les was appointed to the Music Editorial Department and I became the National Bandmaster.

The next few years were very fruitful for Leslie Condon so far as composing music for the Army was concerned and among the excellent pieces he wrote for us was one called 'The Call Of The Righteous', in which he really broke new ground.

With typical modesty he referred to this work as a 'festival arrangement' and when I asked him why he had not called it a tone poem (which sounds grander), he replied that the piece was not long enough for such a title. He had no answer when I asked him if all poems had to be long to be called poems. Since its publication, many have tried to copy its style but, in my opinion, all have fallen short of the original.

Les proved to be a very good tuba (E flat bass) player and amazed everyone by writing a solo for the instrument entitled 'Celestial Morn', which calls for a high degree of expertise on the part of the soloist. I first heard this work when the International Staff Band (with Les as soloist) premiered it at the band's annual Regent Hall Festival. In true Condon style, he brought forward his own chair and music stand before sitting down to play his new solo. When it was over he then took them back to his place in the band. There was just nothing of the prima donna about him.

The year 1965 saw the celebration of the first 100 years of The Salvation Army and, to mark the occasion, Leslie and Catherine Baird collaborated in the writing of the magnificent 'A Song Of Praise'.

The original setting for songsters has different melodies for each verse but the main tune 'Eternal God' (tune book number 492) is the one that is used for the song as it now appears as number 5 in the song book. The opening verse says:

International Staff Songsters

General Arnold Brown with the International Staff Songsters at their
inauguration at Croydon's Fairfield Halls on 8 March 1980

Marching As To War

The International Staff Songsters filming *Marching As To War* (1988)

Butlin's

Norman riding into the
Gaiety Theatre after joining
the French Foreign Legion
– at Butlin's

Willing Helpers

Ray Steadman-
Allen and Ray
Bowes are
enlisted by the
International
Staff Songsters
for a song
about sailing
to Heaven

As a Guest at the 2002 Councils for Bandmasters

Interview with Ray Steadman-Allen, celebrating his 80th birthday

Norman with
Maisie Wiggins
and Muriel
Yendell – two
great supporters

Victors Acclaimed

Bramwell Coles

Emil Söderström

Leslie Condon

Erik Leidzén

Interviewing Colonel Albert Jakeway during his 90th birthday celebrations

Eternal God, our song we raise
In thankful, overflowing praise,
For men of faith whose power was thine,
Whose love no barrier could confine;
They humbly offered Christ their bread,
And lo, the multitudes were fed!

The music matches the words perfectly and has proved to be one of the finest songs in our book. It has became traditional to sing this song at the conclusion of the annual councils for bandmasters and songster leaders held at the training college, where so many Spirit-filled musicians raise their voices in this mighty song of praise, concluding with the final verse:

Our great redeemer liveth still,
His love sustains us in thy will;
Because he conquered, we shall win,
His cross before, his joy within;
Our cheerful banners are unfurled,
For Christ has overcome the world.

Leslie followed me into the appointment of National Bandmaster when I was posted to Canada in 1968. He later told me his years in the Bands Department were the happiest and most fulfilling of his service. Leslie not only inspired bandsmen and songsters with his musical prowess but also proved his love for them in his caring ministry. Unsolicited stories of his generous care came to me from people all over the territory when, in 1976, I returned to Britain and succeeded him as Secrètary for Bands and Songster Brigades. Leslie returned to the Music Editorial Department and became deputy bandmaster of the ISB.

His interest was not restricted to music for larger bands and the *Triumph Series* contains many excellent pieces from his pen – 'The Front Line', 'Blyth Heritage' and the scintillating 'Bognor Regis' to name but a few.

213

The last time Leslie conducted at the Royal Albert Hall was when we had the Canadian Staff Band as our special guests. The CSB, along with the ISB and Festival Chorus, concluded the programme with his great march 'Celebration'.

Les had written a vocal part for the occasion so the singers could rise and sing 'We'll keep the old flag flying' when the trio of the march had been reached.

Wanting the item to have some surprise for him, we let him lift up his bass to play with the bands before inviting him to come forward and conduct his famous march. The massive crowd of listeners left him in no doubt of their delight as he came and took the baton. As the march neared the familiar chorus Les gave the signal for the chorus to rise and sing. This they did and, with faces beaming at the joy of the celebration, reaffirmed their determination to work for God and the Army.

> We'll keep the old flag flying,
> Flying round the world;
> We'll keep the old flag flying
> In every land unfurled.
> Keep the old flag flying,
> Keep the old flag flying,
> Flying round the world.

I think Leslie treasured the fact that I chose this same march for the inauguration of the Canadian Staff Band in 1969 and that of the International Staff Songsters in 1980.

Joy and Ray Steadman-Allen invited a number of officer-friends to their home on the night prior to Christmas Eve in 1983. Among the guests were to be Leslie and his wife Ruth and my wife Jill and me. Ruth and Jill were unable to accept the invitation but Les said he would come 'after Christmas carolling with Croydon Citadel Band'.

The event turned out to be a very happy one with lots of laughter, which increased further when Les arrived around 10 o'clock wearing

214

full uniform and carrying a collecting box, which he promptly passed round the assembled guests!

When the party began to break up Ray whispered to me, 'Don't go yet. Stop and have some time with Les.' This I did and it wasn't until late in the night that we finally took our leave of our generous hosts. We did not expect that the very next morning, while out carolling with Croydon Citadel Band, Les would take his final promotion and go to Heaven.

The news shocked the Army world and I spent most of the day receiving telephone calls from all parts of the world from people anxious to get news concerning their friend and comrade.

His funeral was the largest I ever attended, with by far the larger part of the congregation unable to get into the hall at Fakenham. (Fakenham was the corps Les attended when he was evacuated there in the Second World War and from which he entered training in 1950.)

Major John Mott (then the National Bandmaster) had the foresight to expect that there would be bandsmen travelling from all parts of the territory, bringing their instruments in the hope of playing in what turned out to be a 100-strong band. John had made copies of two Condon marches, 'Duke Street' (his first published composition) and 'Fakenham Temple', which the band played alternately for the entire mile-and-a-quarter procession to the cemetery. As this progressed, a fellow officer who had been in the same session as Leslie and me said, 'Les would never believe all this!'

Among the tributes given at the thanksgiving service at Croydon Citadel was one from a close friend, who told of the time when his wife Ruth took Les to task for making a lot of noise when he returned home very late from some of his duties. She suggested that he should creep in very quietly so as not to disturb the sleeping household.

The next time Les arrived home in the early hours of the morning he crept in, undressed downstairs then made his way to the bedroom where his wife was sleeping. Getting into bed, he lay very quietly for some moments then, gently tapping her on the shoulder said, 'This *is* number 77, isn't it?'

John Mott recalls the first morning he arrived at National Headquarters to take up his position as National Bandmaster. He was just taking off his coat when the office door opened and Les, clad in leather motorcycle overcoat, helmet and goggles, looked in and said, 'I just wanted to wish you well in your new job,' then added, 'it was the best job I ever had,' then was gone.

To deliver this message personally, Les had to travel a different and longer route to his new place of work, had to park in the IHQ car park and climb to the fourth floor. Of course, he could have just picked up the phone and relayed his message without any effort, but the more I think about Leslie Condon, the more I realise this was the way to do it!

Chapter 20

MARCHING THROUGH THE YEARS

On the Halls

Like the previous chapter on the composers, the following contains articles I wrote for *Salvationist* as well as other material not included then.

Over the years, The Salvation Army has used all kinds of halls for meetings of one sort or another. The title is borrowed from the one-time popular entertainment known as 'music hall' – in which singers and artists of all kinds would perform – which had a marked influence on the style of meetings and music used by early-day Salvationists. It is centred on the halls we've used for our music events and the many people and personalities who have helped in the production of the same.

The halls range from the biggest and best concert halls in the country to some which no longer exist. From theatres to cathedrals, large tents to civic halls, dance halls to hotel conference rooms – you name it, the Army has been there!

The remarkable fact is that, once the Army has moved in, and whatever the previous use of the hall, after a prayer for the Lord's presence has been uttered, the place becomes God's house and, for a couple of hours or so, the dwelling of his people.

An early-day song reflects this statement:

> First in the street and then in a tent,
> > Glory, Hallelujah!
> With the word of life to the crowds it went,
> > Sing Glory, Hallelujah!
> And then we got a dancing room,

Glory, Hallelujah!
Where our hearts soon danced to a heavenly tune,
Sing Glory, Hallelujah!

Clapton Congress Hall

Being the son of officers, I was introduced to halls very early in life. My first recollection of a big hall is of a Christmas party for officers' children in Clapton Congress Hall in east London. The special guest was General Evangeline Booth.

Towards the end of the party, the General called for a large (cardboard) pie to be brought into the hall and we were told the pie contained a surprise for every child. We were invited to sing the following refrain (written for the occasion), to the tune of the chorus 'When He Has Come To You'. Just imagine what seemed like hundreds of children singing:

> What's in the pie for me?
> What's in the pie for me?
> Tell me, dear cook,
> With a wink and a look,
> What's in the pie for me?

The General then took a large knife and, after cutting a hole in the pie, pulled out a present for each of us!

Shortly after that memorable occasion, I journeyed to Clapton Congress Hall with my brother Bram and fellow members of the junior band (that is what we were called in those days) for what had been billed as 'A Day Of Instruction And Participation'. (As if we knew what that meant!)

The National Secretary for Bands and Songster Brigades – none other than Brigadier Wilfred Kitching (known to us as a composer of Salvation Army music and who later became the General) – was in charge and the activities included instruction in marching, then marching while playing our instruments, and how to give gospel shots (verses of Scripture shouted loudly in open-air meetings).

The body of the hall was cleared of chairs and became the 'square' on which we were drilled by the brigadier as we marched and counter-marched to the strains of 'The Gloryland'.

The day concluded with each band playing its special piece, after which the brigadier gave his comments on the performance. Then, as massed bands, we played our final piece. This was conducted by the brigadier who, in bringing the meeting to a close, asked the Lord to bless us all and make us worthy Army bandsmen of the future.

At one time, Clapton Congress Hall was the most famous hall in The Salvation Army. It was where cadets were trained to be Salvation Army officers, it was the place of great gatherings in the time of our Founder, William Booth, and it was a splendid hall for bandmasters councils and music festivals.

It was at Clapton Congress Hall where, in 1966, I conducted a performance of Handel's *Messiah*. The soloists were June Mingay (soprano), Susan Stevens (contralto), Norman Heath (tenor) and Lawrence Mallyon (bass). It also featured Michael Clack (organ), Frank Parris (pianoforte), Max Weaver (trumpet) and musicians from the Red Shield Band. The Chorus was formed from 14 songster brigades: Cambridge Heath, Clapton Congress Hall, Leigh-on-Sea, Leytonstone, Harlesden, Harrow, Luton Citadel, Catford, Croydon Citadel, Sutton, Thornton Heath, Kingston-on-Thames, Staines and Twickenham.

At a similar event at the De Montfort Hall in Leicester I received a last-minute call from the person who was to play the trumpet in the aria 'The Trumpet Shall Sound', saying he could not be there. Someone suggested that a certain Deryck Diffey (then unknown to me) would be a good substitute. I contacted Deryck and he agreed to come but he did not own a trumpet. He said he would get one and went to Boosey and Hawkes in London to hire the same. When the time came for the aria Deryck stood to play with a large price tag still dangling and twirling from the end of the trumpet! He sounded great!

Westminster Central Hall

Westminster Central Hall, the lovely building set in the heart of London just a stone's throw from Westminster Abbey, has been a meeting place for Salvationists for many years. Not only is it a headquarters and central hall for the Methodist Church, it is also used for civic occasions, political meetings and many other events requiring a large hall in the centre of the British capital.

During my years in the Bands and Songster Brigades Department, Westminster Central Hall was used at least twice a year – firstly for the Day With God meetings (as they were called from the Founder's day and through to recent years), led by the General, and the annual Christmas festival with the International Staff Band and (later) the International Staff Songsters.

For a few years the Christmas festival at Westminster Central Hall was organised by the Public Relations Department with Major Jorge Booth as the producer. It was always an exciting and adventurous affair.

Many 'showbiz' artists appeared, including Thora Hird who, for a time, starred in a television comedy series called *Hallelujah!* in which she played the part of a Salvation Army captain. Thora obviously felt very much at home with us (I always felt that she came as 'the captain') and we were equally at home with her.

Another guest was Roy Castle who, fresh from making the television series *Marching As To War*, was likewise at home with Army folk. On one occasion it was requested that Roy lead the congregation in a carol that was to be accompanied by the Staff Band (playing under its bandmaster, Lieut-Colonel Ray Bowes). After the first verse Roy suggested that Ray and he change places, so that Ray would lead the congregation and Roy conduct the band. 'After all,' quipped Roy, 'you have more power leading the band.' The suggestion took Ray by surprise but seeing the congregation was clapping its approval he felt he should agree to the request of the special guest. As Ray exchanged his baton for the carol sheet he reminded Roy that it is the leader of the singing who sets the tempo!

One remarkable year, Princess Diana was the special guest and Major Jorge Booth accepted the challenge to produce an evening to remember. Those responsible for the carol concert were invited to join the General in meeting the Princess in a private room before the festival began. Ray Bowes and I were among those present. We were all given a short lecture on what to do if the Princess should single anyone out for a 'little chat' and how to respond if she should want to shake our hand. Ray seemed a bit nervous and suggested he and I stick together. After greeting the General, the Princess made her way straight to where Ray and I were standing and I became aware that Ray had shifted even closer to me. Actually he was leaning on me!

As we were introduced to her as the 'music people' (not a rank I was familiar with!), the Princess shook my hand and then offered her hand to Ray. In his excitement Ray, forgetting the previous instructions, continued to hold her hand and it was only after I nudged him a couple of times that he finally let go! After she had left the room I asked Ray why he had held her hand so long. His only reply was, 'Norman, I think you're jealous!'

Major Jorge Booth had done a lot of work to make the evening a spectacular success, even arranging for laser beams to signal the warmest of welcomes to the Princess. At the given signal a voice was heard to declare, 'Ladies and gentlemen, Her Royal Highness, the Princess of Wales.' Simultaneously with a fanfare from the International Staff Band the 'smoke' required for the lasers was released. Alas! A little too much 'smoke' was released and the whole room was filled with it. It was quite a few moments before it subsided and the audience got their first glimpse of the Princess who, realising what had happened, was almost helpless with laughter!

For one Christmas festival at Westminster Central Hall, Major Booth wanted the Staff Songsters to appear as the Dickensian Singers and requested we be dressed in appropriate costumes. From the Butlin's store (kept at THQ for the annual Holiday-plus-Fellowship Week) and a few visits to charity shops, the songsters were able to appear in the manner requested by Jorge. He suggested the songsters enter the hall from the entrances used by the public and sing as they made their way to the platform.

This we did, singing 'Praise Ye The Lord' to the melody of 'Hail, Smiling Morn', but the hooped skirts worn by the women songsters filled the aisles and swept up all the plastic containers placed at the end of each row in readiness for the collection later in the festival. As we climbed the steps to the platform we left behind what looked like a pile of plastic boxes at a recycling centre! Amid the laughter I had not noticed that our pianist, Howard Parris, had not yet arrived. He should have entered by another door but unfortunately managed to get on the wrong level so was unable to find his way in time to play the introduction to our first carol.

For what seemed like an eternity we stood and waited but still no pianist appeared, so there was nothing else to do but tell the songsters to sing the piano introduction. There were cheers and shouts of welcome when our pianist eventually arrived at the piano in time for the final couple of bars of the carol.

At another Christmas festival in Westminster Central Hall, a stable had been built for a Mary, a Joseph and a baby Jesus. The actual mother of the baby was playing the part of the Angel Gabriel and was standing on the roof of the stable with trumpet in hand. When the baby began to cry, the acting mother Mary, try though she did, could not soothe him and, in the end, had to pass the baby Jesus up to his real mother (acting as Gabriel) for his evening meal!

The annual Day With God meetings held at Westminster Central Hall always included a singing item by cadets from the training college. My lasting memory of such a day is when, back in 1950, I joined with fellow cadets in the singing of a song by General Albert Orsborn, who was leading the three meetings.

The afternoon meeting became a challenge to Salvationists to do something in the Spirit of Christ to help the lost and those who had been wounded by the world. The Good Samaritan parable was the basis of the General's message and he made an impassioned appeal for Salvationists to respond to Christ's call. The General then requested that the cadets sing his song, which has as its chorus:

> From the dark side of the road,
> Where the weak and wounded lie,
> They are calling for help and mercy
> And how can we pass them by?

For the Saviour asks thy love,
In the service of want and pain,
And anything more that thou spendest
He'll repay when he comes again.

It really was a Day With God, with a message as needful today as it was then.

Westminster Abbey

General Eva Burrows asked Jill and me to represent her at Westminster Abbey for a united music service in the days when the ordination of women in the Anglican Church was still being considered.

We were happy to do so and duly arrived at the Abbey to be greeted most warmly and taken to the robing room, where we encountered a large number of clergy – all of whom were male. As they were changing into their clerical clothing, Jill suggested she and I go and sit in the Abbey. A spokesman for the clergy asked us not to do so, seeing that we would not be sitting with the congregation but with the rest of the clergy at their appointed place at the front of the Abbey.

He explained that Jill and I were required to lead the procession of the clergy through the Abbey and that we were most welcome to share the robing room in preparation for this. At this point Jill thought she had better take her overcoat and bonnet off and tidy her hair. The ministers laughed heartily as Jill, pointing to her handbag on the table, remarked, 'I don't suppose you get many of those in here!'

The service was wonderful! There was lovely singing, superb hymns and the Abbey was full to overflowing. During one choir item I noticed one of the clergymen looking at Jill and smiling – he was probably still thinking about that handbag!

Wembley

It's hard to get the best out of a 1,000-voice chorus when the stage on which you're rehearsing is still being built! Such a chorus had been brought together for the 1978 International Congress and the hall chosen for the opening meeting was the Wembley Arena, with His Royal Highness, the Prince of Wales as the special guest.

Although the congress chorus had been well rehearsed in scattered groups all over Britain, it was mid-morning on the day the congress was due to start before I first met the whole chorus together. Whatever had taken place in the Wembley Arena the previous evening had certainly not included a stage which could seat 1,000 singers and the International Staff Band.

On my arrival, the main stage was in place but the risers were still being built. The workmen understood my predicament and were happy for us to commence singing on the stage so long as they could work round us, so, to the accompaniment of hammers, drills and saws, we began to sing a special arrangement of the song 'We're Bound For The Land Of The Pure And The Holy'.

I explained to the songsters that, seeing this song was sung as William Booth and his company made their way through noisy London streets, we ought to manage with a bit of hammering in the background. The task became harder as the workmen began to paint the stage a deep shade of red, at the same time issuing loud warnings to 'Mind the wet paint!' which included some questionable language!

Whatever one might think about the vast arena at Wembley, it can hardly be classed as a holy building, but once the crowd had gathered and a prayer had been offered for God's blessing on the congress, we were in God's house – fresh with the smell of new paint!

Among many musicians featured in the Composers Festival held on the following Saturday evening was my good friend Herbert Mountain. I particularly asked that he conduct his excellent march 'Sheffield Citadel'. This march, which appeared in the band journal in the early 1940s, had a number of special features which marked it out as a 'winner'.

The first feature was in the part of the march usually referred to as the 'bass solo', at which point Herbert had introduced a very interesting florid passage for the cornets, which the massed bands played in sparkling style. The march then concludes with the kind of finish that makes you feel glad you joined the Army.

Herbert had not been well prior to the festival and his daughter Freda, who had been looking after him, told me that he would have been very cross if the Lord had called him Home before he had taken his part with the other composers!

In fact, the Composers Festival took place just a few weeks prior to his promotion to Glory, which, incidentally, he received while conducting a band at a divisional music school. What a way to go!

I was asked to conduct his funeral service, which was preceded by the band marching to the hall in front of the coffin. It so happened that the route to the hall took us past a field full of cows, which, on hearing the band playing, all rushed to the fence to observe the proceedings. I am sure that Herbert would have seen the funny side of this. The service was one of joy and thanksgiving for a life spent in the service of his Saviour and Friend.

Sunbury Court

Sunbury Court, venue for many historic events in the life of the Army, has also hosted a number of music events including music schools and the yearly conference for bandmasters or songster leaders (following the music leaders councils held the previous weekend).

These were originally called refresher courses, where bandmasters or songster leaders could have the opportunity to hone their skills in a week of instruction and fellowship. The courses attracted large numbers of bandmasters and songster leaders, mostly from the British Territory, with a few coming from overseas.

During the bandmasters' course, each delegate was invited to conduct the large band formed from the delegates, then take part in discussion relating to his performance. It often proved to be a hilarious affair with much laughter and good-humoured criticism.

One bandmaster was asked why, at the beginning of each bar, he stood on his toes. As he vigorously denied doing so, it was suggested I kneel behind him and hold his ankles so he could feel the pull at the first beat of each bar. This I did, causing him to admit to his action and saying: 'It's a well-known fact that even Arturo Toscanini had some mannerisms all his own!'

Another year we were very privileged to have Dr Thomas Rive (a New Zealander who had written a number of very fine works for bands) as a delegate, and to have him talk about his magnificent variations on 'I Know A Fount' (my personal favourite set of variations).

Eric Ball came most years, even staying for a few days and bringing the wealth of experience that was his to share with the bandmasters.

Dean Goffin led the first refresher course I attended and, as I had served in the Brigade of Guards a few years previously, he thought it a good idea for me to give some marching drill to the bandmasters. 'You know,' he said, 'like you did on the barrack square.'

Not wishing to be uncooperative, I agreed and we duly formed up on the lawn in the Sunbury Court grounds (not really the ideal place for marching drill!), complete with instruments and music for the march 'Neath The Flag'. Using language a little softer than that of the barrack square, I gave the following instructions:

'On the command: "Baaand",' you take a long time to say that word! 'By the left,' short pause in which you say, 'Wait for it. Wait for it!' (I have no idea why, but drill sergeants always said it), then, 'Quick march!' (ordered in the desired speed of the march). At this point, everyone steps out on the left foot and the drums begin a two-three beat signal (boom, boom, boom! Boom, boom, boom!). At which point, the band strikes up the music.

Now the lawns at Sunbury were not really large enough or suitable for a drill parade. Hardly had we got through the opening bars of the march before we were up to the rose beds. The delegates purposely did not hear me shout 'Halt!' and we all finished up in a heap – still playing!

Bandmaster Bram Williams (then of Birmingham Citadel) suggested, 'If we were to counter-march when we got near the rose beds, we could go on marching all day!'

To confess my ignorance of the manoeuvre at this point of the proceedings did not seem a good idea so I said, 'We will counter-march when we are six feet from the rose bed.' (That certainly did not sound like the loud drill sergeant at Windsor Barracks!)

Bram suggested I should stand some 12 feet from the rose beds then, after marching backwards for six feet, give the command 'Counter-march!' Unable to come up with any better suggestion, I agreed so to do.

Off we went, picking up the music at the point at which the melody of 'Old Soldiers Never Die' appears. In my excitement, I was nearer three than six feet from the rose bed and, as the band closed in on me while I was trying to march backwards, I landed up on my back in the rose bushes, to the accompaniment of uproarious laughter! Dean was laughing but was not impressed!

The International Staff Band came every year to give a private programme which always included some new music about to be published. In later years the International Staff Songsters followed the same pattern.

The life of a bandmaster or a songster leader is not an easy one. The conducting of the band or songsters on a Sunday is probably the easiest part of the job. Dealing with people and problems is another matter! Being a music leader in a corps can be a bit lonely at times, and the Sunbury week was an opportunity to get things into perspective and then, after a time of sharing with leaders of like calling, return to the corps refreshed and ready for the work.

Cory Hall – Cardiff

To many people the mere mention of Cory Hall in Cardiff will conjure up the sound of Welsh male-voice choirs, orchestral concerts and music events of all kinds. The hall, now no longer standing, was used for Salvation Army events for many years – none more joyous than the final weekend of the annual Welsh School of Music.

The school was held in a YMCA complex called Coleg Y Fro, situated near Cardiff (Rhoose) Airport. During the years I was musical director of the school, I wrote a march called 'Coleg Y Fro' which was later published under the title of 'Land Of Song' as a concession to English-speaking people. The march contains the tune 'The Ash Grove', with references to 'Men Of Harlech' and 'Cwm Rhondda', thus leaving no doubt in which part of the British Isles the music school was held.

It was the first co-ed school to be held in the British Territory and, although not restricted to Welsh young people, it was a very musical school with lovely singing from predominantly young Welsh voices.

Unlike most British SA music schools, the course included two weekends, the second one being spent at the Cory Hall in Cardiff, with public meetings led by the staff and students. Dean Goffin had the honour of being the first Music Director of the Welsh school and I had the joy of so being for the next two years.

Major John (Jack) Izzard, the Divisional Young People's Secretary, brought the school into being and remained as Director for a number of years. The music staff consisted of Bandmaster and Mrs Ivor Bosanko, Bandmaster Brian Bowen, M. Denney, Howard Roberts, Joan Clothier, Songster Leader J. Murray, David Mallett and Singing Company Leader A. Davies. My wife Jill was the matron and Doctor John Lowther the medical adviser.

Doctor Lowther proved to be very useful on the occasion that my son Bram (one of the students) broke his collarbone having tripped and fallen while chasing one of the girls. Jill was called to the scene and, seeing Bram lying on the ground, told him to 'Get up and stop being so silly.' This he did but overnight was in a lot of pain, so Doctor Lowther took him into Cardiff for an X-ray that proved a bone was broken. Bram, with his arm in a sling, really enjoyed all the comfort and fuss the female students showered on him during the remainder of the school!

My other two sons were there, Norrie playing trombone and Mark, though too young to be in the bands, enjoyed climbing the parallel bars in the room used for band practice. On one occasion, Jill came to me saying that she could not find Mark anywhere – we discovered him sitting on one of the beams in the ceiling to which he had climbed from the parallel bars!

Many boy-girl friendships were formed during the week and I conducted the marriage ceremony of a couple who fell in love at Coleg Y Fro. Sadness always followed the final Sunday night meeting when the time came to say goodbye. Young sweethearts could be seen, with tears in their eyes, speaking their fond farewells and pledging undying love against the wall of the Cory Hall. It came to be known to staff members as the Wailing Wall.

I always felt very much at home in Wales where their love of music and singing always gets right to your heart. Eric and Nancy Lear of Morriston Corps in Wales were a couple in whose home we were welcomed on many occasions. Eric was the songster leader of a very fine brigade of singers and maintained the highest of standards both in deportment and singing.

Graham and Beryl Smith, who live near Swansea in Wales, have also been very welcoming. I remember staying with them when I was with the Canadian Staff Band on a visit to Swansea. Beryl told me that if a Welsh congregation really do enjoy a programme given by visitors from outside Wales, at the close the audience will stand and sing the Welsh National Anthem (which English people call 'Land Of My Fathers'). It is always sung in the Welsh language and is a very moving experience. The Canadian Staff Band were the recipients on this occasion and I still remember the experience.

Surprise Item

I was more than a little surprised when looking in the 5 September 1998 copy of *Salvationist* for the latest of my 'On The Halls' series, to find that Jill had responded to another request from the editor to write an article herself about me.

The Editor's introduction read: 'For one week only, Mrs Colonel Jill Bearcroft takes over the typewriter.' Here is what she had written:

When I was 14 and Norman Bearcroft was 17 he wrote to his sister Nancy saying he had found the girl he was going to marry and her name was Jill. He neglected to tell me, but four years later he met me off the train when I was coming home for weekend leave from the Women's Land Army, and took me straight into Bravingtons the Jewellers, and bought me a ring! I was dating somebody else at that time but I knew Norman was right for me.

After a little persuasion my parents agreed to us getting married when I was 19 and Norman was 22.

It was just after the war – 11 September 1948 – and the world was a drab, grey place, so the families decided the wedding should be a return to long dresses and bridesmaids and be as colourful as possible. I hired a beautiful dress from Rank Film Studios and the six girls in both families spent time, money and, more importantly, precious clothing coupons on lovely dresses, and it all began to shape up.

I asked Norman what he was going to wear and he replied, 'My uniform.' As he was in the Life Guards I could see him in his 'dress' uniform, smart and adding to the splendour of it all – even if I hoped he wouldn't wear the spurs!

The great day dawned and I finally arrived on my father's arm. All the bridesmaids looked lovely as we formed up to process in. As we entered the Southall Citadel hall to music arranged by Norman there he was, waiting for me – not in his smart Guards uniform as I expected but in an old red 'lion-tamer' festival tunic with blue and white stripes, which obviously wasn't made for him as it was pre-war and he had found it in the band-room cupboard!

There was nothing to do but to laugh – which I managed to control fairly well. But then I knew life was never going to be 'ordinary' with this man. He fixed our honeymoon and we went on the Royal Blue coach to a bed-and-breakfast house in Bournemouth, arriving quite late.

On Sunday morning we followed Boscombe Band to their open-air meeting and spent all day at the Army. We swam during the day, but every evening bar one (when we went to a Bournemouth Symphony Orchestra concert) we spent at the Army, in halls or outside. One evening we stood outside Boscombe hall listening to Herbert Mountain conducting band practice!

I had confirmed to me in the first week of our marriage the strong faith and trust that Norman had in the grace of our Lord. His great love for music, the Army and me, have become so much part of each other over the years, all to be used in the service and love of God.

So as I can no longer get out to buy an anniversary card:

Dear Norman, happy anniversary! It has been a wonderful 50 years. Forgive me for this surprise but I wanted to share my laughter with our many friends.

As always, Your Jill.

PS – Thanks for the TLC.

Birmingham Town Hall

Birmingham Town Hall is another building used by great orchestras of the world and is the hall in which Mendelssohn conducted the first performance of his great oratorio *Elijah* in the year before he died at the age of 38. The fact that Mendelssohn conducted there had a marked effect on Dean Goffin, whose arrangement for brass band of themes from Mendelssohn's 'Italian Symphony' had recently been published for SA bands.

I had just climbed on to the conducting rostrum to rehearse the massed bands when Dean came over to me and, with a very wistful look in his eyes, said, 'Just imagine, Norm,' slight pause, 'you are standing on the very spot where Mendelssohn stood and conducted.' I was about to reply with, 'Yes, but he didn't conduct the "Red Shield March",' when I remembered that it was Dean's father who had written that march!

The next day (Sunday) was the occasion of Bandsmen's Councils held in Birmingham Town Hall. *The Musician* (dated 4 March 1961) reported that there were 1,500 bandsmen in attendance.

During the evening meeting Retired Corps Secretary William Rudd of Longton Corps (who had composed a new melody for the words of 'The Saviour's Name' which had become known to thousands of Salvationists the world over) was called to the platform. He was given a standing ovation as the commissioner warmly greeted him. Then the great congregation, without any instruction, began to sing:

> There is a name I love to hear,
> I love to sing its worth;
> It sounds like music in mine ear,
> The sweetest name on earth.

It seemed to me that all Heaven was rejoicing as the great crowd of male voices soared into the chorus, '*O how I love the Saviour's name!*' William Rudd was so overcome that he sat down in the commissioner's chair and stayed there until the end of the meeting!

The Royal Albert Hall

A story has it that, when an American band arrived at the Royal Albert Hall to rehearse for a congress festival, one of the bandsmen, being overawed at the size and setting of the place, became very vocal in his expressions of wonder. One of his fellow bandsmen (having been to the Albert Hall before) was heard to remark, 'If you're so impressed with this, just wait till you see the senior hall!'

The Royal Albert Hall in London – for Salvationists a building inextricably linked with The Salvation Army – has been the scene of hundreds of Army meetings and festivals through its exciting history.

Built in 1871, just six years after the birth of the Army (then known as The Christian Mission), the massive Royal Albert Hall has hosted events of many kinds including exhibitions, orchestral and choral concerts, beauty contests, the annual Festival of Remembrance, New Year parties, the annual brass band contest (which attracts band enthusiasts from all parts of the world), boxing matches and a host of other events.

It was at the Royal Albert Hall that William Booth is thought to have given his last message to the Army with his 'I'll fight' address, which clearly laid out the path that Salvationists should continue to take in their mission to save the lost.

It is worth noting that this message would have been given in that vast hall without the aid of amplification.

Army events have included congress meetings – with the hall being filled with delegates from all parts of the world – women's rallies, youth events, welcomes and farewells of Generals, the yearly commissioning of cadets as officers, the annual music festival in connection with the bandmasters or songster leaders councils and the occasional meetings called for by our leaders to encourage and inspire our people in salvation warfare. The hall, with its seating for some 7,000 people and its massive stage which can hold 1,000 participants, is ideal for many Army purposes. (In 1986 the hall was renovated and the seating reduced to 5,222.)

My personal involvement with the RAH began in May 1951 when my wife Jill and I marched, with a host of other cadets, to the apron of the stage to receive our commissions as Salvation Army officers. Although we had been taught not to be anxious, I was conscious of a little apprehension as Jill and I stepped forward to receive our commissions and to discover the corps to which we were being appointed.

I suppose my previous involvement in Army music was the reason the International Staff Band played a few extra notes when our names were called. Anyway, we received our appointment to Alderney in the Channel Islands. As we made our way back to our seats, someone whispered, 'You will have to go by aeroplane,' which we did. It was the first of many flights on Army service.

The evening meeting of commissioning day took the form of a pageant in which Jill was a Greek dancing girl and I was a monk! She looked great and, had we not already been married, I would have proposed to her there and then!

I thought I had been miscast as a monk but when I was asked to write a chant and lead the other monks in singing it my musical career at the RAH was launched.

Following my appointment in 1960 as National Bandmaster for the British Territory my visits to the RAH became very frequent. Not only were there the annual music festivals in connection with the bandmasters and songster leaders councils, in which I worked alongside Dean Goffin, there were also charitable concerts and other events in which Army musicians were involved.

In 1965, the International Congress called by General Frederick Coutts celebrated the fact that the Army had been in existence for 100 years. Although other buildings such as Westminster Abbey, St Paul's Cathedral, Westminster Central Hall and Crystal Palace were used, the main venue for the Centenary Congress was the Royal Albert Hall.

Her Majesty, Queen Elizabeth was the principal guest at the opening ceremony led by General Coutts. A massive chorus, accompanied by the International Staff Band and Bandmaster Michael Clack at the grand organ, gave a magnificent rendering of the National Anthem in recognition of Her Majesty's presence.

For many years the acoustic properties of the Albert Hall had caused slight problems for orchestras and concert-goers alike. Sir Thomas Beecham, the famous English conductor, is on record as saying, 'The Royal Albert Hall is the place where you can get two concerts for the price of one!' It was true that in certain seats you got an echo, especially in brass band concerts, where short staccato notes would bounce off somewhere and you could hear two such notes instead of the offered one. Some improvement was made, when the canopy situated over the stage was raised or lowered according to the type of concert being given. We discovered that, for bands, it was better to have the canopy lowered, but if the festival was featuring singers situated in the seats above the canopy, then those voices were completely lost.

I was always very grateful that the canopy could not be moved during a festival; otherwise half the time would have been taken up with moving it. I can just hear the General, or whoever was leading the occasion, saying, 'Let's have a chorus, while the canopy is raised.' Several suitable ones come to mind: 'I'd Rather Be A Little Thing Climbing Up' would please the singers, while 'Oh, The Crowning Day Is Coming, Hallelujah!' would make the bandsmen a little apprehensive.

Well, the whole acoustic problem was solved when, a few years later, large mushroom-shaped domes were suspended from the ceiling, resulting in every voice being heard and notes intended to be heard only once, being heard only once! In these days a good singer can be heard without the aid of electronic microphones.

I remember a time during one of our festivals when the mighty chorus was singing and a note on the grand organ got stuck. No matter what Michael did he was unable to stop it sounding or even switch the organ off. There was some good-hearted laughter as the song was abandoned.

Marching visiting groups or bands into the Royal Albert Hall has become a tradition but is not without its problems. The first is found in the fact that the steps leading into the arena from the back of the hall are not continuous. After every few steps there is a flat area before more stairs are encountered. This means that those marching into the hall must look down to see where the steps are while keeping their heads up in a military fashion. Add to this the excitement of entering the hall to lively band music and the cheering and applause of the crowd (causing the heart to beat faster than usual) and you have the ingredients for a disaster, which somehow was always overcome.

In the days before the acoustic problems were solved, there was one other problem – the time delay of the music coming from the stage to the point of entry. With an empty hall there was almost a beat in delay. With these problems in mind it was always advisable to have a practice run at entering during the afternoon rehearsal. Some visiting bands have informed me that such a practice was not needed, and my insistence has caused a little murmuring at times.

I well remember a woman officer accompanying an overseas group of female singers who were rehearsing the required traditional entry telling me that the band was not in time with the marchers. From the back of the hall, she said she could see that the band was playing a long time behind the bandmaster's beat and not keeping in time with the marchers. I advised her not to watch the bandmaster but just to listen to the music.

As they got closer to the stage she shouted to me, 'The band is doing better now so why couldn't they have done it right from the start?' It was one of those times when a smile is better than a spoken answer.

It was during an unrehearsed home league marching entrance that my wife Jill and I stood at the bottom of the same steps and caught a number of ladies who, looking up to see the special guest – the Queen Mother – missed their footing altogether and landed in our arms! One woman, finding herself in my arms, said she enjoyed the experience as much as the meeting. There's no answer to that!

On one occasion, a very agitated secretary came to the Green Room at the back of the RAH stage with news that the audience were

235

still without programmes. Seeing that the opening congregational song was printed on these, General Kitching said he would not go to the stage until they were found and distributed. Even as he was saying this, Dean Goffin saw a huge package containing the programmes. Now the problem was how to get them to the thousands of people already seated in the hall itself. Grabbing the programmes, Dean enlisted the aid of songsters sitting nearest the door but, even as he was asking them to distribute the same, realised this would take at least 20 minutes. 'Quick,' he said, 'get up to the top balcony and throw handfuls of programmes as far out as you can.' This they did and it was quite a sight to see hundreds of programmes falling as if from the sky. On seeing this, the General remarked to the audience, 'All good gifts around us are sent from Heaven above.'

We always had excellent co-operation from the RAH authorities, never more so than on the occasion when, as the producer of the festival, I wanted the audience to refrain from giving applause at the end of a piece I had written as a tribute to Colonel Catherine Baird. It was a setting of three of her poems under the title 'Reflections'. The third and final poem has the following words:

> I would go silently,
> Lord, when I come to thee;
> Glide as some gallant barque
> Into the mighty dark.
> Softly and gently ride
> O'er the receding tide;
> Steer from the shores of time
> T'ward an eternal clime.
> Lord, on a quiet sea
> Let me sail home to thee.

I began to hope that the final reflective moments would not be lost in applause. The RAH lighting technician must have had the same feelings as me for, when the last bars were being sung, and without any previous instruction from me or anybody else, he began to slowly fade down the lights until there was only the faintest glimmer of light remaining for the final chord. There was no sound from the audience. He came to me at the end of the programme and said he hoped I didn't mind him dimming the lights, but just felt he had to prevent any applause. In thanking him, I expressed the hope that he would always be there for Army programmes.

As stated earlier, Eric Ball was very happy for me to vocalise some of his music for bands, such as 'The Kingdom Triumphant', 'The Eternal Presence' or 'The King Of Kings', feeling that the words added greatly to the impact of the music. These pieces, along with many others presented by the International Staff Band (or massed bands if other bands were there), organ and voices, make a grand finish to the programme.

I realised at an early stage in my work with Army music programmes that it was essential to time every item to the second. The more individual items a programme contains, the more pitfalls will be encountered with regard to timing.

The length of an RAH programme is usually two-and-a-half hours, from 6.30 to 9 pm. If the compère was to be one of the Army leaders (usually the General in my earlier days), I found it a good idea to let them have a copy of the programme with all the timings set beside the items and another column showing where we should be at any given time.

It was always with a smile that succeeding Generals accepted the programme during a private briefing a few days before the event. I well remember such a meeting with General Arnold Brown, a superb chairman, who, looking at the programme and quickly calculating the time allotted to him for comments, said with a twinkle in his eye, 'Well, Norman, I see your pieces are getting longer and my time is getting shorter!'

The Royal Albert Hall holds different memories for all the Salvationists who have been there: officers – some in lonely and difficult appointments – bandsmen and songsters who have had the privilege of playing or singing there, Generals and commissioners who have led meetings there, people who got saved there, people who just like to be with Army folk, and maybe you, just reading this book.

I cannot say which was my highest moment at the RAH but one such moment was when, during the 1965 Centenary Congress, I conducted the massive chorus in a piece written especially for the Congress called 'A Song Of Praise'. As stated earlier, the words were by Catherine Baird and the music by Leslie Condon. As we sang the final verse, with the trumpets sounding out and the voices repeating the final line, it seemed as if all Heaven opened up to us:

> Our great redeemer liveth still,
> His love sustains us in thy will;
> Because he conquered, we shall win,
> His cross before, his joy within;
> Our cheerful banners are unfurled,
> For Christ has overcome the world.

The last statement, 'Christ has overcome the world', is repeated three times.

As has happened so many times when Salvationists have pledged themselves to Christ and his work, the Lord himself came and stood among us.

Whether in a tent or dancing room, theatre or town hall, humble barn or the magnificent Royal Albert Hall, on so many occasions, in response to a prayer from his people, God has taken possession of the place and, for a few hours, made it a dwelling for himself and for those who want to meet him there. As the old song says:

> Jesus, where'er thy people meet,
> There they behold the mercy seat;
> Where'er they seek thee thou art found,
> And every place is hallowed ground.

The setting of 'Crown Him With Many Crowns' by Colonel Charles Skinner is a particular favourite of mine. It was commissioned for one of the song festivals held in the Royal Albert Hall and written for a massive chorus accompanied by the International Staff Band, with their newly acquired fanfare trumpets – decorated with Salvation Army banners. The trumpeters stood in line just in front of the grand organ and the spotlights picked them out as Charles raised his baton to commence this magnificent hymn of praise to our risen Lord.

Well may the song state, 'Hark! how the heavenly anthem drowns all music but its own', because that is just what it did. The women's voices in unison sang the verse, which commemorates Christ as the 'Lord of peace', then, following a brief interlude, the full company of musicians, singers, trumpeters, band, grand organ and the assembled congregation proclaimed:

All hail, redeemer, hail!
For thou hast died for me;
Thy praise and glory shall not fail
Throughout eternity.

Then it was time to go home!

The smaller bands and songster brigades of the territory have been featured in these festivals. On one occasion the bandmaster led his band of nine players while playing the E flat bass himself! Smaller brigades were included in the festival chorus – after all, each makes an invaluable contribution to his or her own corps life, as well as on the special occasion at the RAH.

At one event – during the singing of a song by the whole congregation, accompanied by the organ – firemen, resplendent in helmets and carrying axes, appeared on the stage to put out a fire, which was reported to be in the organ.

As one would expect at an Army event, the song carried on, even as the chief fireman and his men, watched by the singing congregation, climbed inside the organ loft to investigate the problem. Nothing amiss was found and the firemen left as they had entered, with the song being stretched out to allow for the firemen's withdrawal. Good old Army!

239

During the last 10 or 12 years of my responsibility for RAH programmes I always followed the final 'big' piece with a verse and two choruses of 'Give To Jesus Glory', inviting the congregation to join in the second chorus. Sometimes it was simply sung with organ accompaniment. At other times it involved massed bands, organ and fanfare trumpets making a mighty paean of praise to the Lord. This song signifies that the glory is Christ's alone, with the second line being a reminder to all Salvationists that to 'proclaim redemption's wondrous plan' is what we are all called to do.

> To save the world the Saviour came;
> It was for this in mercy
> He gave his life; the news proclaim
> And give to Jesus glory.

> *Give to Jesus glory,*
> *Give to Jesus glory,*
> *Proclaim redemption's wondrous plan*
> *And give to Jesus glory.*

I doubt there could be a more glorious sound to the ear of a Salvationist than when a congregation of thousands join in the second chorus with its divine instruction to:

> *Proclaim redemption's wondrous plan*
> *And give to Jesus glory!*

On one occasion, as I was about to enter the Albert Hall, a man came up to me and said, 'Hello Norman,' to which I responded in like manner. Looking a bit surprised, he said in a questioning tone, 'You do remember me?' Now, this is always a little embarrassing and, while I was trying to think of an answer, he said, 'Look at me! Go on, look, look!' I looked but still had no idea who he was and again, even more excited, he invited to, 'Look at me. Go on, look!' After a few seconds or so and having no response from me, he said, 'Wallsend-on-Tyne,

1926!' (I was born in Wallsend-on-Tyne in 1926 and my parents moved to another corps a few weeks later.) Seeing the expectant look on his face, I could do no other than reply, 'Oh yes! That's right.' He smiled, shook my hand vigorously and then walked away looking very happy!

Chapter 21

SHARE YOUR FAITH

Songs Of Praise

Regent Hall

It was my privilege to work with the BBC in four productions of the much-loved television series *Songs Of Praise*. The first I did was in 1968 and was held in Regent Hall in London, featuring the students from the National School of Music and the New Jersey Youth Band from the USA, who, with their bandmaster Alf Swenarton, were concluding a tour of Britain.

The New Jersey Youth Band provided a cornet trio, 'Sweetest Name', and the girls from the National School of Music, conducted by Major Brindley Boon, sang 'It's New' and Catherine Baird's lovely song 'When Jesus Looked O'er Galilee'.

Leeds Town Hall

My second venture into *Songs Of Praise* was when the BBC asked me to conduct a programme from Leeds Town Hall. Unlike the more usual programmes, this one was to feature a chorus of 500 voices drawn from songster brigades in the Leeds area.

The rehearsal caused much merriment as the make-up girls kept coming to mop my brow and apply powder and rouge to my face to make me 'look my best' in the close-up camera shots.

We were well into the evening before the programme was complete and it was quite late when Jill and I started our car journey back to London down the motorway. We had been going quite some time when I momentarily dozed off to sleep. We came to a halt on the bank of a field adjoining the motorway! Jill's comment was, 'If you want to

keep working for the Army we had better book into the next motel!'
And that we gratefully did!

Camberwell Citadel
Camberwell Citadel was the venue for the next *Songs Of Praise* programme I was to conduct. This time the large congregation was made up of whoever wished to come and included my mother and other officers from Glebelands, a retirement residence for Salvation Army officers situated in Camberwell.

Sutton Band, under Bandmaster Reg Jobson, provided the accompaniment for the songs. The now familiar stops and starts that one encounters in these productions didn't worry me in the least but my mother – who was well into her 90s – thinking I had more power than I actually had, called me over and said in a loud voice, 'For goodness' sake tell them to get on with it. We've sung this song three times already!'

Just before the final song, 'And can it be that I should gain an interest in the Saviour's blood?', Commissioner Stanley Cottrill, then the Army's Chief of the Staff, led the congregation in four statements of faith.

The BBC producer, Christian Forssander, thanked all the people for their patience and hard work, and then told us that we would be 'going out' on the second verse of the final song. It was with real conviction that the congregation sang the lines so well loved by Salvationists:

> My chains fell off, my heart was free,
> I rose, went forth, and followed thee.

As we were singing I thought, 'What can be better than this!' (It is number 283 in song book and will be well worth the time you spend in looking it up!)

Butlin's
My last *Songs Of Praise* was at the Army week in the Butlin's holiday camp near Skegness. With well over 1,500 enthusiastic people singing

244

and being accompanied by the band which Bram Williams had formed for the week, I knew we were on to a good thing.

Although we were well into September the congregation was asked to attend in summer dress as far as possible so the programme could have a holiday atmosphere. We had to ask one or two who had come wearing extra-large sunglasses to take them off.

This BBC team seemed much more accustomed than earlier ones to producing *Songs Of Praise*, completing the whole recording within two hours.

The presenter was the well-known Pam Rhodes who, having requested that the programme should conclude with 'I'll Go In The Strength Of The Lord' (to Ivor Bosanko's melody), said she was amazed at the power and joy expressed by the singing of the holidaymakers. What she did not know was that, every evening during the Army week, we had concluded the day with community singing in which we had rehearsed the songs we were going to sing on *Songs Of Praise*. Ask yourself: can we ever measure the power of real songs of salvation and praise?

Chapter 22

ZIMBABWE

Some years ago I received an invitation from Commissioner Alan Coles (then Territorial Commander for Zimbabwe) to attend the national councils for bandmasters and songster leaders to be held at the training college in Harare and then to be a guest at a music camp for young Salvationists from all parts of that territory.

I readily accepted and in a few weeks was on an airplane taking me to Africa for the first time. The journey was not without problems – the worst being an emergency landing in the dead of night somewhere in Africa, to check there was 'nothing sinister' in the luggage compartment!

The first Saturday was the occasion for me to meet the bandmasters and songster leaders and, as we made our way to the college assembly hall, I could hear the music leaders singing. The sound fair took my breath away!

The rich, sonorous sound of African voices is something I shall never forget. I had, of course, heard African singing at various International Congress meetings when 20 or so singers were able to fill the Royal Albert Hall without electronic amplification.

About 40 delegates were present and, following the commissioner's welcome, we were into the opening song. I was immediately struck by the fact that all the singing was unaccompanied, even though there was a piano in the hall. The meeting leader simply hummed a note (they all appeared to have a good sense of pitch) and off they went – singing in lovely, full, rich harmony with natural rhythm.

The bandmasters formed themselves into a well-balanced band for the technical part of the councils and then joined with the songster leaders in making a very acceptable choir.

Early-day Christian missionaries taught the African people to sing by the tonic sol-fa method using (mostly) only the diatonic notes of the seven primary scales, so the appearance of (say) F sharp in a melody in the key of B flat causes a real problem.

This was very evident when we began to rehearse the setting by Chris Mallett of 'To God Be The Glory'. All went well until the men were required to repeat the line 'And opened the life gate' a semitone higher (F sharp). I could get them to sing an F and then an F sharp but when it came in the line of the song with no break (F followed by F sharp) we were in real trouble and it became almost impossible.

In the end I got the men to repeat the line sung by the women on F using the same note F, then all rising a full tone to the G with which the next line begins. One delegate asked, 'Why didn't Chris Mallett write it like that?'

I do realise that a comprehensive study of the tonic sol-fa system will reveal how to negotiate notes outside the diatonic scale (that is, sharps and flats not in the given scale) but the African delegates had not been taught that this was so. However, we did manage to sing the song in a public meeting held later in the day in the Harare City Corps hall and, judging by the response, the assembled company really enjoyed it – F sharp or no F sharp!

Monday saw the arrival of the music camp students. Most of them arrived in band or songster uniform, some having walked very many miles to be there. They brought an assortment of brass instruments, some of which were in need of repair.

Sticky tape and string held many instruments together and I wondered what kind of sound to expect from them. I did not have to wait very long for we were soon at work on a suite by Leslie Condon called 'Blyth Heritage', which became our star piece.

I soon discovered that the students had a great appetite for making music and things like tea breaks (for which everyone washed their hands in a communal bowl and in which ritual I was always given the honour of being the first with my hands in the bowl and first to use the towel!) were inconvenient interruptions to the great joy of making music together. They just did not want to stop!

In his first letter to me, Commissioner Coles had suggested I might write a march to mark the occasion, which could be featured at the Zimbabwe Congress meetings immediately following the music camp.

He asked me to remember the African peoples' great love of drums and then remarked that the march 'will be judged by its drum part'! He also sent me a tape recording of some African singers enjoying some of their favourite Salvation Army songs, in the hope that I might use them in the new march.

The tape included two songs which were new to me, both of which I was able to feature in the march using their own harmonies. Also included were 'Soldiers Fighting Round The Cross' and the tune 'Auld Lang Syne'.

The tunes seemed right for a Zimbabwe march so I used them all. Our first encounter with this new piece was well received by the students, who kept reminding me that the music was theirs! I heeded the advice about the drum part and wrote a whole section devoted entirely to the percussionists, which could be repeated ad infinitum.

We had just two drummers in the band, both of whom worked very hard to produce what was written but who (alas!) were quite unable to curb their natural instinct when required to 'solo' on the drums in front of an audience. I quickly decided that their version was better than mine and gladly let them have free rein.

This section of the march tended to grow with each performance so I devised a plan by which they could drum away to their heart's content until I gave a nod to the bass drummer who, at the next convenient spot, would give a five beat indication louder than any drumming hitherto (similar to that used by our bands when on the march) and the band would take up from where they had left the printed copy.

When we played the march for a second time in each of the Congress meetings I suggested that any other drummers who were present might like to join us in the allotted solo part and – as if from nowhere – drummers of all kinds, carrying what looked like tom-toms, appeared and, unrehearsed, launched into the drum break with a fervour you would find hard to believe!

I felt so happy that these few bars of music brought so much joy to the Zimbabwean Salvationists, including those who were sitting listening, those who were drumming and those who were dancing.

The training college in Harare would be a credit to any territory in the world and it was a great joy for me to have the cadets join us for the various evening activities. The married women cadets came with their babies strapped on their backs and I found it strangely moving to see the baby fast asleep while mother was joining in some chorus in which she felt the need to add some dancing to the singing.

The spirit of the camp was epitomised by the young man who took it upon himself to be 'duty trumpeter' for the week and who – each morning – dressed in faded blue jeans and a red upright-collared festival tunic, sounded Reveille! Then, as an unrequested encore, proceeded to play the second cornet part of 'Soldiers Fighting Round The Cross' from the Zimbabwe march before a final reprise of Reveille!

What lovely young Salvationists I found them to be – so courteous and well-mannered and a credit to The Salvation Army in Zimbabwe.

The final festival for the music school coincided with the opening of the new Harare Citadel Corps hall. The lovely, large hall was filled to overflowing by people giving thanks to God for this new place in which to gather to sing his praises and in which to lead sinners to Jesus.

I was struck by the fact that the hall was just a hall. No anterooms, no kitchen, but yes, there was tea to drink! This was prepared in a very large, black kettle over a blazing fire just outside the hall, by a woman wearing Harare Citadel uniform and with a baby strapped on her back. I just had to go and talk to her. What else could I say other than, 'There's nothing like an Army cup of tea!'

She told me she felt everybody had work to do for Jesus and it just so happened that making tea was what he wanted her to do – and he wanted her to make it good. I can testify that she was living up to her calling, just like so many other tea-makers in this Army of ours.

I found it most moving as I stood and watched the people arriving for the Congress meetings, most of them having walked many, many miles to be there.

The Congress meetings were held in the International Conference Centre, a lovely, large civic building, and (just like other halls all round the world that the Army takes over) the Lord came and filled it with his glory!

Chapter 23

SPIRIT OF ENDEAVOUR

Writing Music

People often ask, 'How do you write music?' I have to answer, 'I really don't know!' I do know how to write notes down on paper (anyone can do that!). I do know the laws of harmony and counterpoint (anyone can learn those!). I have a good supply of manuscript paper, pencils, erasers, and a large waste-paper basket (anyone can get those!).

But then what? Where do you start? How long will it take? (People often ask that.) All I can say is that from somewhere an idea comes (not always at convenient times so, if you are married, you do need an understanding spouse!). Sometimes you come across some words that immediately appeal as they present musical shapes and phrasing. Some words may be perfectly good but do not ring a bell for me. I have, once or twice, seen words that did not capture me only to find that another composer has produced a beautiful song with them.

This is how it happened in the writing of 'The City Of God' for the International Staff Songsters:

The Psalms abound in an imagery that you can both see and feel and, for some inexplicable reason, Psalm 46 seemed to reach out and grab me. That was it and for the purpose of a new setting I used the wording from the *King James Bible*. I have heard people say that the old *King James* version is difficult to read. Having now read many other translations, I find the wording and style of the old version is so much more conducive to musical settings. However, I did also use verses from the *New English Bible* for this piece.

The opening statement, 'God is our refuge and strength, a very present help in trouble', had (for me) to be expressed with lively and vigorous music. I suppose you could whisper 'God is our refuge and strength', but, to me, the obvious thing was to declare it loudly with big dramatic leaps, ablaze with fire as (I think) did the Psalmist as he continued:

'Therefore will not we fear, though the earth be removed, and though the mountains be carried into the midst of the sea; though the waters thereof roar and be troubled, though the mountains shake with the swelling thereof.'

Even as I was writing, I felt that my setting needed a sudden interjection of quiet majesty – the majesty that makes you bow your head in adoration and reflection.

Then back, with renewed vigour, to 'God is our refuge and strength', to which you can add a loud 'Hallelujah!' – which, incidentally, is a wonderful word to sing! (No wonder Handel, in his *Messiah*, used it 54 times in one chorus!)

I have no idea how long this piece took to write but there would have been a few meal interruptions and constant cups of tea. It's hard to even remember what or when you last ate when the inspiration takes over!

Contrast in music is a must, so the second movement needs a different style altogether. The psalm continues with: 'There is a river, the streams whereof shall make glad the city of God, the holy place of the tabernacles of the most High.' In the *New English Bible* this verse reads: 'There is a river whose streams gladden the city of God, which the Most High has made his holy dwelling.'

Again the picture becomes clear. It now needs to be quietly flowing like a stream in a meadow and, as I read it, I knew how the second movement had to sound as it continued:

There is a river whose streams make glad the City of God,
The City of God, which the Most High has made his dwelling;
There is a river whose streams make glad the City of our God,
He is in the midst of her, she shall not be moved,

254

And he will help her at the break of day.
Be still, be still and know that I am God.
Be still, be still, be still!

As we sat in our little caravan (where I was writing this setting) it seemed as if the psalm was writing the music for me! High soprano notes and low chords in the other parts, then fading into nothing. (What a message of hope in this troubled world, 'Be still and know that I am God!')

As Christian people we need to find the place where the Old Testament meets and joins with the New Testament. As I was searching for where this could happen, 'Come and see what the Lord has done' leapt from the page! What a gift from Heaven! What has the Lord done? I know he gave his Son. (I have quoted John 3:16 for as long as I can remember!) Then I needed the help of someone who could express God's greatest gift in such beautiful and simple language that everyone can understand. So, as I have done many times before, I turned to Catherine Baird and found her words (verses four, five and six in number 36 in the song book) to be perfect for my need.

O loving, living Lord,
Thou hast in Jesus given
A purpose and a way
For travellers to Heaven!

Then let us dwell in him
Whose dwelling is above,
And seek until we know,
And love until we love.

O ever-living Lord,
Our hearts and lips shall prove
The beauty of thy house,
The glory of thy love!

Her song about creation, about thunder and fire, about sacred thought, about a loving, living Lord, about a purpose and a way, about a place to live, and about love (which Catherine Baird once told me was the only theme for her sermons) finishes with another gift from Heaven:

> The beauty of thy house,
> The glory of thy love!

To me, such words need a strong melodic line with trumpet-like sounds to convey the wonder of the message. There are certain chords and styles that belong to trumpets that will have to be used and which may be hard to sing – but how can you measure the amount of effort and time needed if the words and music call for such an effort? (Well, that's my theory on music for singing.) This setting was sung as the final piece at our retirement at Regent Hall by the International Staff Songsters, with whom my service came to an end.

The writing of 'The City Of God' took place in our little caravan on the campsite at Holmsley in the New Forest and some of the music was tried out on the piano in the Winton Corps hall while we were on holiday there in June 1991. 'Some holiday!' you might say. Yet I never had a better one!

The Sunday morning at Winton (when their songsters sang 'The City Of God') will, for me, remain something very special because they took my musical signs on the paper and, by their love and sheer hard work, made them live. You can't ask for anything better than that!

Peter Cooke, then the singing company leader at Twickenham Corps, gave me these incredible words, asking if I would write music to them.

> Thou hast no weapons, lowly Christ,
> No sword nor buckler dost thou wield,
> And yet my heart, beholding thee,
> Immediately is forced to yield.

The Spirit's sword, my trusty blade,
Will be my weapon for the fight;
And in thy strength, O Son of God,
Thine enemies I'll put to flight.

Thou hast no beauty in thy face,
No comeliness thy form adorns;
Thy visage is with suffering marred,
Thy brow is pierced by sin's sharp thorns.
But clad in raiment white as light
I see thee, and in awe I bow,
For thou art Sharon's rose indeed,
The fairest of ten thousand now.

Thou hast no glory, humble Christ,
But just a simple village home;
A workman's bench, a lowly cot,
And hills whereon thy feet can roam;
But thou art Christ, the Son of God,
From highest Heaven to earth come down;
The velvet sky thy mantle is,
The stars are diamonds in thy crown.

O Christ, can I transformed be
By thy most wonder-working power?
Then take me as I am, I pray,
The miracle perform this hour.
And shaking off the former man,
On faith's strong pinions I will rise
To greet thee who hast set the course
And giv'st the everlasting prize!

               (Published as 'The Divine Paradox',
           The Musical Salvationist, January 1962)

Peter named this 'The Divine Paradox' and it became clear to me
that the first half of each verse had to be in a minor key with the

paradox in the major key. Whenever I look into the heavens and see the stars I always remember his line, 'The stars are diamonds in thy crown.'

My old friend Harry Read, whose last appointment was that of British Commissioner, retired and, with his wife Win, came to live in Bournemouth. They became soldiers of Winton Corps, the same corps at which we soldiered. He gave me some words entitled 'Song Of Renewal', which has this chorus:

> *O Holy Spirit, come to me again,*
> *My every gift and power refresh, restore;*
> *My heart is open, come to me again*
> *And fill me with your love and grace once more.*
>
> (Published in *Sing To The Lord*, 1998)

Another unexpected experience came when my son Mark sent me some music and asked me to write some words for it. His request came as a bit of a shock but, as I played the music, the following words for the chorus came to me.

> *His love still flows in boundless measure*
> *For a world all lost in sin,*
> *O Jesus, Son of God most holy,*
> *Come and make me pure within.*
>
> (Published as 'Boundless Love' in
> *The Musical Salvationist*, July 1984)

Whence does inspiration come? Sometimes from a verse such as those printed above. Sometimes from something someone says. Who can tell?

Chapter 24

TIMEPIECE

Retirement

The thought of retirement was not a welcome one for me. I had conducted my last Royal Albert Hall festival and was awaiting the day to vacate my office at National Headquarters when Lieut-Colonel Ivor Rich (Executive Officer of the International Staff Songsters) came to see me, just to let me know that a farewell festival for Jill and me had been arranged and would be in Regent Hall in London.

He then confessed that all the plans were now completed, the soloists and speakers chosen and that General Arnold Brown was coming from Canada to officiate as chairman. The plot got thicker when Ivor said that the demand for seats had been so great that a decision was made to do the festival twice, afternoon and evening, and that all seats were now sold for the two occasions. He then added, 'Your three sons, their wives and family will be there, and all you and Jill have to do is come.'

A report in *Salvationist* by Lieut-Colonel Max Ryan of our retirement headed 'Bearcroft Bonanza' was as follows:

The Army's musical fraternity was out in full force to honour one of its own during two festivals given by the International Staff Songsters at Regent Hall. The occasion was the 'Bearcroft Bonanza', a retirement salute for the founding conductor of the ISS who has laid down his baton after more than 12 years' leadership of the UK's premier vocal group.

Originally planned as an evening event only, the demand for tickets necessitated an afternoon meeting as well. Both meetings were under the guidance of General Arnold Brown (R), whose anecdotal leadership suited the nostalgic pot-pourri of music and reminiscences.

To brilliant music by the Cobham A Band, the 31 members of the ISS marched to the platform. They joined in a standing ovation given to the Bearcrofts who were accompanied by General Brown and the ISS Executive Officer, Lieut-Colonel Ivor Rich.

Also greeted (in the evening meeting) were three retired Chiefs of the Staff (Commissioners Stanley Cottrill, Caughey Gauntlett and Ron Cox), two former executive officers (Colonel Ken Bridge, who had travelled from New Zealand, and Colonel Will Clark), as well as Commissioner (TC) John Larsson.

The music – all by Norman Bearcroft – ranged from his setting of 'Onward, Christian Soldiers', with which the ISS commenced the programmes, to the brigade's concluding piece 'The City Of God'. Memories were stirred and interest was sustained by such vocal music as: 'Grieve My Lord No More', 'This Train', 'Reflections' and 'The Well Is Deep'.

The colonel's brass compositions were represented by 'The Seafarer', 'Better World' (a euphonium solo played by Derick Kane), 'Song Of Exultation' (a cornet solo played by Kevin Ashman) and 'A Bearcroft Bouquet' – a medley of Bearcroft music which was arranged and conducted by Lieut-Colonel Ray Steadman-Allen (R), and which included congregational chorus singing.

Words of appreciation were brought by Canadian Staff Bandmaster Brian Burditt (Lieut-Colonel Bearcroft recommenced the CSB during his eight years in Canada). The bandmaster also led the territorial music school band in Bearcroft's 'Songs Of Newfoundland'. Other speakers were Bandmaster Alan Laing and Retired Bandmaster Bram Williams, Retired Songster Leaders Mrs Joyce Jones and Mrs Muriel Yendell, former International Staff Songster Gerald Boniface and Songster Sergeant Dennis Anderson. The common theme of these tributes was the humanity, good humour, pastoral interest and sheer hard work of the Bearcrofts.

Staff Songster Jonathan Forrest (afternoon) and Mrs Jacqui Proctor (a former member of the ISS who had travelled from

Australia) brought vocal solos. Jacqui's soaring soprano had provided the first note from the ISS to be broadcast. The strong voice of Deputy Staff Songster Leader Mrs Susan Turner was tested successfully in 'Sweet Chariot', as were the vocal capabilities of Cadet Mrs Tracy Bearcroft in the demanding 'Hallelujah City'.

There were recollections of the Army's Butlin's weeks – in which over the years the Bearcrofts had played a prominent part – with Majors John Mott and Peter Mylechreest and others (including the Bearcrofts) providing a hilarious comedy sketch, which was matched later by the entry of two 'senior citizens' who welcomed the guests of honour to their world.

Retirement certificates were presented by the Territorial Commander, who thanked the Bearcrofts for 41 years' active service as officers, and dedicated them in prayer under the flag of the ISS. In their chatty and informal response the recipients of the certificates acknowledged the joy of service, and in particular the privilege of commencing two major music groups within the Army.

The afternoon and evening meetings drew to a close with the ISS gathering around their former leader singing their 'trademark' benediction, 'Let nothing disturb thee... alone God sufficeth.' And in the solemn poignancy of the moment there was the recognition that an era had passed and, for some, life would never be the same again.

A few days later, Jill and I packed our belongings and moved to Christchurch, where for many years we had spent our summer holidays. By the next Sunday we were welcomed into Winton Corps in Bournemouth by the corps officers, Major and Mrs Steve Russell, and very soon I was made the songster leader and the timpanist and bass drummer of the band.

Winton Songster Brigade had high standards, good singers and were always ready to work hard. They were on duty for the three meetings every Sunday and were also required to sing at the Pier-head meetings every Sunday evening in the summer months. This really is a hard-working corps!

The band (Bandmaster Stan Randell) rehearsed for two hours every Tuesday evening and the songsters for two hours every Thursday evening, so that made two evenings a week out of retirement. Jill and I also became members of the meal-run team, led by Mary Randell, which operated every Monday evening so, for me, this made three evenings a week in which 'retirement' was forgotten!

The men and women we served on the meal run were mostly very pleasant and grateful people. One exception was a man who was queuing for the tea I was serving. He asked me for some more milk but, unfortunately, I didn't quite hear his request and asked him to repeat it. He then said in a very loud voice, 'MILK, MILK,' then, in case I had not got the message, spelt out, 'M-I-L-K.' As he walked away, I heard him say to his friend, 'These people don't seem to be able to get the right staff!' The other members of the team were helpless with laughter.

The house into which we retired backed on to some lovely woodland which, at any time of the year, was a joy to see. It was also a real pleasure to walk through these woods from which, when the summit was reached, a lovely view of the New Forest could be had. Often we would make the climb, then sit and have tea and biscuits, which Jill would produce from the bag she always carried.

We also had a nice garden with a greenhouse, which proved to be a great delight for Jill and in which she would spend many hours cultivating plants and flowers. Another joy was to take a ride into the New Forest and to call into one of the places serving cream teas. Having spent most of our holidays 'caravanning' in the Forest, we really felt a sense of belonging.

Unknown to me, Jill had been arranging a special treat to mark the end of our active service. This was to take place about a month after we had retired and was to be a trip to Canada for the 25th anniversary of the Canadian Staff Band, followed by a holiday in Florida. Not knowing I would be there, I had written a Festival March for the anniversary celebrations and called it 'Day Of Jubilee'. It contains the melody called 'Cleansing For Me' (not to be mistaken for the 'Long, Long Ago' tune to which we usually sing to these words) and concludes with 'When we all get to Heaven, what a day of rejoicing that will be.'

The Monday morning found us with our very dear friends Tom and Joyce LeGrow as we loaded Tom's snow-covered car and set out for the sunshine of Florida. The trip took us through many interesting places, including an area that crossed the Swanee River. Remembering Stephen Foster's immortal song that commences with 'Way down upon the Swanee River', we stopped and took a trip on this very river. Next day we passed a museum dedicated to Stephen Foster so, once again, we stopped and had a good look round. It was fascinating to see the manuscripts of the songs I had known since boyhood and to play a verse of 'Old Black Joe' on Stephen Foster's piano.

By the time we had come this far, the weather was now quite warm with the promise of even warmer weather when we arrived in Florida. It was here that we stayed in a house in the grounds of the divisional headquarters. A note left for us invited us to help ourselves to the grapefruit from the trees in the grounds.

It was while we were here that we had some discussion with the Divisional Commander, Lieut-Colonel Philip Swyers, about the festival of my music at Clearwater on the coming Saturday. This featured the Florida Divisional Band and Timbrels, the united songster brigades from Tampa, St Petersburg, Lakeland and Clearwater and the Divisional Youth Band.

For a bit of light relief, during the playing of the 'Zimbabwe Centenary' march, I called upon Colonel Swyers to play the bass drum. He gladly accepted the invitation on the understanding that the Divisional Youth Secretary would play the side drum. This he agreed to do and it so turned out that he had been a professional drummer so, instead of a humorous item, we had a drumming display which was as good as I have ever seen!

The holiday in Florida was lovely and, on arrival back home in Christchurch, we found our house decorated with streamers and flags welcoming us back home and back to Winton Corps.

I very much enjoyed being in the percussion section of Winton Band and, although I understood all the principles of drumming, I did need to do some serious private study and practice in order to be an acceptable member of the band.

As a conductor and being so used to reading the full score where every bar is accounted for, my biggest problem now, as the timpanist, was counting all the bars where the timpani would be at rest. There would be some pieces in which one would need to count 30 or 40 bars' rest before entry. It so happened at a Christmas programme, when the band was playing 'The Kingdom Triumphant', my mind wandered for a very brief moment and I lost count of the bars prior to a very dramatic entry for the timpani and came in with a very loud timpani entrance – a bar too soon! Fortunately, I was sitting very near to the stage curtains behind which I was able to hide. Unfortunately, my nephew (composer Brian Bowen) was in the audience and still likes to remind me of the incident!

Stan Randell, the Winton bandmaster, thought that carrying and playing the bass drum on the march was asking too much of me, so one of the other bandsmen, Chris Launn, played the drum on the march and I was promoted to the cymbals.

The December 1996 edition of *The Sword And Trowel* (the Winton Corps monthly magazine) contained the story of my concertina, which had been such a useful instrument in the days when I was leading meetings in the street or somewhere where there was no band or piano. The reporter for the corps magazine must have interviewed my wife Jill, and this was the result:

No doubt about it! Jill Bearcroft has a heart of gold. A warm, generous lady who, when she hears of any real need or learns of any good cause, is restless until she has been able to make some response.

So it was when she read in the late, much-lamented *Musician*, that the Army's School for the Blind in Thika, East Africa, was sorely in need of a concertina that her thoughts immediately flew to the fine instrument owned by her husband.

'He doesn't really need it,' she told herself. 'He doesn't often play it and besides he's not really very good on it to say the least.

264

It would be a godsend to our wonderful missionaries in Africa, toiling so bravely in trying to help those dear children.'

The more Jill thought about it, the more convinced she became that just as Dr Livingstone had sacrificed so much for Africa, so could Norman spare his little-used concertina. 'He'll not miss it at all,' she told herself.

But Norman did miss it, though not for some two years after Jill had dispatched the concertina with love and prayers. Jill could hear him going from room to room, muttering to himself, looking in cupboards, getting a stepladder to rummage among the things in the attic and peering under the beds. But all to no avail. The concertina was nowhere to be found.

'Jill!' Norman called out in some desperation from the small bedroom. 'Do you know where my concertina is?' Knowing the moment of truth had come, and putting on her well-known, most innocent, matter-of-fact look, said, 'It's at the Army's School for the Blind in Thika.'

Norman's eyes grew wide as he asked, 'What's it doing there?' 'Well, you hardly looked at it from one year to the next,' replied Jill, in the tone of a wife who has every right to part with her husband's possessions, then continued, 'Much better for it to be doing some good at the Army's School for the Blind than just cluttering up our house.' As Norm sat down on the bed he said, 'Well, my old squeeze box is in Africa, and you didn't tell me.'

Hardly ever was the missing concertina mentioned again – that is, not until Wednesday 13 November 1996, during the retired officers fellowship meeting at Boscombe, when Brigadier Ivor Howells led the 'retireds' in some choruses on his concertina. From the expert way he played, following his introductory remarks about the value of the concertina to the Army in days gone by, one could tell how much he loved the instrument.

Suddenly, Jill Bearcroft stood to her feet and said, 'My husband used to have a concertina but I sent it to the School for the Blind in Thika.' A strange silence followed until up stood Mrs Lieut-Colonel Letisha Mason, another retired officer who, looking at Jill, said, 'Here is something you ought to know. We were in a meeting led by the then Colonel Geoffrey Dalziel (home from East Africa where he was Territorial Commander) who spoke about the great work at the Thika School for the Blind and told how badly they needed a teacher with music skills. On hearing this, Band Leader Kenneth Doney stood to his feet and, addressing the colonel, offered himself to the School for the Blind, adding, "If you will have me."

'Soon after arrival in Thika, Kenneth decided that a priority would be to form a choir from the young people. Wondering what musical instrument was available to help him in teaching them to sing, he was delighted to find an excellent concertina – the one donated by Mrs Jill Bearcroft. The concertina proved to be vital in teaching them to sing and, some time later, helped them to gain first prize in an important choir competition.'

As Mrs Mason took her seat again, a whimsical smile appeared on the face of Norman Bearcroft and there was a look on Jill's face which said, 'There, now you should be glad!'

Kenneth Doney (a nephew of the Masons) served for three years at Thika. He is now the Principal of the School for the Blind in Sheffield.

Worthing Band

It was in a billet, during a tour of Norway with Worthing Band, that I was invited to look through a bookshelf while waiting for supper. It seemed to be a pointless invitation seeing that the books would be in a language which I did not understand. However, I did find a book by William Booth (the founder of The Salvation Army) in which he was writing about facing hardship and opposition.

Now, seeing that I was on tour with Worthing Band, I was more than a bit surprised to discover that there, right on the first page was an artist's impression of the early-day Worthing Band and Salvationists marching from the hall to meet some violent opposition from what was known as 'the Skeleton Army'. How strange that I should find this book in which Worthing Band was showing such courage! Right there and then I sketched a few bars of a new march which I would call 'Wreath Of Courage'. The march, published in December 1999, has the following comments in the score:

General William Booth, in his book about the fierce opposition that early-day Salvationists were facing, has a chapter about the riots in Worthing and the courage of the soldiers of that corps as they marched out to meet the mobs who were intent on the Army's destruction.

The march includes the chorus:

Launch out into the deep,
O let the shore lines go!
Launch out, launch out in the ocean divine,
Out where the full tides flow.

It seems to me to be good advice for present-day Salvationists.

Incidentally, I seemed to have a spring in my step while on the march with Worthing Band the very next day!

Chapter 25

CAMP VICTORY

We were in a meeting in Boscombe, Bournemouth, in which the Moscow Singing Company were taking part, when a visiting captain, Sven Ljungholm, took the opportunity to announce a forthcoming music school which he was arranging in Kiev in Ukraine and said, 'Norman Bearcroft will be coming as the Music Director.' This was quite a surprise seeing that I was not aware that The Salvation Army had even started work in Kiev, let alone had plans to hold a music camp!

I later discovered that the captain had been in touch with a few Winton Corps soldiers about the possibility of such a camp and that they had agreed to undertake the staffing of the same.

Came the time to leave for Kiev and Major Steve Russell (our corps officer) and I, a group of bandsmen and songsters and Major John Mott left London Airport for this new adventure. On arrival at Kiev Airport, while I was waiting in a long queue to clear the customs, Major Kathleen Ljungholm – the first Salvation Army officer sent there to open the Army's work – suddenly appeared at the entrance and I was whisked through the customs and taken to a concert given by the National Capitol Band from the USA, led by Bandmaster Stephen Bulla.

The next morning, on arrival at the camp, we discovered that there were 150 new Salvationist young people, all in Salvation Army uniform, eager to learn how to play a brass instrument, improve their singing or further their skills with the timbrel.

David Ramsey, one of our adventurous bandsmen, had previously contacted dozens of corps in England asking if they could supply a brass instrument for the Kiev adventure and had secured 60 or so instruments of one sort or another. These were waiting for us when we arrived at Camp Victory, an ex-Red Army camp which had been hired for the music school. Other gifts sent to the camp included 80 tambourines, several portable organs, three pianos, food for the 190 persons participating in the camp and T-shirts for everyone. These and many other things were all sent to Kiev in a 38-ton truck and trailer, driven by a Church of England priest, Geoff Stickland from Gloucester, and Brian Hart from Exeter.

Auditions for the brass players proved to be difficult seeing that all but five of the students had never played a brass instrument before. So, looking at a student, I would say, 'You look like a bass player,' then hand him a bass, or I would say to another student, 'You look like a cornet player,' and he would get a cornet. It went on like this until all the brass students had something to play.

Our instructors each took a small group and slowly got them to play more than one note in reasonable sound. Low C seemed to be the favourite note, some students finding it very hard to get any higher, but with many gesticulations (an upward movement of the shoulder by the instructor) new sounds at a higher pitch emerged.

On the third day, the instrumental students were brought together for what was listed as Massed Bands Rehearsal, which was conducted by John Mott. The look on the face of Major Steve Russell as the sound increased said it all!

The hard work of the instructors was rewarded when, on the final day of the camp, the band managed to play the march I had written for them called 'Camp Victory'.

The singers had no such problems. The Winton Singing Company Leader, Billie Smith, and her helpers did a remarkable job with the girls and boys, both with singing and with the timbrels. The young people seemed to be able to sing in both English and Ukrainian without any difficulty and they had a real capacity to learn. The drama class was doing well and our instructors had the happy knack of making them work even through the language barrier.

Among the students were about ten young men who were members of what had been the Young Communists Band. John Mott

270

took this group and, with a few of the beginners, formed the A Band. It was quite an experience watching and listening to John as he tried, through an interpreter, to get the required results. In the final festival they played the march 'The Glory Land' and 'Songs Of Testimony' – truly an amazing feat!

It was when I was giving out the instruments that one small boy received a baritone which also had a very nice leather case – the only instrument handed out that had a case. In a day or so he was still only making a hooting sound and I thought that, perhaps, the baritone was too big for him. Through an interpreter I informed him of my opinion and gave him a smaller E flat horn. He did not look too pleased as he walked away with his new horn, which was without a case.

Two days later he was back with the interpreter asking if he could revert to the baritone and saying that playing the E flat horn gave him a headache! I asked the interpreter to tell him that when he played the baritone it gave me a headache then, repenting of my action, gave him back the baritone with the case! In the final festival he was still making the funny hooting sound but he gave me the thumbs-up sign just to let me know that I had done the right thing by giving him back the baritone with the case!

A group of Salvationists from the USA Western Territory joined us for the second week, taking on responsibility for entertaining the children when the music classes ended. This special service group did one of the fun nights, as did the British instructors.

The evening in which the young people entertained us with their Russian-style music was quite outstanding. There were some excellent pianists and when they sang in their own language in true Russian style it was just lovely.

A highlight for many was the visit to an orphanage located in the vicinity of our camp. It was here that the students entertained the children while the instructors distributed several dozen boxes of medicines, children's clothing and other gifts.

On the first Sunday morning, the whole camp went to Kiev Central Corps for a meeting where more than 400 people were present, some visiting the Army for the first time. Our students sang a couple of solo items and the instructors accompanied the congregational singing. At night Major Stephen Russell, with the help of a translator, led a songs of praise meeting.

The second Sunday morning was spent at the camp, where we witnessed the enrolment of 13 junior soldiers and 26 senior soldiers. Among them was the bandmaster of the former Young Communists Band. What a miracle of grace!

Knowing that we would be with beginners, I had written a march in which, for the first cornets, only the first valve was needed. It was impossible to do this for all parts, but I did my best to make it as simple as possible. By the end of the week we were able to give a fair performance of the march and a mini-concert along with the singers and timbrelists.

The whole experience was a very moving one and to see so many young people new to the Christian faith trying so hard to become good Salvationists was inspiring to say the least.

Incidentally, when we were going through the customs at Kiev Airport prior to our departure for London, an official, seeing me carrying an old bass trombone (the one with the handle and quite beyond repair), asked if I had purchased the same in Kiev. After my telling him that it was one that we had brought from England he asked for proof of my statement or some payment. He was quite surprised when, handing him the trombone, I said, 'Please accept this as a gift and I hope you become a good player.' Looking somewhat bewildered, he let me through.

A very warm welcome was ours on arrival back at Winton Corps!

In complete contrast to Camp Victory, Jill and I journeyed to Louth in the Northampton Division where our son Mark and his wife Tracy were the corps officers. The corps, needing a new building, had been raising money for many years and it was my privilege on 10 July 1999 to cut the ribbon and declare this new house of God 'well and truly open'. We were very honoured to be invited to conduct the weekend celebrations along with the divisional leaders, Majors John and Elizabeth Matear. The march I wrote for the occasion contains the song:

Glory, glory, hallelujah!
I have given my all to God;
And I now have full salvation
Through the precious blood.

The Household Troops Band, with Major John Mott, brought their own spirit and enthusiasm to the occasion, especially as they were seen marching through the town.

Incidentally, it was a bit strange to see my face on hundreds of oven gloves, which were being sold to raise money for the new hall!

Chapter 26

WREATH OF COURAGE

Unwelcome News

Some years after our retirement, Jill was confirmed as having cancer and we had to make a daily trip to the neighbouring town of Poole for special treatment. This helped for a time but in April 2002 she was admitted to the Macmillan unit back in Christchurch. If ever there were caring people, this is where they were. Jill kept a high and positive spirit throughout her days there.

On one occasion a minister from one of the local churches came visiting the people in the ward. As he came to Jill, who was having a blood transfusion, he said, in an attempt to get her into conversation, 'Powerful stuff this blood.' 'Yes,' she replied, 'there is power in the blood,' and began to sing the old chorus,

> *There is power, power, wonder-working power,*
> *In the precious blood of the Lamb.*

She then told the minister, 'It is number 281 in the Salvation Army song book,' and added, 'It is a good song to read and even better to believe!' As I followed the minister to the door he said, 'Your wife is a truly remarkable woman.' 'She certainly is!' was my reply.

I was at her bedside daily from early morning until late at night and witnessed her giving comfort and solace to the other ladies in the same ward – and some to me!

The Winton corps officers, Majors David and Judith Bennett, came to see Jill on most days and, on the night before Jill left us for Heaven, they came to the hospital, thus giving my sons and me a chance to get a quick meal. On our return, Judith told me that they had had a little

275

meeting together in which they had sung a song and read from the Psalms and finally sung a verse of Albert Orsborn's song, 'I Know Thee, Who Thou Art'. As they were about to sing the last verse, Jill whispered the opening lines:

> Let nothing draw me back
> Or turn my heart from thee.

These were Jill's final words.

The remainder of the verse is:

> But by the Calvary track
> Bring me at last to see
> The courts of God, that city fair,
> And find my name is written there.

A meeting of thanksgiving for the life and work of Jill Bearcroft was celebrated at Winton Corps with my sons taking part. Mark's wife Tracy, with Norrie's son Andrew playing a trumpet obbligato, sang 'When We All Get To Heaven'. Sitting with me were Bram and his wife Jennifer with daughters Naomi and Hannah, Norrie and his wife Julie with their children, Andrew and Georgia, and Mark and his wife Tracy, with Matthew and Elanor.

Stephen Cobb, Head of the Army's Music Ministries in the UK and Ireland, spoke about Jill and Major Judith Bennett recounted some of her conversations at the Macmillan hospital. My son Mark presented some thoughts prepared by our family and our first-born son, Bramwell, read from Paul's letter to the Romans chapter 8. The band played 'They'll Sing A Welcome Home' and the songsters sang 'In The Secret Of Thy Presence'. The last two lines of the third verse became fact for Jill as, a few days before, we saw her take leave of her earthly life:

> First to know thee, then to serve thee,
> Then to see thee as thou art.

Surprise Item

Norman and Jill's wedding (11 September 1948)

Writing Music

Writing music helped by Mozart (the cat)

Retirement

Retirement – June
1992 at Regent Hall

The Bearcroft Family in 1998 at Norman and Jill's 50th wedding
anniversary party

Profile Night – New York, USA, 2002

Norman joining Kathleen's family on the occasion of their marriage in
December 2002

Norman
and
Kathleen

80th Birthday Celebrations

Kathleen reads from the Bible during a festival at Regent Hall with the International Staff Songsters and the Household Troops Band celebrating Norman's 80th birthday

Life Guards at Windsor

Norman with the Life Guards Band at Windsor Castle (2007)

A complete surprise was ours when a group from the International Staff Songsters arrived and sang, after which everybody joined in singing Jill's favourite song:

> All creatures of our God and King,
> Lift up your voice and with us sing
> Alleluia, alleluia!
> Thou burning sun with golden beam,
> Thou silver moon with softer gleam:
>
> *O praise him, O praise him,*
> *Alleluia, alleluia, alleluia!*

Jill had made one request, and that was for everyone to sing the old song 'I Have A Home That Is Fairer Than Day'. This request was made because she knew how much I liked the Erik Leidzén selection entitled 'On The Way Home' in which, after presenting 'I have a home that is fairer than day', the following old chorus is heard as the final message of the piece:

> *He will keep you from falling,*
> *He will keep to the end,*
> *What a wonderful Saviour!*
> *What a wonderful Friend!*

The following day, as a devastated family we all made our way to Jill's favourite spot in the New Forest and, following a short service of thanksgiving, scattered her ashes in accordance with her request. Jill had made me promise that there would not be a stone or any markings signifying her death, but to just to believe the verse of the Catherine Baird song (*SASB* 874) I had so often quoted to others in time of parting:

> With Jesus' name upon their lips,
> The vale of death his servants tread;

In him they dared believe; in him
They dare depart; nor sigh, nor dread;
To love committing all their loves,
All counted good through peace or strife,
Content to die believing still
In Jesus, everlasting life.

This is what gave me hope in my now desolate world.

Chapter 27

THE SEAFARER

As a Guest at the 2002 Councils for Bandmasters

I was about to write and cancel my acceptance of taking part in the June Councils for Bandmasters when I realised this would be the last thing Jill would want me to do. So the next month, being June, found me back in London for the Bandmasters Councils. Seeing it was around the time of Ray Steadman-Allen's 80th birthday, I was asked if I would interview him in the afternoon session. For this they had erected a small platform in the Assembly Hall of the William Booth College on which were placed two armchairs so the two 'old boys' could have a good old chat with the assembled host listening in to their conversation.

I reminded him about the time when he was Editor of *The Musician*. Attending the Thursday morning prayer meeting, he heard some of the people from one department expressing publicly some disparaging remarks about our bands. Ray was so incensed that, following the meeting, he went and kicked all the doors on that departmental floor. I saw him looking very red and took him down to my office, where Joy Webb, making us a cup of tea, helped to calm him down. When I asked him, 'Do you remember that, Ray?' He said he remembered the tea but not what it was for!

One year, Ray's contribution to an Albert Hall festival was in the form of a piano concerto with the Festival Chorus in an orchestral-type accompaniment. It was entitled 'A Childhood Suite' and contained songs we had learned as children in Sunday school. For this year, I wanted Ray to conduct the piece on the night of the festival, which meant he would have to come to the rehearsals. On the way to the first one he suggested that, for this rehearsal, I should conduct and he would play the piano solo part. All went well.

279

On the journey home he expressed the thought that, on the night of the festival, we should do the same thing, him play and me conduct. I explained that I had already secured a soloist and he would have to conduct as previously arranged. On the afternoon of the event, following the final rehearsal, Joy, Ray's wife, asked me, 'Seeing that today is our wedding anniversary, could I put a little message in the front of the score so that when he opens it tonight he will see it and remember.' Came the time for Ray to enter the stage and, following his acknowledgement of the loud applause that greeted him, he opened the score and saw Joy's note. Appearing not to know quite what to do, he turned to the vast audience and having no idea where she was sitting said, 'Er, er, thank you for that!' Only Joy and I knew what he was talking about but it was a very nice idea.

The Bramwell Booth Hall, which was in the basement of International Headquarters, was used for various meetings such as welcomes and farewells, the Thursday morning prayer meeting for International Headquarters personnel and on Fridays for the members of British National Headquarters. It was during one of these meetings that Ray, looking around at the paintings of all the Salvation Army Generals (on display in the Bramwell Booth hall), began to think of the songs that some of them had written. By now, unaware of what was happening in the meeting, he began to jot down a few ideas for the next Albert Hall festival in response to my annual request. As he looked at the paintings he remembered songs by William Booth, Bramwell Booth, Evangeline Booth, Albert Orsborn and Wilfred Kitching (at that time this completed the list of songwriting Generals).

The work arrived in good time for the festival and I noticed a melody which was not the work of any of the Generals, so I asked Ray about this. His reply was, 'Oh well, it was the kind of tune that one of them could have written.' The piece was called 'Inspirations From The Bramwell Booth Memorial Hall' and was a great success.

I then reminded him of the time we went for a rehearsal to the town of Margate where, seeing it was at the seaside, we took our wives along for a picnic. The fact that it was the middle of winter and bitterly cold didn't stop Ray, on arrival, jumping out of the car and running down to the sea, where he had a paddle in the icy waters. On his arrival back to the car, I suggested that perhaps his escapade in the ocean was not the wisest thing he had ever done! He answered that he had been in the Navy and the sea, cold or otherwise, had a special attraction for him.

Our 'chat' went on for an hour and, judging by the applause, everyone seemed very happy with our effort. The commissioner leading the councils suggested that, 'Now would be a good time for a cup of tea!'

Chapter 28

SAVED TO SERVE

Profile Night – New York, USA, 2002

My very dear friends Den and Bet Lewis were having a short holiday with me in Christchurch when I told them I had received an invitation to go to New York in the USA for what is called a Profile Night (a yearly series in which well-known composers are featured and their music played by the New York Staff Band and other sections and soloists). I had received a similar request some years before but, owing to duties in Britain, was unable to accept. Knowing that I had mixed feelings about the invitation, both Den and Bet thought I should accept and they agreed to come back to Christchurch during my visit to look after my cat, Mozart. I took up their kind offer and accepted the assignment.

Arriving at New York Airport, I was met by Captain Arthur Henry (solo horn player in the New York Staff Band) who drove me to the Greater New York Divisional Headquarters where we met Gordon Ward who, as the Divisional Director of Music, was responsible for the Profile Night. Gordon and I then made our way to Territorial Headquarters for a rehearsal with the Staff Band.

As we were going up the stairs to the Music Department, I met Major Kathleen Ljungholm (whom I remembered meeting in Kiev when she drove me from the airport to the music school at Camp Victory in Ukraine). Gordon took me in to meet Staff Bandmaster Ron Waiksnoris and, while he and Gordon were in conversation, I went back to see Kathleen in her office (Eastern Territory Heritage Museum) where she kindly presented me with an old song book. It was good to meet up with the New York Staff Band again and to rehearse the pieces I was to conduct at the Profile Night.

Captain Henry had been asked to take me on a tour of New York City during the next day but sickness prevented him from so doing. Kathleen Ljungholm then agreed to take me to see the city and asked Gordon Ward for his telephone number in case we needed to be in touch. Gordon replied, 'Nah, do what you want with him. Just bring him back happy!' Kathleen then asked me if there was anything I particularly wanted to see in New York. I said I would like to see the sight of the terrorist attack (where the two aircraft flew into the World Trade Center) so Kathleen took me to the scene known as Ground Zero, where there was little else but a large hole in the ground. She then took me to the mortuary where she had worked beside the police, the firemen and emergency teams with whom she prayed as the bodies from this disaster were brought in. I then met the Chief Medical Examiner who told me of the wonderful work Kathleen and other Salvationists had done during this horrific time.

As we took the elevator to another floor, it was very strange to see my picture on the mortuary wall advertising the coming Profile Night. Kathleen then explained that she had put the advert there hoping some of the workers (who had become her great friends) would come to the concert.

Following dinner in an American diner (an experience I will never forget, with a menu of hundreds of items to eat), Kathleen asked if I would like to see the Salvation Army section at the Kensico Cemetery. She said that many Salvationist musicians and officers were buried there, so there we went. I saw names of composers like Bearchell, Holz and Evangeline and Herbert Booth, as well as the name of my old friend John Bloethe, who was at the International College for Officers at the same time as me back in 1965. In another part of the cemetery we found a memorial to the famous composer Sergei Rachmaninov.

The next evening (Friday) was the Profile Night with the venue being the Centennial Memorial Temple in New York (the Temple wasn't new to me seeing I had been there with the Canadian Staff Band and with the International Staff Songsters on previous occasions).

Following a rehearsal we went to another part of the building for a meal with the band. Kathleen was about to sit with some other people when I grabbed her arm and said, 'Stop with me.' She pointed out that the top table was for special guests only but I hung on to her and she sat beside me. In the conversation that followed, someone asked me where Kathie (as she was known by all) had taken me. I replied, in all innocence, 'Well, first she took me to the morgue and then to a cemetery.' My reply caused gales of laughter!

A very large crowd had gathered at the Temple for the Profile Night, where the opening number was 'Spirit Of The Army'. The printed programme revealed:

This march was written for the 1988 International Leaders Conference and features tunes with historical significance, the first being, 'We're Bound For The Land Of The Pure And The Holy', which was sung by William Booth and his followers as they made their way to Mile End Waste for the first Army open-air meeting.

Other items the New York Staff Band played included 'Just Like John', 'Fantasia On Three Spirituals' and 'The Londonderry Air'. Guest cornet soloist Mark Ridenour played 'Song Of Exultation' and 'The Call Of Christ'.

The Greater New York Youth Band played 'Bells Of Heaven' and 'Temple 85' and the Youth Chorus sang 'I'm Goin' To Sing' and 'Just As I Am'. The New York Staff Band Chorus sang 'The Calvary Track'.

The programme also included a welcome to Commissioners Lawrence and Nancy Moretz, their first appearance as the new territorial leaders.

It so happened that my Profile Night was the 24th in the series, the previous guests being: Eric Ball, Albert Jakeway, Brindley Boon, Philip Catelinet, Richard Holz, Ray Steadman-Allen, Leslie Condon, Stanley Ditmer, Ray Bowes, Robert Redhead, William Himes, James Curnow, Michael Kenyon, Erik Silfverberg, Howard Davies, Ivor Bosanko, William and Bruce Broughton, Noel Jones, Peter Graham, Stephen Bulla, Kenneth Downie, Kevin Norbury and Trevor Davis.

The New York Staff Band was in great form, as were the other sections and soloists. It was certainly a night I will never forget!

285

I had been told how good American ice cream is and, at my request, Kathleen and I ventured into the streets of New York in search of the perfect ice cream cone. We found an ice cream parlour where dozens of flavours were available, including strawberry, vanilla, peppermint, rum and raisin and goodness knows what else! It was a very late hour when we said goodbye!

The following evening found me again with the Staff Band, this time in the town of Kingston, where I was invited to be the compère and guest conductor in a number of pieces we had used the previous night. Kathleen agreed to make the journey to Kingston on the Saturday, and made it again on the Sunday. The Sunday morning meeting, with its songs, the playing of the Staff Band and the spoken message, had very real meaning for me and I realised that I really should start to live again. Kathleen drove me to the airport for my journey home and this gave us a little more time to discuss the future, and time for her to agree to marry me.

Following the flight and a bus journey back to Bournemouth, I arrived at the bus station to find Den and Bet Lewis there to meet me. They were able to sense something about my demeanour that brought me to tell them my good news. One month later, with the blessing of my three sons, Kathleen and I were married in a service led by her brother, Lieut-Colonel Jack Getz, in the Centennial Memorial Temple in New York. My son Norman (Norrie), with his wife Julie and their children Andrew and Georgia represented my family, with Norrie as my best man.

A good number of Staff Bandsmen, plus a few other players, were conducted by Staff Bandmaster Ron Waiksnoris in the playing of the march 'Wreath Of Courage', as Kathleen's nine grandchildren – Jacob, Kelton, Erik, Reid, Van, Sydney, Grayson, Annika and Kaja – entered waving British flags. Five more grandchildren have been born since this event – Ryder, Lillemor, Sofie, Ellexa and Otto. The Scottish folksong 'My Love Is Like A Red, Red Rose' was played by the band for the entry of the bride, escorted by her brother, Bob Getz.

A group of songsters, led by Bandmaster Gordon Ward, sang number of songs before and during the service. My son Mark and his family were represented by the singing of his song 'Boundless Love', beautifully sung by Captain Margaret Davies. Colonel Henry Gariepy kindly officiated for the actual wedding vows.

Kathleen's two daughters, Katrina Bender and Kaarina Owens, with their husbands Michael and Jason, and her two sons, Lars – and his wife Kellie – and Sven Ljungholm (who later married Tanya), were present at the ceremony. Kathleen's sister, Sharon Lundstrom (who organised an English tea reception, with her husband Jim who videoed everything) read from the Bible. Kathleen's sister-in-law, Lieut-Colonel Barbara Getz, played the piano. A message from my son Bram and his family was read at the reception.

Considering the English march and British flags, plus a Scottish song, an English best man and a British leader of the songsters, to say nothing of the English bridegroom, one could have expected to hear 'God Save The Queen' at any moment!

It was during the wedding ceremony that Kathleen's brother Jack made reference to the fact that we had both lived colourful lives in our work for The Salvation Army. I later learned that in the winter of 1993 Kathleen had journeyed from Moscow on a 15-hour train ride to start the Army's work in Ukraine on her own. There was no house to go to and the Army was completely unknown. Her first job was to find somewhere to live, somewhere to work and to look for some willing helpers, then to find a hall for meetings. A few months later 60 young people attended a music camp, with guest Captain Donna Peterson, and two months after that I went with some Winton Corps comrades to lead a second music camp, attended this time by 150 young people, all in Salvation Army uniform! (See chapter 25.)

Chapter 29

TO REGIONS FAIR

On We March!

I received a very warm welcome at Territorial Headquarters in New York, where Kathleen is the Director of the Heritage Museum and Historical Society. Ron Waiksnoris, Territorial Music Secretary, has been particularly kind in including me in musical events and making me an honorary member of the New York Staff Band.

Our travels have taken us as far afield as Melbourne, Australia, in response to a request for us to lead an Easter weekend at Waverley Corps. This was a very happy occasion for us, seeing that we could stay with my son and daughter-in-law Mark and Tracy and their children Matthew and Elanor. Mark and Tracy were then the officers at Greensborough Corps in Melbourne. Next it was off to California in the west, to Florida in the south, to Canada in the north, then to Holland and France.

Back at Star Lake Music Camp, I was invited to conduct a group of young Salvationists from Korea. There were enough of them to make a complete band and they were a perfect delight to be with. They had an interpreter who, at my saying, 'Letter A', would take what seemed like several sentences to explain just where we would be starting, but it proved to be an unforgettable experience.

Kathleen was invited to lead the class for those who had come for timbrel instruction. It was during one of the classes that a lady came and said that a bear was nearby and Kathleen, thinking she meant me, just smiled and said 'OK'. Her smile changed when a real bear appeared, looked at her and then ambled away into the woods!

An invitation to be the guests at the annual retired officers camp meetings in California proved to be a very pleasant and exciting few days. We were required to lead all the meetings, and it was a pleasure to meet a number of those who had been in the 1950 Ambassadors Session of cadets. One of the officers, a lady known to me as Bunty Robinson, had been in the Ambassadors Session with Jill and me back in England.

A very tuneful band, formed from the officers, required a rehearsal every day, as did a very good group of singers. I almost felt as if I were back at Butlin's, especially on the day that Lieut-Colonels Doug and Diane O'Brien came for the day (Diane, née Lillicrap, was a member of the Butlin's entertainments team for a number of years). They both joined Kathleen and me in a Butlin's type sketch and we sang a few light-hearted songs.

At the close of a weekend spent in Ithaca (New York State) the corps officer came to thank us for leading the weekend's meetings and then, turning to me, said, 'I'm so glad to have met you. I thought you were dead!'

During a weekend spent at Rockford (Illinois) Corps, a lady came to Kathleen saying how much she had enjoyed playing and singing my music. She then asked Kathleen to introduce her to me. After Kathleen had done so, the lady, holding my hand, said, 'Oh Colonel, it is so good to meet you. I have *endured* your music for years!'

80th Birthday Celebrations

Unexpected celebrations for my 80th birthday began in January 2006 with a few close friends surprising me with a party on my actual birthday, and there was another that evening. A few days later, New York Staff Bandmaster Ron Waiksnoris asked me to go to the USA Eastern Territorial Headquarters to speak to a number of 'musical people' and suggested it would be best to wear my uniform. I was totally surprised when it turned out to be a birthday party for me, hosted by the territorial leaders, Commissioners Lawrence and Nancy Moretz, with lots of musicians and friends.

In June of the same year a birthday festival at Regent Hall in London was arranged by Staff Bandmaster Stephen Cobb, Kevin Ashman, Major John Mott and others. The Household Troops Band

and the International Staff Songsters were in attendance, playing and singing some of my music. *Salvationist* carried the following account by Major Dean Pallant:

'The best thing I ever did was to become a Salvation Army officer,' said Norman Bearcroft at the conclusion of a tribute evening on the occasion of his 80th birthday. On a warm summer's evening, Regent Hall was packed to capacity with well-wishers who enjoyed an evening of quality Bearcroft music provided by the International Staff Songsters and the Household Troops Band. Three soloists, who had all worked closely with Norman, gave outstanding performances: Jacqui Proctor (vocal, Australia Southern), Derick Kane (euphonium) and Songster Leader Kevin Ashman with a premiere performance of a new Bearcroft cornet solo, 'Stories Of Jesus'. The evening had a strong international flavour with former Canadian Staff Bandmaster Brian Burditt sending a video tribute from Canada, Captain Mark Bearcroft (Australia Southern) bringing a word from the Scriptures and Bram Bearcroft coming from his home in France to deliver a humour-filled tribute to his father. Personal, joyful tributes were also given by Lieut-Colonel Ray Steadman-Allen OF and Bandmaster Howard Evans (Boscombe), who both stressed Norman's impact on people through his music and personality. Norman, who was the first leader of the ISS when it was reformed in 1980, presented the current leader, Dorothy Nancekievill, with a new flag. He reflected: 'It has been a wonderful life. I give God all the glory.'

Not reported was a touch of Butlin's, when Major John Mott joined me in a comedy sketch in which we recounted some of the productions we had done in years past. We finished with a duet which featured the names of a number of persons present, including my sister Nancy, Tom and Joyce LeGrow (friends from Canada), Stephen Cobb, Derick Kane, and Kevin Ashman. One verse caused my three sons, seated in the gallery, to stand and sing, 'And we love our dear old Dad!'

Owing to the fact that these events were completely sold out at Regent Hall, Major George Whittingham, with the South London Fellowship Band, arranged a similar event to a packed house at Bromley Temple two weeks later. Items on the programme included 'To Regions Fair', 'Joyous Proclamation' and 'Temple 85'. Featured soloists were David Daws, in a flawless performance of 'Golden Slippers', and Derick Kane in 'Better World', accompanied by the band. Bromley Songsters sang two numbers and my old friend and colleague Colonel Brindley Boon offered a prayer of thanksgiving. Fellow Ambassador Colonel Ray Holdstock (we were in training together back in 1950) offered the final prayer. I left thinking how kind and generous everybody had been in these two events.

Florida

It was in Clearwater, Florida, that Kathleen and I received a very warm welcome when we went for an occasion with the many retired officers living there. First it was a rehearsal with the very good corps songster brigade (leader Debi Forde) and their pianist, Commissioner Ron Irwin, and then with a fine band conducted by Bandmaster Max Wood. The Sunday evening meeting, a mini Royal Albert Hall occasion, featured the band, the songsters and male voices. All forces joined in the old war song 'Storm The Forts'. For the congregational singing, Major Mae Anderson played the piano and Commissioner Raymond Cooper played the organ. Everyone present joined in 'Sing Along With The Band' – and did they sing! Monday evening was spent with the retired officers, many of whom we knew from years gone by. What a happy and active crowd they are!

Back in New York, Kathleen and I, along with two friends, Hans Knutzen and his wife Catherine, formed a vocal quartet and have accepted a number of requests to conduct meetings. We have a standing order for the retired officers' summer picnic for those living in and around Asbury Park, New Jersey, where we have been the entertainment for the past seven years. We have also done programmes at the Adult Rehabilitation Centre in New York, and have led musical meetings at corps and senior citizens residences.

Life Guards at Windsor

A letter arrived from Martin Whybrow (a former Salvationist now serving in the Life Guards Band) inviting us to the Life Guards Band reunion with a request that I write a march for the band in which I served during and just after the Second World War. The reunion was on a date soon after we arrived back in New York from the 85th birthday celebrations for Ray Steadman-Allen, thus making it too difficult for me to be present at the Life Guards Band reunion. A second letter arrived saying they were sorry I could not be at the reunion, but they would still like me to write a march and could I attend a rehearsal while in London for the Ray Steadman-Allen festival? I accepted the invitation for the rehearsal but did not have the time to write a new march. I said I would re-orchestrate one of my Salvation Army marches which had been published some years previously and contained two secular tunes, 'Widecombe Fair' and 'Dashing Away With A Smoothing Iron'.

On arrival we were warmly greeted and taken to the band room where the march was rehearsed and sounded OK, though a little different with the additional woodwind, flutes, piccolos, clarinets and saxophones. We were then invited to travel with the band to another barracks in Windsor, where the band was to march the Coldstream Guards to Windsor Castle for the Changing of the Guard. Obeying the request to keep very near to the band as they were marching to the Castle, we were allowed to go in along with the band to the actual parade ground in the Castle grounds, where the traditional Changing of the Guard was to take place.

At one point in the ceremony, the band is required to play some music and their choice was my march 'Westward Ho!', which we had just heard them rehearsing. Imagine my feeling when, following the two secular tunes contained in the march, the next melody was 'Oh, Yes, There's Salvation For You'. I wondered how many in the crowd of hundreds of people watching and listening to all that was going on would be Salvationists and what would they think, hearing one of their songs being played on the parade ground in Windsor Castle. The march goes on with two more 'Army' songs, 'No Retreating, Hell

Defeating' and 'Are You Washed In The Blood Of The Lamb?'. As I stood there listening to all this I realised what a great privilege it is to be a Salvationist!

We marched back to the Coldstream Barracks with the band and then had a bus ride to Combermere Barracks for a thank you to and from the band. As we walked out of the gates, I said to Kathleen, 'It is just 60 years since I last walked out of these gates with the prospect of going to the International Training College to become a Salvation Army officer.'

Looking back, I thank God for all the wonderful experiences and opportunities that have come my way. I would like to begin all over again but the Lord, I am sure, has other plans for me.

A Methodist minister, with whom I was billeted while on an engagement with the International Staff Songsters in Plymouth, England, gave me a book of poems by Charles Wesley. Of all the wonderful verses contained in the book, this one verse, all on its own, stood out from all the rest:

> Saviour, the mystery of thy grace
> Shall be the matter of my praise,
> That grace which fills the hosts above
> With joy, astonishment and love!

This is why my little book is called *In Good Company*. With my family and loved ones, with musicians both in the Army and outside, with the countless Salvationists throughout the world who have shown me such kindness, I seem to have been in good company all my life!

Music by N.B. Published for Band (to 2009)

FS = *Festival Series*; GS = *General Series*; TS = *Triumph Series*;
US = *Unity Series*; ABJ = *American Band Journal*;
Triumphonic (USA British Scoring)

Argyle Citadel	GS 1696	March
Bedford	GS 1558	Hymn arrangement
Bells Of Heaven, The	FS 460	Double quartet
Better World, The	FS 418	Euphonium solo
Bournemouth Centennial	GS 1877	March
Brightlingsea	TS 483	March
Call Of Christ, The	GS 1699	Cornet solo
Camp Fellowship	GS 1588	March
Camp Victory	TS 1044	March
City Of God	Triumphonic	Scripture setting
Cobham Hall	GS 1757	March
Coventry Carol	GS 2007	
Cross, The Victory, The	GS 1536	Selection
Day Of Jubilee	FS 515	Festival march
Dear Lord And Father	GS 2047	Hymn setting
Fantasia On The Sussex Carol	ABJ 256	
First Nowell, The	ABJ 171	Carol arrangement
Flower Duet, The	FS 521	Duet for cornet & flugelhorn
Golden Slippers	FS 402	Cornet solo
Good Cheer	TS 922	Selection
Great Adventure, The	FS 581	Euphonium solo
Great Day	2010	March
Great Physician	GS 1976	Song setting
Harbour Light	FS 478	Euphonium solo
High Fidelity	GS 1852	Soprano cornet solo
In Dulci Jubilo	GS 1876	Carol arrangement

It Came Upon The Midnight	Special	Carol arrangement
Jesus I Come To Thee	GS 1871	Euphonium solo
Jingle Bells	FS 445	Carol arrangement
Joyous Carillon	300	Double trio
Joyous Proclamation	GS 1704	Cornet quartet
Just Like John	FS 360	Festival arrangement
King Of Love, The	GS 1995	Hymn setting
King's Trumpeters, The	FS 498	Cornet ensemble
Land Of Song	GS 1608	March
Locomotion	FS 570	Euphonium solo
Long Point	1661	March
Louth 99	TS 1081	March
Marching Thro' The Years	FS 404	Selection of marches
Masters In This Hall	GS 1820	Festival arrangement
Merry Christmas	2020	Carols in march time
Nicaea	TS 1104	Hymn setting
Richmond	GS 1783	Hymn setting
Redeeming Grace	GS 1990	Selection
Reflections	FS 553	Suite
Riverside	TS 1072	March
SASA 120	GS 2056	March
Saved By Grace	GS 1584	Selection
Saved To Serve	Triumphonic	March
Seafarer, The	1736	March
Share Your Faith	GS 1748	March
Shout Aloud Salvation	GS 1542	Festival arrangement
Sing Along With The Band	GS 1714	Selection
Song Of Exultation	FS 433	Cornet solo
Songs Of Assurance	US 64	Selection
Songs Of Newfoundland	FS 504	Suite
Songs Of Testimony	TS 621	Selection
Sound Of Britain	FS 429	Suite
Sounds Like Christmas	ABJ 247	March
Sounds Of Christmas	SPS	Suite
Southall One Hundred	GS 1798	March

Spirit Of Endeavour	TS 1085	March
Spirit Of The Army	GS 1845	March
Stories Of Jesus	TS 1158	Cornet solo
Stracathro	TS 935	Hymn setting
Suite Of Carols	GS 1922	Suite
Sussex Carol	ABJ 256	Fantasia
Temple 85	GS 1642	March
Tenderly Calling	ABJ 253	Cornet solo
There Is A Green Hill	GS 2000	Horn solo
They'll Sing A Welcome	GS 1994	Song setting
Three Spirituals	SPS	Suite
Timepiece	Judd St	Euphonium duet
To Regions Fair	GS 1458	March
Travelling Home	GS 1543	Selection
True Courage	GS 2024	March
Valor Camaradas!	TS 1013	March
Vanguard	TS 636	March
Westward Ho!	GS 1949	March
Whiter Than The Snow	GS 2078	Euphonium solo
Winton-Bournemouth	GS 1929	March
With Gladsome Mind	GS 1796	Hymn setting
Wonderful Story Of Love	GS 1723	Selection
Wondrous Love	US 117	Selection
Word Of Grace	FS 376	Trombone solo
Wreath Of Courage	GS 1962	March
Zambia	TS 1148	March
Zimbabwe	TS 993	March

Vocal Music Published by The Salvation Army (to 2009)

MS = *Musical Salvationist*;
STL = *Sing To The Lord*; SFMV = *Songs For Male Voices*; AUS = Australia

All Is Well	MS Oct	1985
At Thy Throne	MS Oct	1952
Bound For The Promised Land	MS Oct	1981
Carol Of The Bells	MS Oct, Jan	1965
Charm Of The Cross, The	MS Jan	1982
Christ Of Calvary, The	STL	2009
Cleansing For Me	MS Jan	1966
Divine Paradox, The	MS Jan	1962
Ever Is The War Cry, Victory!	MS Apr	1978
Faith And Trust	STL	2003
God Will Find You	MS July	1951
Gospel Feast, The	MS July	1950
Happy Song	MS July	1968
Holy, Holy, Holy	MS Apr	1992
How Wonderful To Walk With God	MS Apr	1983
I'm Goin' To Sing	MS Jan	1989
In Good Company	MS July	1991
In Jesus' Steps	MS Jan	1991
Jesus, The Name High Over All	STL	1995
Jesus, The Very Thought Of Thee	STL	1999
Just As I Am	MS Jan	1988
Lord Is King, The	STL	2001
Lullaby For The Little Lord	MS Oct	1968
Mid All The Traffic	AUS	2006
Morning Has Broken	STL	2007
My Jesus, I Love Thee	MS Apr	1966
My Solemn Vow	MS Apr	1979
Nothing But Thy Blood	MS July	1977
Our Blest Redeemer	MS Oct	1987

Passport To Heaven	MS Oct	1986
Psalm 23	MS July	1982
Reckon On	MS July	1990
Reflections	MS Jan	1986
Shout Aloud Salvation	MS Oct	1964
Song Of Renewal	STL	1998
Still The Night	STL	1994
Storm The Forts	MS Oct	1965
Sweet Land Of Light	AUS	2007
There Is A Green Hill	STL Feb	1997
There Is Mercy In Jesus	MS Apr	1986
This Joyful Eastertide	MS Oct	1989
Vamos Pastorcitos	MS July	1988
Wasted Years	MS Jan	1968
Well Is Deep, The	MS Apr	1981
When We All Get To Heaven	MS Oct	1991

MALE VOICES

Happy Song	SFMV	1968
He Careth For Me	SFMV	1988
I Know Thee Who Thou Art	SFMV	1992
Simply Trusting	SFMV	1967
That Kind Of Lord	SFMV	2001
What Will You Do With Jesus?	SFMV	1976

INDEX

303

H

Hackney 45
Hadleigh 117, 164
Haines, Don and Mrs 101
Hair, Susan 189
Halifax NS 90
'Hallelujah City' 261
Hallelujah! 220
Hamburg 10
Hamilton Argyle 85
Hammond, Capt David 80
Hammond, Dep SL Jean 46
Hammond, Mrs Maj David 88, 111
Hammond, William 182
Hansen, Charles 153
Hanwell 206
Harare 247, 248, 250
'Harbour Light' 32, 89
Harlesden 219
Harrow 194, 219
Hart, Brian 270
Hartford Songster Brigade 94
Hawkes, Frederick 46, 208
Hazell, Andrea 161
Heath, Norman 219
Heaton, Wilfred 39, 89
Heckmondwike 2
Henderson, Maj Stephen 13
Henry, Capt Arthur 283, 284
High Wycombe 44
High, Colin 161
Hill, Edward (Ted) 206
Himes, BM William 139, 285
Hird, Thora 220
Hiscock, Maj and Mrs Edwin 113
Hoboken Singing Company 94
Hodgetts, Olive 151
Holbrook, Olive 173, 179, 180, 181
Holdstock, Ray 115, 292
Holland 15, 161, 289
Holmsley 256
Holz, BM Ronald 153
Holz, Richard (Dick) 48, 99, 102, 103, 285
Hook (Hampshire) 52

Hopkin, BM Jim 52
Horrabin, Roy 42
Hosty, Maj Bill 92
Household Troops Band 126, 273, 290, 291
Howe, Norman 120, 122
Howe, Mrs (Marian) 122
Howells, Brig Ivor (R) 265
Hubbard, Sidney 182
Huke, Brian 161
Hunt, Col Stanley 115
Hunter, Denis 55, 117, 172
Hutchinson, Shirley 156
Hynd, Margaret 162

I

'I'm Goin' To Sing' 285
Ilford 8, 9, 148
'In Jesus' Steps' 177
International College for Officers 205, 284
International (Centenary) Congress (1965) 57, 233, 238
International Congress (1978) 115, 143, 150, 151, 223
International Congress (1990) 126, 169, 197
International Headquarters (IHQ) 9, 10, 45, 55, 113, 115, 155, 158, 177, 210, 216, 280
International Music Board 42, 44, 45, 99, 139, 206
International Staff Band (ISB) x, 23, 44, 45, 46, 49, 57, 78, 105, 106, 117, 121, 125, 127, 132, 133, 137, 138, 140, 143, 146, 147, 149, 159, 166, 170, 185, 187, 188, 193, 195, 199, 207, 212, 213, 214, 220, 221, 224, 227, 233, 234, 237, 239
International Staff Songsters (ISS) x, 127, 128, 137, 155, 158, 160, 161, 162, 163, 164, 165, 166, 170, 187, 188, 189, 214, 220, 221, 227, 253, 256, 259, 260, 261, 277, 284, 291, 294

306

International Training College (William Booth College) 21, 34, 45, 99, 137, 139, 174, 180, 211, 213, 222, 279, 294
International Youth Congress 22
Irwin, Comr Ron 292
Ithaca (USA) 290
Izzard, Maj John (Jack) 177, 228

J

Jackson, BM William 38
Jacobs, BM Bramwell 46
Jakeway, Albert 148, 170, 194, 195, 196, 197, 198, 285
Japan 153
Jenkins, Don 141
Jerrett, Frances 80
Jerrett, Jack 81
'Jesus, The Very Thought Of Thee' 158
Jobson, BM Reg 52, 244
Johnson, Carol 162
Jones, Delia 138
Jones, Noel 285
Jones, Rtd SL Joyce 260
Jorgensen, Chris 25, 26
'Joyous Carillon' 182
'Joyous Proclamation' 292
Joystrings 60
Judd Street (King's Cross) 3
Juno Beach 14
'Just As I Am' 184, 285
'Just Like John' x, 89, 149, 188, 285

K

Kane, Derick 117, 146, 260, 291, 292
Keep Singing! 84, 116
Kendrick, Comr Kathleen 115, 175
Kensico Cemetery 58, 284
Kenyon, Michael 86, 129, 149, 170, 171, 285
Kerr, Maj William (Bill) 82, 93
Kiev 269, 270, 271, 272, 283

Kimmins, Edwin 80
Kingston (USA) 286
Kingston-on-Thames 5, 6, 219
Kitchen, June 50, 115, 122
Kitchen, Maj Eric 80
Kitchener 85, 88
Kitching, Gen Wilfred 43, 44, 47, 49, 105, 197, 206, 218, 236, 280
Kitney, Marvin 80
Knapman, Col Arthur 27, 28
Knightsbridge Barracks 109
Knutzen, Catherine 292
Knutzen, Hans 292
Korea 145, 289

L

Laing, BM Alan 260
Lakeland 263
'Land Of Song' 88, 227
Larsson, John 83, 89, 90, 106, 117, 166, 170, 188, 260
Latham, Philip 166, 167
Launceston (Australia) 101
Launn, Chris 264
Lawson, Martyn 157
Lear, Eric and Nancy 229
Leeds Town Hall 243
LeGrow, Joyce 135, 263, 291
LeGrow, Tom 82, 93, 106, 111, 135, 136, 263, 291
Leidzén, Erik 11, 12, 24, 43, 48, 53, 81, 86, 88, 89, 95, 109, 144, 151, 194, 198, 199, 200, 201, 202, 203, 204, 277
Leidzén, Mrs Maria 199, 201
Leigh-on-Sea 219
Leighton Buzzard 59
Lemoine, Capt Albert 12, 15
Leopoldville Band 59
Les Andelys 14
Lewis, Betty (Bet) 33, 34, 283, 286
Lewis, Dennis (Den) 33, 34, 39, 211, 283, 286
Leytonstone 219

307

Salvationist 187, 191, 217, 229, 259, 291
Salvationist Publishing & Supplies
  (SP&S) 3, 49, 122, 191, 195
Sampson, Lily 173
Sanders, Margaret 156
Sandford, Kevin 156, 161
Saunders, Brig Doris 115
Scarborough (Canada) 85
School for the Blind, Thika 264, 265,
  266
Scotney, Harold 144
'Seafarer, The' 260
Second World War 7, 31, 95, 135, 215,
  293
Seddon, Yvonne 156
Sewell, David 156, 157, 161
Sheffield 39, 266
Shipley 2
Showboat (Butlin's) 123
Silfverberg, Erik 148, 285
Silver Birches 76
Sing To The Lord 258
Six Nations North American Indian
  Reserve 87
Skegness 124, 244
Skinner, Celestine (Cissie) 41, 50, 134
Skinner, Charles 9, 44, 49, 86, 187, 238,
  239
Skinner, Isobel 156
Smith, BM Derek 95, 109
Smith, Graham and Beryl 229
Smith, Margaret 156
Smith, SCL Billie 270
Snape, Col William 122
Snell, Maj Malcolm 123
Snook, BM George 52
Söderström, Emil 144, 198, 199, 202,
  203, 204, 205
Song Book Council 115
Song Book Of The Salvation Army, The 84,
  94, 115
'Song Of Exultation' 260, 285
'Song Of Renewal' 258
Songs Of Faith 82, 83, 84, 116
'Songs Of Newfoundland' 90, 260
Songs Of Praise 243, 244, 245

'Songs Of Testimony' 85
'Sound Of Britain, The' 106, 109, 119
Southall 3, 11, 109, 199
Southall Band 3, 11, 13
Southall Citadel (Southall 1 Corps) 13,
  14, 21, 44, 65, 106, 108, 148, 149,
  182, 194, 205, 206, 209, 230
South London Fellowship Band 292
Southsea 108
Southwood, Brig Charles 200
Southwood, Mrs Col 200
Spencer, Joan 162
'Spirit Of The Army' 285
Springate, BM Alf 52, 54, 117, 129
St Catherines (Canada) 85
St John's (Newfoundland) 90, 114
St Paul's Cathedral 16, 17, 233
St Petersburg (USA) 263
Staines 5, 140, 219
Stapleford 46
Star Lake (USA) 152, 153, 199, 200, 289
Stead, William 165
Steadman-Allen, Joy ix, x, 127, 214, 280
Steadman-Allen, Ray xi, 39, 46, 47, 49,
  81, 86, 88, 89, 90, 93, 120, 126, 127,
  133, 134, 138, 139, 143, 147, 148,
  160, 170, 188, 209, 214, 215, 260,
  279, 280, 285, 291, 293
Stevens, Susan 219
Stickland, Geoff 270
'Stories Of Jesus' 291
Sudbury 211, 212
Sunbury Court 55, 116, 117, 118, 139,
  140, 175, 179, 208, 225, 226, 227
Sunderland Monkwearmouth 42
Sutton 6, 52, 219, 244
Swaddling, George 79
Swansea 108, 229
Swanwick 62
Sweden 59, 152, 161, 198
'Sweet Chariot' 261
Swenarton, Alf 243
Swindon 52
Switzerland 140
Swyers, Lieut-Col Philip 263
Sydney 102

311

313